THAT'S LIFE

WITH ILLUSTRATIONS BY

BILL TIDY, HEATH
AND LARRY

TREASURE PRESS

First published in Great Britain as four separate titles by
Octopus Books Limited

I Wish I'd Said That
Text and illustrations © 1984 Octopus Books Limited

I Don't Believe It
Text © 1986 Octopus Books Limited
Illustrations © 1986 Bill Tidy

What a Mistake
Text and illustrations © 1983 Octopus Books Limited

It Can't be True
Text and illustrations © 1983 Octopus Books Limited

This omnibus edition first published in Great Britain in 1989 by
Treasure Press
Michelin House
81 Fulham Road
London SW3 6RB

Reprinted 1990

ISBN 1 85051 478 X

Printed in Czechoslovakia
50509/2

Acknowledgement
The extracts from Dorothy Parker's works are reproduced by
permission of Duckworth.

I WISH I'D SAID THAT!

ILLUSTRATED BY HEATH

CONTENTS

INSTANT QUIPS

A collection of witty epigrams and wisecracks.

*There is nothing more satisfying than a witty riposte.
Unfortunately, most of us think of the perfect
response only hours later – usually in the bath! The
following collection of verbal gems was spoken or
written by people whose instant wit is a constant
source of envy – and delight!*

With A Twist

*Be warned! You are about to read some distinctly **warped**
pieces of wisdom which make hay with familiar phrases
and ideas*

Essayist **Charles Lamb**:

> *'The greatest pleasure I know is to do good by stealth, and to
> have it found out by accident.'*

Jerome K. Jerome, author of *Three Men in a Boat*, argued that

> *'It is always the best policy to speak the truth, unless of course
> you are an exceptionally good liar.'*

According to **Sir Winston Churchill**:

> *'Men occasionally stumble over the truth, but most of them
> pick themselves up and hurry off as if nothing had happened.'*

The American satirist **Mark Twain** was responsible for the following highly moral reflections:

'To be good is noble, but to teach others to be good is nobler – and less trouble.'

'The holy passion of Friendship is of so sweet and steady and loyal and enduring a nature that it will last through a whole lifetime, if not asked to lend money.'

'Always do right: this will gratify some people and astonish the rest.'

The wily French statesman Talleyrand, mastermind behind the favourable peace terms of the Congress of Vienna in 1815, was – perhaps understandably – a confirmed cynic:

'Mistrust first impulses, they are always good.'

When Shakespeare wrote the immortal 'Brevity is the soul of wit' he couldn't know that **Dorothy Parker** would cap it with:

'Brevity is the soul of lingerie.' *BOOM!*

BOOM!

Austrian novelist **Robert Musil** on the modern world and its problems:

'Progress would be wonderful – if only it would stop.'

Damon Runyon adapted the Bible to the outlook of gambling guys and dolls, advising:

> *'The race is not always to the swift, nor the battle to the strong, but that's the way to bet.'*

Worldly wisdom from American humorist **Artemus Ward**:

> *'Thrice is he armed that hath his quarrel just – and four times he who gets his fist in fust.'*

Crackerbarrel philosophy from **Edward Noyes Westcott**:

> *'Do unto the other feller the way he'd like to do unto you, an' do it fust.'*

Immoral moral reflections were a speciality of Irish playwright **George Bernard Shaw**:

> *'Do not do unto others as you would they should do unto you. Their tastes may not be the same.'*

> *'The British churchgoer prefers a severe preacher because he thinks a few home truths will do his neighbours no harm.'*

> *'Martyrdom . . . is the only way in which a man can become famous without ability.'*

Heinrich Heine, German poet:

'One should forgive one's enemies, but not before they are hanged.'

Lord Melbourne, British prime minister and friend of Queen Victoria, was religious – when he was in a church. Shocked by a sermon, he once remarked:

'Things have come to a pretty pass when religion is allowed to invade the sphere of private life.'

Will Rogers, American humorist:

'Everything is funny as long as it is happening to somebody else.'

NICE ONE

C. E. Montague, a journalist, served at the front in the First World War but found that there was more hysteria *behind* the lines. He wrote:

'War hath no fury like a non-combatant.'

American novelist **James Branch Cabell**:

'The optimist proclaims that we live in the best of all possible worlds, and the pessimist fears this is true.'

Arthur Bloch, shrewd commentator on contemporary society, calls this Jones's Law:

'The man who can smile when things go wrong has thought of someone he can blame it on.'

The American poet **Robert Frost** showed perfect understanding of the psychology of work:

'The brain is a wonderful organ. It starts working the moment you get up in the morning and does not stop until you get into the office.'

Poul Anderson, writer of science fiction, expressed his confidence in the power of the human mind, writing:

'I have yet to see any problem, however complicated, which, when looked at in the right way, did not become more complicated.'

G. K. Chesterton, English master of paradox, noted the social revolution that occurred when the invention of the typewriter created new job opportunities for women:

'Twenty million young women rose to their feet with the cry "We will not be dictated to," and promptly became stenographers.'

The American scientist **Paul Ehrlich** on technology, ancient and modern:

'To err is human but to really foul things up requires a computer.'

The film comedian **W. C. Fields,** bumbling and bad-tempered, came up with this inspiring thought:

'If at first you don't succeed, try, try again. Then give up. No use being a damn fool about it.'

Old-fashioned morality — according to **Robert Benchley**:

'A dog teaches a boy fidelity, perseverance, and to turn around three times before lying down.'

Oscar Wilde on how to secure a stable relationship:

'To love oneself is the beginning of a lifelong romance.'

Benjamin Franklin, American revolutionary leader and writer, identified one of the drawbacks of self-love:

'He that falls in love with himself will have no rivals.'

Film actress **Lily Tomlin** on the human condition:

'We're all in this together — by ourselves.'

A profoundly self-critical thought from film star **Ava Gardner**:

'Deep down, I'm pretty superficial.'

The flamboyant Irish dramatist **Oscar Wilde** made his own publicity. He believed that

'There is only one thing in the world worse than being talked about, and that is not being talked about.'

American art historian **Bernard Berenson**:

> *'Consistency requires you to be as ignorant today as you were a year ago.'*

Labour firebrand **Aneurin Bevan** had little time for compromise:

> *'We know what happens to people who stay in the middle of the road. They get run over.'*

BOOM!
BOOM!

The American comedienne **Phyllis Diller** has this advice to give on the subject of domestic relations:

> *'Never go to bed mad. Stay up and fight.'*

Sir James Barrie was the author of *Peter Pan*, the sentimental story of a boy who refused to grow up. But Barrie could still be irritated by his juniors, snapping:

> *'I am not young enough to know everything.'*

Oscar Wilde noted the freedom enjoyed by children in the United States:

> *'In America, the young are always ready to give to those who are older than themselves the benefit of their inexperience.'*

The Duke of Windsor (ex-King Edward VIII) put it another way:

'The thing that impresses me most about America is the way parents obey their children.'

Hollywood star **John Barrymore** didn't believe that virtue was its own reward. In fact –

'The good die young – because they see it's no use living if you've got to be good.'

Bernard Shaw:

'Youth is a wonderful thing; what a crime to waste it on children.'

Oscar Wilde doubted whether age brought wisdom, saying of an acquaintance:

'He is old enough to know worse.'

American essayist **Logan Pearsall Smith**:

'There is more felicity on the far side of baldness than young men can possibly imagine.'

16

William Feather, American author:

'Setting a good example for your children takes all the fun out of middle age.'

American humorist **Kin Hubbard** thought being 'grown up' and good was a delusion:

'Boys will be boys, and so will a lot of middle-aged men.'

French film star **Maurice Chevalier**:

> *'Old age isn't so bad when you consider the alternative.'*

Of one of his characters, American novelist **Joseph Heller** writes:

> *'He had decided to live forever, or die in the attempt.'*

GROAN!

In the French film *Breathless*, a smooth and successful writer is asked whether he has any ambition still to be fulfilled. Indeed he does:

> *'To become immortal, and then to die.'*

American comedian **Woody Allen**:

> *'It's not that I'm afraid to die. I just don't want to be there when it happens.'*

Summing up the meaning of human existence, writer-performer **Quentin Crisp** says:

> *'Life was a funny thing that happened to me on the way to the grave.'*

MONEY MATTERS.

The possession or acquisition of wealth has yielded a glittering crop of wisecracks and ironic remarks over the years, as the following examples bear witness:

Conversation recorded by the novelist **Scott Fitzgerald**, who was dazzled by the glamour of the rich:

FITZGERALD: *The rich are different from us.*
ERNEST HEMINGWAY: *Yes, they have more money.*

The American critic **John Leonard** made the same point with more sophistication:

'The rich are different from you and me because they have more credit.'

'Red Hot Momma' blues singer **Sophie Tucker** summed up her own experience:

'I have been poor and I have been rich. Rich is better.'

The rich, although more fortunate than many, may yet behave decently. One of the dukes of **Argyll** remarked:

'As far as I'm concerned there are only two kinds of people in the world. Those who are nice to their servants and those who aren't.'

How rich is rich? According to multi-millionaire **John Jacob Astor III**:

'A man who has a million dollars is as well off as if he were rich.'

Wealth is a shield against even the harshest criticisms, as the glittering showman **Liberace** pointed out:

'What you said hurt me very much. I cried all the way to the bank.'

TAKE THAT!

American journalist **Earl Wilson**:

'Success is just a matter of luck. Ask any failure.'

American comedian **Jack Benny**, famed for his supposed meanness, is said to have been held up one day by a gangster.

GANGSTER: *Your money or your life!*

Pause.

BENNY: *I'm thinking it over.*

In the bad old days, when the husband controlled all the money in a family, there were many male fortune hunters. The novelist **Henry Fielding** described one scoundrel like this:

> *'His designs were strictly honourable, as the saying is; that is, to rob a lady of her fortune by way of marriage.'*

Girls too can be shrewd when it comes to romance — like Anita Loos's blonde heroine **Lorelei Lee** in *Gentlemen Prefer Blondes*:

> *'Kissing your hand may make you feel very good, but a diamond bracelet lasts for ever.'*

Dorothy Parker bemoaned her failure as a gold-digger:

> *Why is it no one ever sent me yet*
> *One perfect limousine, do you suppose?*
> *Ah no, it's always just my luck to get*
> *One perfect rose.*

Much loved and often married, Hollywood star **Zsa Zsa Gabor** remembered that:

> *'I never hated a man enough to give him his diamonds back.'*

21

One of the United States' Founding Fathers, **Benjamin Franklin**, handed out much solid practical advice, including this:

'If you would know the value of money, go and try to borrow some.'

Film star **Lana Turner** describes the perfect marriage:

'A successful man is one who makes more money than his wife can spend. A successful woman is one who can find such a man.'

In the movie *The Producers*, **Bialystok (Zero Mostel)** urges Leo (Gene Wilder) to seize his (crooked) opportunity while he can:

'Leo, he who hesitates is poor!'

Quentin Crisp's view of social mobility:

'Never keep up with the Joneses. Drag them down to your level. It's cheaper.'

The famous 18th century playwright **Sheridan** was never out of debt, but still managed to take a fine town house and furnish it. He told a friend that everything was 'going like clockwork'.
    'Yes, I know what you mean,' answered the friend:

'Tick! Tick! Tick!'

When pressed for payment by one of his many creditors, **Sheridan** said:

'You know it is not in my interest to pay the principal; nor is it my principle to pay the interest.'

Sheridan was an Irishman. When asked why his name did not begin with 'O', the ever-penurious playwright answered:

'No family has a better right to an O than our family, for in truth we owe everybody.'

SHOW STOPPERS

The larger-than-life figures of the entertainment business have been known to inspire and produce off-the-cuff lines which would make any scriptwriter green with envy:

The great showman **Phineas T. Barnum** knew that there were fortunes to be made in show business, since

'Every crowd has a silver lining.'

Columbia executive **Harry Cohn** hints at how Hollywood got its results in this description of a budding actress of the silver screen:

'She's got talent and personality. Give me two years and I'll make her an overnight star.'

Hollywood producer **Sam Goldwyn** was famous for making gaffes in his own brand of mangled English. But some of his remarks were shrewder than they seemed:

'Anyone who goes to a psychiatrist should have his head examined.'

'What we want is a story that starts with an earthquake and works its way up to a climax.'

Pianist and mordant wit **Oscar Levant**:

'Strip away the phoney tinsel of Hollywood and you find the real tinsel underneath.'

In the 1930s **Mae West** played the bad girl who gloried in a lurid past – and present – as the following remarks demonstrate:

'I used to be Snow White, but I drifted.'

GIRL: *Goodness, what beautiful diamonds you're wearing!*

MAE WEST: *Goodness had nothing to do with it, dearie.*

——— *NICE ONE* ———

Comedian **Will Rogers** found that the cinema possessed one overwhelming advantage for the performer:

'The movies are the only business where you can go out front and applaud yourself.'

In his films, bottle-nosed comedian W. C. Fields played The Man You Love To Hate; but author **Leo Rosten** took a charitable view of him:

'Anybody who hates children and dogs can't be all bad.'

Screen hero **Errol Flynn**, whose private life was expensively wild, confessed:

> *'My problem lies in reconciling my gross habits with my net income.'*

Veteran star **Mickey Rooney**'s marital career has been extraordinary even by showbiz standards, as he himself recognizes:

> *'I'm the only man who has a marriage licence made out To Whom It May Concern.'*

In *I'm No Angel*, a reporter asks **Mae West** why she told a court all about the men in her life. Her classic retort:

> *'It's not the men in your life that counts, it's the life in your men.'*

In the Marx Brothers' films **Groucho** was blatantly a crook, a fake, or both at once. Hence this supposed letter to a certain Membership Secretary:

> *'Please accept my resignation. I don't care to belong to a club that will have me as a member.'*

INSTANT QUIPS

Sam Goldwyn explains why competition from television damaged the film industry so badly:

'Why should people go out and pay money to see bad films when they can stay at home and see bad television for nothing?'

Suave film star **George Sanders**:

'An actor is not quite a human being – but then, who is?'

TAKE THAT!

Dr Samuel Johnson, undisputed king of 18th century English talkers, restrained his usual ferocity when he received a visit from the great actress Mrs Siddons. Since his servant proved slow in bringing her a chair, Johnson made the incident the occasion for a compliment:

'You see, madam, wherever you go, there are no seats to be had.'

D. W. Griffith, director of the epoch-making *Birth of a Nation*, is universally recognized as a pioneer of early film-making. Strangely, he was never invited to leave his footprints in cement outside Grauman's Chinese Restaurant – Hollywood's way of conferring immortality.

Columnist **Hedda Hopper** commented on this oversight in this subtle tribute to a movie giant:

'His footprints were never asked for, yet no one has ever filled his shoes.'

28

SPOKEN FROM THE ARTS

Critics and playwrights, novelists and poets, painters, composers and dancers all have, in their time, coined or elicited some highly quotable remarks:

A friend found the 18th century playwright **R. B. Sheridan** in the street, glass in hand, watching as his theatre, the Drury Lane, burned down. Sheridan remarked calmly:

> *'A man may surely be allowed to take a glass of wine by his own fireside.'*

The witty **Sydney Smith** claimed that, in his work as a critic:

> *'I never read a book before reviewing it; it prejudices a man so.'*

Drama critic **James Agate** on theatre audiences:

> *'Long experience has taught me that in England nobody goes to the theatre unless he or she has bronchitis.'*

James Agate on actors:

> *'A professional is a man who can do his job when he doesn't feel like it. An amateur is a man who can't do his job when he does feel like it.'*

George Bernard Shaw:

'A drama critic is a man who leaves no turn unstoned.'

The book you are now reading is a work of research, as **Wilson Mizner** kindly points out:

'When you take stuff from one writer, it's plagiarism; but when you take it from many writers, it's research.'

Oscar Wilde remained unruffled by the failure of his early play *The Duchess of Padua*:

'The play itself was a profound success. But the audience was a profound failure.'

The biographer is even worse than a critic or an audience, according to **Oscar Wilde**:

'Every great man nowadays has his disciples, and it is always Judas who writes the biography.'

Playwright **John Osborne** turns on the critics:

'Asking a working writer what he thinks about critics is like asking a lamp-post what it thinks about dogs.'

Novelist **Joseph Heller** describes a rugged individualist:

'He was a self-made man who owed his lack of success to nobody.'

Journalist **J. Alfred Spender**:

'The misfortune of the "artistic temperament" is that so many people have the temperament and so few the art.'

Artistic integrity is hard on mothers. **Bernard Shaw** boasted that he allowed his aged parent to support him while he wrote novels that no one would publish:

'I did not throw myself into the battle of life: I threw my mother into it.'

The American writer **William Faulkner** scorned the less sensational art of an earlier American novelist:

'Henry James was one of the nicest old ladies I ever met.'

TAKE THAT!

Confronted with US Customs, **Oscar Wilde** exclaimed with magnificent bravado:

'I have nothing to declare — except my genius!'

SHUCKS!

'Cowboy' humorist **Will Rogers** was the original author of this immortal comment on the Venus de Milo:

'See what'll happen to you if you don't stop biting your finger nails!'

The booklover's worst enemy is the book-borrower. **Sir Walter Scott**:

'I find that though many of my friends are poor arithmeticians, they are nearly all good book-keepers.'

Musician **Pete Seeger**:

> *'Education is when you read the fine print. Experience is what you get if you don't.'*

A character in one of **Christopher Morley**'s novels took an extremely practical view of the dancer's art:

> *'Dancing is a wonderful training for girls; it's the first way you learn to guess what a man is going to do before he does it.'*

Music critic **Ernest Newman** argued that in the arts justice was eventually done:

> *'The good composer is slowly discovered, the bad composer is slowly found out.'*

The American painter **James McNeil Whistler** was witty and also waspish; he wrote a treatise on *The Gentle Art of Making Enemies*. Towards the end of his life he was heard to complain:

> *'I'm lonesome. They are all dying. I have hardly a warm personal enemy left.'*

Dancer and choreographer **Sir Robert Helpman** on the difference between audacity and art:

> *'The trouble with nude dancing is that not everything stops when the music does.'*

LIFE LINES

Reflections on the meaning of life, the universe and everything to do with human behaviour are by no means always serious subjects of conversation, as the following examples illustrate:

Playwright **Tom Stoppard**:

'I think age is a very high price to pay for maturity.'

American **Cardinal Spellman** on old age . . . and beyond:

'You've heard of the three ages of man: youth, age, and ''you are looking wonderful''.'

One day Dr Johnson happened to meet **Oliver Edwards**, a man he had known at college many years before. Unusually, it was not the Sage of Fleet Street who said the memorable thing, but the otherwise unknown Edwards:

'You are a philosopher, Dr Johnson. I have tried, too, in my time to be a philosopher; but, I don't know how, cheerfulness was always breaking in.'

Dean Swift, scathing as ever on the subject of human follies:

'Old men and comets have been reverenced for the same reason: their long beards, and pretences to foretell events.'

Woody Allen:

'I don't want to achieve immortality through my work. I want to achieve it through not dying.'

NICE ONE

The artist **Aubrey Beardsley**, darling of the 'camp' 1890s, was consumptive but made light of it:

'Really I believe I'm so affected, even my lungs are affected.'

Premature obituaries get published somehow from time to time. In a cable sent from Europe to the Associated Press news agency after reading of his own demise, **Mark Twain** commented drily:

'The reports of my death are greatly exaggerated.'

American writer **W. D. Howells** anticipated modern science by discovering the time-warp:

'Some people can stay longer in an hour than others can in a week.'

Despite his gift for comedy, **Mark Twain** was a savage pessimist, as is shown by observations such as:

'If you pick up a starving dog and make him prosperous, he will not bite you; that is the principal difference between a dog and a man.'

Apparently the great Greek thinker **Socrates** also believed that philosophy and cheerfulness were incompatible. He advised:

'By all means marry: if you get a good wife, you'll be happy; if you get a bad one, you'll become a philosopher.'

Bernard Shaw on English puritanism:

'Morality consists in suspecting other people of not being legally married.'

Dialogue across the centuries:

FRANCIS BACON: *Silence is the virtue of fools.*

ABRAHAM LINCOLN: *Better to remain silent and be thought a fool than to speak out and remove all doubt.*

The quest for universal peace, as seen by **Woody Allen**:

'The lion and the calf shall lie down together, but the calf won't get much sleep.'

Benjamin Disraeli identified a vital symptom of decay:

'When a man fell into his anecdotage it was a sign for him to retire from the world.'

TALKING POLITICS

Politicians are often on the receiving end of wisecracks, but sometimes too they can give as good as they get:

Simon Cameron, a 19th century American politician whose own reputation was somewhat doubtful, took a cynical view of his trade:

'An honest politician is one who when he is bought will stay bought.'

Mark Twain's opinion of his elected representatives was clear enough:

'Reader, suppose you were an idiot; and suppose you were a member of Congress; but I repeat myself . . .'

A man told **Coolidge** that he'd bet a friend he could get more than two words out of the President. Said Coolidge:

'You lose.'

Sir Winston Churchill on the hazards of political life:

'Politics are almost as exciting as war. In war you can only be killed once, but in politics many times.'

Good advice for politicians from American humorist **Josh Billings**:

'To enjoy a good reputation, give publicly and steal privately.'

Calvin Coolidge, President of the United States, was often ridiculed for his taciturn personality. He defended himself by saying that

'I have noticed that nothing I never said ever did me any harm.'

GROAN!

American comedian **George Burns**:

'Too bad all the people who know how to run the country are busy driving taxi cabs and cutting hair.'

Aneurin Bevan, hero of the Left during the 1950s and '60s:

'I read the newspaper avidly. It is my one form of continuous fiction.'

F. E. Smith on Churchillian eloquence:

'Winston has devoted the best years of his life to preparing his impromptu speeches.'

Newspaper reporting has inspired little confidence in those best qualified to judge. American editor **Erwin Knoll**:

> *'Everything you read in the newspapers is absolutely true except for the rare story of which you happen to have first-hand knowledge.'*

Curmudgeonly comedian **W. C. Fields** had a ready answer when asked who he would vote for:

> *'Hell, I never vote for anybody; I always vote against.'*

American President **Harry S. Truman** tells it like it is:

> *'It's a recession when your neighbour loses his job; it's a depression when you lose your own.'*

The American vice-presidency sounds an important office, but in reality the vice-president has virtually no power and few responsibilities. One vice-president, **Thomas R. Marshall**, told the following story:

> *'Once there were two brothers. One ran away to sea, the other was elected vice-president, and nothing was ever heard of either of them again.'*

Will Rogers on income tax:

> *'It has made more liars out of the American people than Golf.'*

Most of the world's monarchies have disappeared during the 20th century. On being deposed, **King Farouk** of Egypt remarked:

'There will soon be only five kings left: the Kings of England, Diamonds, Hearts, Spades and Clubs.'

Jean Baptiste Colbert was probably the first minister of finance in the modern sense. He knew exactly what he was doing:

'The art of taxation consists in so plucking the goose as to obtain the largest amount of feathers with the least amount of hissing.'

PROFESSIONAL OPINIONS

The learned professions have us at their mercy. It is hardly surprising, therefore, if they have occasionally been the targets as well as the authors of various well-chosen words:

Lord Brougham, who became Lord Chancellor, did not think particularly well of his fellow practitioners:

> *'A lawyer is a learned gentleman who rescues your estate from your enemies and keeps it himself.'*

Sir Winston Churchill gives a politician's view of the most prestigious modern profession:

> *'Scientists should be on tap but not on top.'*

Benjamin Franklin warned darkly:

> *'He's a fool that makes his doctor his heir.'*

17th century writer **Francis Quarles** on 'covering up your mistakes':

> *'Physicians of all men are most happy; what good success soever they have, the world proclaimeth, and what faults they commit, the earth covereth.'*

Quarles's contemporary, the physician **Sir Samuel Garth,** admitted in a spirit of self-criticism:

*Whilst others meanly asked whole months to slay,
I oft dispatched the patient in a day.*

Education. By the 1770s, **Dr Johnson** (himself an ex-schoolmaster) was lamenting the passing of 'the good old days':

'There is less flogging in our great schools than formerly, but then less is learned there; so that what the boys get at one end they lose at the other.'

In the good/bad old days, a man's eldest son inherited his estate, another son went into the army – and the dunce went into the Church. The **Reverend Sydney Smith** pointed out how absurd this was:

'When a man is a fool, in England we only trust him with the immortal concerns of human beings.'

WIT'S END

There have always been people whose every remembered word seems a gem of verbal wizardry. The following enviable quotations are gleaned from the works of such giants of humour:

Sydney Smith was one of the great English wits. One of his typically playful remarks was:

> *'Gout is the only enemy which I don't wish to have at my feet.'*

Smith's wit had a strong vein of fantasy, one example being the way in which he expressed his disapproval of an acquaintance:

> *'He deserves to be preached to death by wild curates.'*

Washington Irving, author of 'Rip Van Winkle':

> *'A sharp tongue is the only edged tool that grows keener with constant use.'*

G. K. Chesterton explains the link between wit and cruelty:

> *'Wit is a sword; it is meant to make people feel the point as well as see it.'*

Sydney Smith was often exasperated by Lord Macaulay, who was a non-stop talker. Smith once told him:

'You know, when I am gone you will be sorry you never heard me speak.'

Smith on Macaulay:

'He has occasional flashes of silence that make his conversation perfectly delightful.'

Sydney Smith on Sydney Smith:

'The whole of my life has been passed like a razor – in hot water or a scrape!'
— *NICE ONE*

17th century humour. Daniel Purcell, 'the famous punster', was challenged to make a new pun on the spot.

'Upon what subject?' asked Purcell.
'The King,' ventured his challenger.
'The King, sir,' said Purcell, 'is not a subject.'

The Irish playwright Oscar Wilde remains the most famous of all wits, as one of his modern competitors, Dorothy Parker, conceded:

If, with the literate, I am
Impelled to try an epigram,
I never seek to take the credit;
We all assume that Oscar said it.

When a friend gave birth, **Dorothy Parker** sent her a telegram:

'Congratulations: we all knew you had it in you.'

Wilde on travel literature:

'I never travel without my diary. One should always have something sensational to read in the train.'

Oscar Wilde was harshly punished for violating the moral taboos of Victorian England, but his wit remained undimmed. Standing in the pouring rain, handcuffed, on his way to prison, he remarked:

'If this is the way Queen Victoria treats her convicts, she doesn't deserve to have any.'

Oscar Wilde on drink:

'Work is the curse of the drinking classes.'

'Absinthe makes the heart grow fonder.'

Oscar Wilde lectured in the United States – for the money:

'Of course, if one had enough money to go to America, one wouldn't go.'

Wilde found much to entertain him in America, including its myths:

'The youth of America is their oldest tradition. It has been going on now for three hundred years.'

Comic poet **Ogden Nash** knew the way to a girl's heart:

> *Candy is dandy*
> *But liquor is quicker.*

Wilde put this Wildean view of society into the mouth of one of his characters:

> *'To be in it is merely a bore. But to be out of it is simply a tragedy.'*

Much of **Wilde**'s humour is what we should now call 'camp':

> *'I feel that football is all very well as a game for rough girls, but it is hardly suitable for delicate boys.'*

ROMANCE LANGUAGE

The subject of love was bound to come up since it has inspired more speeches than Prime Minister's Question Time – not all of them serious:

American wit Dorothy Parker was disillusioned:

> *By the time you swear you're his,*
> *Shivering and sighing,*
> *And he vows his passion is*
> *Infinite, undying –*
> *Lady, make a note of this:*
> *One of you is lying.*

Readers of a later chapter in this book, 'A Talent to Abuse', will find plenty of ammunition to use against women. **Groucho Marx** answers on their behalf:

> *'Anyone who says he can see through women is missing a lot.'*

Actress **Evelyn Laye** believed that sex should be discreet and private:

> *'Sex, unlike justice, should not be seen to be done.'*

Once, women were supposed to be indifferent to sex. The actress **Cornelia Otis Skinner** told all:

> *'Woman's virtue is man's greatest invention.'*

By the free and easy 1920s, actress **Tallulah Bankhead** felt able to boast:

> *'I'm as pure as the driven slush.'*

Tallulah Bankhead on starting as you mean to go on:

> *'The only thing I regret about my past is the length of it. If I had to live my life again I'd make the same mistakes, only sooner.'*

Bad girls' seminar:

> TALLULAH BANKHEAD: *It's the good girls who keep diaries; the bad girls never have the time.*

> MAE WEST: *Keep a diary and one day it'll keep you.*

Woody Allen provides a reason for remaining cheerful:

> *'Love is the answer, but while you are waiting for the answer, sex raises some pretty good questions.'*

BOOM!
BOOM!

Woody Allen, 20th century *homo neuroticus*:

> *'The difference between sex and death is that with death you can do it alone and no one is going to make fun of you.'*

The Kinsey Report was a pioneering investigation of sexual behaviour – but **Dr Kinsey's wife** complained:

> *'I don't see so much of Alfred any more since he got so interested in sex.'*

Two minds with but a single . . .

GROUCHO MARX: *A man's only as old as the woman he feels.*

JEAN HARLOW: *I like to wake up feeling a new man.*

MARRIAGE LINES

If you're not careful, sex can lead to marriage, an institution which has taken plenty of knocks over the centuries. Here are just a few of them!

American writer **Helen Rowland**, one of the wittiest commentators on the battle of the sexes, gives the girl's-eye view:

'A bachelor never quite gets over the idea that he is a thing of beauty and a boy forever.'

'The hardest task in a girl's life is to prove to a man that his intentions are serious.'

'When you see what some girls marry, you realize how much they must hate to work for a living.'

American humorist **James Thurber**:

'A woman's place is in the wrong.'

Oscar Wilde describes the mating season:

> *'The London season is entirely matrimonial; people are either hunting for husbands or hiding from them.'*

For women, there is only a choice of evils – according to **Oscar Wilde**:

> *'Twenty years of romance makes a woman look like a ruin; but twenty years of marriage makes her something like a public building.'*

A recent attack from writer **David Pryce-Jones**:

> *'When you're bored with yourself, marry and be bored with someone else.'*

The philosophical view, as expounded by 18th century dramatist George Farquhar:

> *'Hanging and marriage, you know, go by Destiny.'*

Professional cynic **H. L. Mencken**:

> *'Bachelors know more about women than married men. If they didn't they'd be married too.'*

> *'It is more blessed to give than to receive; for example, wedding presents.'*

There are many motives for marrying, and especially for 'marrying well'. American comedian **Joey Adams**:

> *'The most popular labour-saving device today is still a husband with money.'*

GROAN!

Robert Louis Stevenson was no enemy to marriage, which was

> *'at its lowest . . . a sort of friendship recognized by the police.'*

Dr Johnson's verdict on matrimony was favourable – just:

> *'Marriage has many pains, but celibacy has no pleasures.'*

But when a man who had been unhappily married decided to take the plunge again immediately after his first wife's death, **Johnson** said that it represented

> *'The triumph of hope over experience.'*

Poet **William Blake**'s version of 'getting to know each other':

> *When a man has married a wife, he finds out whether Her knees and elbows are only glued together.*

Benjamin Franklin advised husbands to take a prudent course:

> *'Keep your eyes wide open before marriage and half-shut afterwards.'*

Zsa Zsa Gabor, speaking from experience:

'A girl must marry for love, and keep on marrying until she finds it.'

Oscar Wilde noted that:

'Woman begins by resisting a man's advances and ends by blocking his retreat.'

Canadian humorist **Stephen Leacock**:

'Many a man in love with a dimple makes the mistake of marrying the whole girl.'

The wit **Sydney Smith** neatly pictured the married state:

> *'It resembles a pair of shears, so joined that they cannot be separated; often moving in opposite directions, yet always punishing anyone who comes between them.'*

Clergyman and writer **Charles Colton** describes the worst of matrimonial disappointments:

> *'Marriage is a feast where the grace is sometimes better than the dinner.'*

The poet **Samuel Rogers**:

> *'It doesn't much signify whom one marries, for one is sure to find next morning it was someone else.'*

The poet **Shelley** and more recent author **Norman Douglas** expressed directly opposing opinions – but both managed to complain:

> SHELLEY: *When a man marries, dies, or turns Hindoo, his best friends hear no more of him.*

> DOUGLAS: *Many a man who thinks to found a home discovers that he has merely opened a tavern for his friends.*

The novelist **Samuel Butler**:

> *'Brigands demand your money or your life; women require both.'*

When Brigham Young founded the Mormon community in Utah, polygamy was permitted. The result, said **Artemus Ward**, was that

'The pretty girls in Utah mostly marry Young.'

The marital adventures of Zsa Zsa Gabor and other members of her family often made the headlines. **Oscar Levant** summed up:

'Marriage is for bores. I mean Gabors.'

American politician **Hubert Humphrey** gave a different slant on an old subject:

'Behind every successful man stands a surprised mother-in-law.' BOOM! BOOM!

Marriage can have serious consequences, as **Mark Twain** observed:

'Familiarity breeds contempt – and children.'

American novelist **Peter De Vries** describes a universal experience:

'There are times when parenthood seems nothing but feeding the mouth that bites you.'

It is said that a man likes nothing better than a 'safely' married woman with whom to indulge in a casual flirtation. That woman's husband may not regard the matter in the same light, however, as **Helen Rowland** observes:

'One man's folly is another man's wife.'

She advised:

'Never trust a husband too far nor a bachelor too near.'

A Mediterranean perspective from **Lord Byron**:

What men call gallantry, and gods adultery
Is much more common where the climate's sultry.

Alexandre Dumas the elder reflects in the urbane French style:

'The chain of wedlock is so heavy that it takes two to carry it, sometimes three.'

Helen Rowland:

'When a girl marries she exchanges the attentions of many men for the inattention of one.'

TAKE THAT!

Lord Mancroft on the properly serviced and run husband:

'Happy the man with a wife to tell him what to do and a secretary to do it for him.'

Dorothy Parker and Robert Benchley only just preserved their virtue — says Parker:

'He and I had an office so tiny that an inch smaller and it would have been adultery.'

The most sophisticated modern society puzzles **Cleveland Amory**:

'Relations between the sexes are so complicated that the only way you can tell if members of the set are "going together" is if they're married. Then, almost certainly, they are not.'

Is it all worth it? **Lord Beaverbrook** thought not:

'Buy old masters. They fetch a better price than old mistresses.'

Hollywood star **John Barrymore** came to see that 'time is money':

'You never realize how short a month is until you pay alimony.'

Anonymous:

'Widows are divided into two classes: the bereaved and the relieved.'

LATE ENTRIES

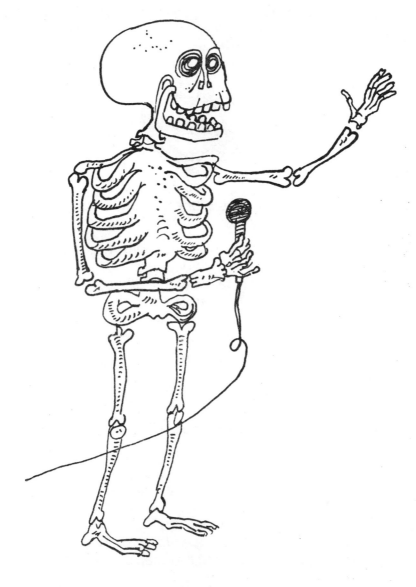

**Epitaphs, inscriptions and verses
in memoriam.**

One of the curses of fame is that someone is sure to score off you by composing a witty epitaph for you . . . even before you're dead.

The Earl of Rochester wrote one on King Charles II, then got drunk and accidentally showed it to his royal master. It read:

> *Here lies our sovereign lord the king*
> *Whose promise none relies on;*
> *Who never said a foolish thing*
> *Nor ever did a wise one.*

The **Merry Monarch** had a ready answer:

> *'This is very true; for my words are my own, and my actions are my ministers.'*

This inscription, commemorating a 17th century author, tells the old, old story of neglected genius:

> *Whilst Butler, needy wretch, was yet alive,*
> *No generous patron would a dinner give.*
> *See him when starved to death and turned to dust*
> *Presented with a monumental bust.*
> *The poet's fate is here in emblem shewn:*
> *He asked for bread, and he received a stone.*

The 18th century writer **Horace Walpole** recorded some verses
that circulated after the death of Frederick, Prince of Wales:

Here lies Fred,
Who was alive and is dead:
Had it been his father,
I had much rather;
Had it been his brother,
Still better than another;
Had it been his sister,
No one would have missed her;
Had it been the whole generation,
Still better for the nation;
But since 'tis only Fred,
Who was alive and is dead —
There's no more to be said.

An anonymous punster commemorated Dr John Potter,
Archbishop of Canterbury:

Alack and well a-day
Potter himself is turned to clay.

GROAN!

Lord Byron savaged prime minister William Pitt the Younger,
who was buried in Westminster Abbey:

With death doomed to grapple,
Beneath this cold slab, he
Who lied in the chapel
Now lies in the Abbey.

The poet **Ben Jonson**, Shakespeare's contemporary, wrote this vitriolic epitaph for a great lord:

> Here lies a valiant warrior
> Who never drew a sword;
> Here lies a noble courtier
> Who never kept his word;
> Here lies the Earl of Leicester
> Who governed the estates
> Whom the earth could never living love
> And the just heaven now hates.

The 'Welsh Wizard', **David Lloyd George**, suggested an epitaph for himself that might have been adopted by many other politicians:

> Count not my broken pledges as a crime,
> I MEANT them, HOW I meant them, at the time.

64

Wisecracking American writer **Dorothy Parker** proposed this simple tombstone inscription for herself:

Excuse my dust.

Hilaire Belloc wrote of himself with the cheerful vanity of an author:

> *When I am dead, I hope it may be said*
> *'His sins were scarlet but his books were read.'*

John Gay, author of *The Beggars' Opera*, composed his own epitaph:

> *Life is a jest, and all things show it.*
> *I thought so once; but now I know it.*

John Gibson Lockhart, Sir Walter Scott's biographer, suggested this intentionally clumsy verse epitaph for a clumsy would-be poet:

> *Here lies that peerless peer Lord Peter,*
> *Who broke the laws of God and man and metre.*

Oliver Goldsmith was a great writer but a notoriously inept conversationalist. On one occasion the actor **David Garrick** improvised this epitaph for his friend 'Noll':

> *Here lies Nolly Goldsmith, for shortness called Noll,*
> *Who wrote like an angel but talked like poor Poll.*

In this epitaph on himself, the 18th century poet **Matthew Prior** claimed a posthumous equality with the great royal families of Europe:

> *Nobles and heralds by your leave,*
> *Here lies what once was Matthew Prior;*
> *The son of Adam and of Eve –*
> *Can Bourbon or Nassau go higher?*

Shakespeare's tomb at Stratford-on-Avon carries this solemn warning:

> *Good friend, for Jesu's sake forbear*
> *To dig the dust enclosèd here;*
> *Blessed be the man that spares these stones,*
> *And cursed be he that moves my bones.*

The 18th century Scottish philosopher **David Hume** was much concerned with the workings of the human mind — to the very end, as his tomb at Edinburgh demonstrates:

> *Within this circular idea,*
> *Called vulgarly a tomb,*
> *The ideas and impressions lie*
> *That constituted Hume.*

As a young man, still unknown to fame, the great American **Benjamin Franklin** composed this elaborate epitaph for himself:

The body of
Benjamin Franklin, printer
(Like the cover of an old book,
Its contents worn out
And stript of its lettering and gilding)
Lies here, food for worms.
Yet the work itself shall not be lost,
For it will, as he believed, appear once more
In a new
And more beautiful edition,
Corrected and amended
By its Author!

William Blake, eccentric poet and painter, detested everything his highly successful fellow-artist, Sir Joshua Reynolds, stood for. Hence this odd little verse:

When Sir Joshua Reynolds died
All Nature was degraded;
The King dropped a tear in the Queen's ear,
And all his pictures faded.

On **Nance Oldfield,** a famous 18th century actress:

> *This we must own in justice to her shade,*
> *'Tis the first bad exit Oldfield ever made.*

Curmudgeonly comic **W. C. Fields** said that his epitaph should
be:

> *On the whole I'd rather be in Philadelphia.*

Groucho Marx had very definite ideas:

> *I want it known here and now that this is what I want on my*
> *tombstone. Here lies Groucho Marx, and Lies and Lies and*
> *Lies and Lies. P. S. He never kissed an ugly girl.*

Versatile Hollywood actor **Lionel Barrymore** told a magazine
that his epitaph should be:

> *Well, I've played everything but a harp.*

The 18th century actor **Samuel Foote**, a brilliant mimic,
inspired two understandably anonymous tributes:

> *Foote from his earthly stage, alas! is hurled;*
> *Death took him off, who took off all the world.*

and

> *Here lies one Foote, whose death rnay thousands serve,*
> *For death has now one foot within the grave.*

LATE ENTRIES

The poet Keats proposed for his epitaph the gloomy 'Here lies one whose name was writ in water.' The scandalous **Robert Ross**, Oscar Wilde's intimate friend, went one better on his own behalf:

Here lies one whose name is writ in hot water!

No guarantee of authenticity is offered for this classically brief gravestone inscription:

Cheerio, see you soon.

Graveyard philosophy from the USA:

> *Once I wasn't*
> *Then I was*
> *Now I ain't again.*

A young person's tale:

> *Came in*
> *Looked about*
> *Didn't like it*
> *Went out*

Silly, but brief:

> *Here lies Ann Mann;*
> *She lived an old maid*
> *And she died an old Mann.*

This 18th century tombstone tribute is unintentionally funny:

> *Today he rises from a Velvet Bed*
> *Tomorrow he's in one that's made of Lead*
>
> *Today perfumed, and sweet as is the Rose,*
> *Tomorrow stinks in ev'ry Body's Nose*

A missionary in India was accidentally shot by his native bearer. His tombstone is said to have included the hardly appropriate Biblical quotation:

> *'Well done thou good and faithful servant.'*

An Irish epitaph:

> *Erected in the memory of*
> *John Philips*
> *Accidentally shot*
> *As a mark of affection by his brother.*

From Dumfries:

> *Here lies Andrew MacPherson,*
> *Who was a peculiar person;*
> *He stood six foot two*
> *Without his shoe,*
> *And he was slew*
> *At Waterloo.*

LATE ENTRIES

These tombstones are less than fulsome in praise of the dear
departed . . .

> *Friend, in your epitaph I'm grieved*
> *So very much is said:*
> *One half will never be believed,*
> *The other never read.*

> *Here lies John Rackett*
> *In his wooden jacket;*
> *He kept neither horses nor mules.*
> *He lived like a hog*
> *And died like a dog,*
> *And left all his money to fools.*

Anna Harrison of Easingwold in Yorkshire had *some* good
qualities:

> *Her tongue and her hands were not governable,*
> *But the rest of her members she kept in subjection.*

From Yarmouth:

> *Owen Moore has gone away,*
> *Owin' more than he can pay.*

From Shrewsbury:

> *Here lies the body of Martha Dias,*
> *Who was always uneasy and not over pious;*
> *She lived to the age of threescore and ten,*
> *And gave that to the worms she refused to the men.*

It would be nice to know just who **Hilaire Belloc** had in mind
when he penned this:

Here richly, with ridiculous display,
The Politician's corpse was laid away.
While all of his acquaintance sneered and slanged,
I wept: for I had longed to see him hanged.

LATE ENTRIES

There are other versions of this one, naming other towns – not surprisingly, since it bursts with civic pride:

> *Here lie the bones of Elizabeth Charlotte,*
> *Born a virgin, died a harlot.*
> *She was aye a virgin at seventeen,*
> *A remarkable thing in Aberdeen.*

Dorothy Parker, bitchy as always, suggested that this should be carved on an actress's tombstone:

> *Her name, cut clear upon this marble cross,*
> *Shines, as it shone when she was still on earth,*
> *While tenderly the mild, agreeable moss*
> *Obscures the figures of her date of birth.*

One American Congressman (**Samuel Cox**) seeing off another:

> *Beneath this stone Owen Lovejoy lies,*
> *Little in everything except in size;*
> *What though his burly body fills the hole,*
> *Yet through Hell's keyhole crept his little soul.*

The journalist **George Augustus Sala** dealt a cruel posthumous blow to a colleague, John Camden Hotten:

> *Hotten*
> *Rotten*
> *Forgotten*

This marital last word has been attributed to the poet **John Dryden**:

> *Here lies my wife: here let her lie!*
> *Now she's at rest, and so am I.*

BOOM!
BOOM!

One version of a popular and vindictive adieu runs as follows:

> *My wife lies dead, yes here she lies;*
> *Nobody laughs and nobody cries.*
> *Where she has gone to and how she fares*
> *Nobody knows and nobody cares.*

A formula for happiness (eventual) in marriage:

> *Underneath this tuft doth lie,*
> *Back to back, my wife and I.*
> *Generous stranger, spare a tear,*
> *For could she speak, I cannot hear.*
> *Happier far than when in life,*
> *Free from noise and free from strife,*
> *When the last trump the air doth fill,*
> *If she gets up then I'll lie still.*

LATE ENTRIES

On tombstones, at least, men seem to get the better of the battle of the sexes. But there are exceptions:

> *Here lies the mother of children seven,*
> *Four on earth and three in heaven;*
> *The three in heaven preferring rather*
> *To die with mother than live with father.*

The moral of this is 'better the devil you *don't* know':

> *Here lies Mary, the wife of John Ford,*
> *We hope her soul is gone to the Lord;*
> *But if for Hell she has changed this life*
> *She had better be there than be John Ford's wife.*

The poet **Lord Byron** wrote a number of harsh epitaphs – and this single kindly one:

> *Near this spot are deposited the remains of one who possessed Beauty without Vanity, Strength without Insolence, Courage without Ferocity, and all the virtues of Man, without his Vices. This Praise, which would be unmeaning Flattery if inscribed over human ashes is but just tribute to the memory of Boatswain, a Dog.*

Graveyard humour is often excruciating – and never more so than in this epitaph for one 'Cookhouse Jake':

> *Peace to his hashes.*

Lament for a Liverpool brewer:

> *Poor John Scott lies buried here,*
> *Though once he was hale and stout;*
> *Death stretched him on his bitter bier:*
> *In another world he hops about.*

Epitaph for a peer caught cheating at cards:

> *Here lies*
> *Henry William, twenty-second Lord _____,*
> *In joyful expectation of the last trump.*

From Ireland:

> *Here lie the remains of John Hall, grocer.*
> *The world is not worth a fig*
> *And I have good raisins for saying so.*

GROAN!

From the USA:

> *Under the sod and under these trees,*
> *Here lies the body of Solomon Pease.*
> *He's not in this hole but only his pod:*
> *He shelled out his soul and went up to God.*

On a dentist:

> *Stranger, approach this spot with gravity:*
> *John Brown is filling his last cavity.*

Epitaph for a hard-drinking carrier, possibly written by **Lord Byron**:

> *John Adams lies here, of the parish of Southwell,*
> *A carrier who carried his can to his mouth well.*
> *He carried so much, and he carried so fast,*
> *He could carry no more – so was carried at last;*
> *For the liquor he drank, being too much for one,*
> *He could not carry off – so he's now carrion.*

If your trade is dyeing cloth – this is the sort of epitaph you can expect:

> *Here lies a man who first did dye*
> *When he was twenty-four;*
> *And yet he lived to reach the age*
> *Of hoary years fourscore.*
> *But now he's gone, and certain 'tis*
> *He'll not dye any more.*

On the tomb of a **Mrs Stone** at Melton Mowbray:

> *Curious enough we all must say,*
> *That what was stone should now be clay;*
> *Most curious still, to own we must,*
> *That what was stone must soon be dust.*

Many epitaphs touch upon the trade followed by the late lamented during his earthly life. This one even includes some discreet advertising:

> *Beneath this stone, in hopes of Zion,*
> *Doth lie the landlord of The Lion.*
> *His son keeps on the business still*
> *Resigned unto the heavenly will.*

A sexton gets his come uppance:

> *Hurrah! My brave boys,*
> *Let's rejoice at his fall!*
> *For if he'd have lived*
> *He'd have buried us all.*

LATE ENTRIES

In folklore, *all* lawyers are crooks. Hence the note of surprise in this memorial:

> *Here lies one, believe it if you can,*
> *Who, though an attorney, was an honest man.*

And in this, of **Sir John Strange**:

> *Here lies an honest lawyer:*
> *That is Strange!*

TAKE THAT!

Of a first lieutenant of marines, off-duty in Yorkshire:

> *Confined in earth in narrow borders,*
> *He rises not till further orders.*

This 17th century locksmith was clearly a conscientious worker:

> *A zealous locksmith died of late,*
> *And did arrive at Heaven's gate.*
> *He stood without, and would not knock,*
> *Because he meant to pick the lock.*

Robert Trollope of Gateshead was an architect:

> *Here lies Robert Trollope,*
> *Who made yon stones roll up.*
> *When Death took his soul up*
> *His body filled this hole up.*

Inscription for a fisherman who . . . exaggerated:

> He angled many a purling brook,
> But lacked the angler's skill:
> He lied about the fish he took,
> And here he's lying still.

Western epitaph for one who knew both sides of a job:

> Here lies Wild Bill Britt.
> Ran for sheriff in '82;
> Ran from sheriff in '83;
> Buried in '84.

A wry, graceful farewell from Ashover in Derbyshire:

> To the memory of
> David Wall,
> whose superior performance on the
> bassoon endeared him to an
> extensive musical acquaintance.
> His social life closed on the
> 4th Dec., 1796, in his 57th year.

From Whitby:

> Sudden and unexpected was the end
> Of our esteemed and beloved friend:
> He gave all his friends a sudden shock
> By one day falling into Sunderland dock.

One of **Leonard Robbins'** *Epitaphs for the Speed Age,* with a
wide potential application:

> *Stranger, pause and shed a tear*
> *For one who leaves no mourners.*
> *D. F. Sapp reposes here:*
> *He would cut corners.*

Mini-novel by the American poet **Carl Sandburg**:

> *Papa loved mamma*
> *Mamma loved men*
> *Mamma's in the graveyard*
> *Papa's in the pen.*

Dr Johnson had no doubts about the final destination of a recently deceased gentleman from Jamaica:

'He will not, whither he is now gone, find much difference, I believe, either in the climate or the company.'

Advice from beyond the grave – to be precise, from Eastwell in Kent:

Fear God
Keep the Commandments
and
Don't attempt to climb a tree,
For that's what caused the death of me.

A comment on 'death after death'; from Kingsbridge in Devon:

Here lie I at the Chancel door.
Here I lie because I'm poor.
The further in the more you pay;
Here lie I as warm as they.

From Leeds:

Angels, grant a trifling boon
To our brother who here lies.
Sound the trumpet after noon,
Earlier doth he never rise.

Epitaph possibly written by **Oliver Goldsmith**:

> *Here lies poor Ned Pardon, from misery freed,*
> *Who long was a bookseller's hack;*
> *He led such a damnable life in this world,*
> *I don't think he'll ever come back.*

Wolverhampton, 1690:

> *Here lies the bones*
> *Of Joseph Jones,*
> *Who ate while he was able;*
> *But once o'erfed,*
> *He dropped down dead*
> *And fell beneathe the table.*
> *When from the tomb*
> *To meet his doom,*
> *He rises amidst the sinners,*
> *Since he must dwell*
> *In Heaven or Hell,*
> *Take him — which gives best dinners.*

A vicar's widow, questioned about her spouse's recent passage from Earth to Elsewhere, replied:

> *'I'm sure my husband is enjoying eternal bliss. But must we talk about such an unpleasant subject?'*

Sad story from Norfolk:

> *Here lie I and my four daughters,*
> *Killed by drinking Cheltenham waters.*
> *Had we but stuck to Epsom Salts,*
> *We wouldn't be lying in these here vaults.*

From Ryde, Isle of Wight:

> *There was an old lady from Ryde*
> *Who ate some apples and died.*
> *The apples fermented inside the lamented*
> *Made cider inside her inside.*

NICE ONE

Bad news from Bideford:

> *The wedding day appointed was,*
> *The wedding clothes provided.*
> *But ere the day did come, alas,*
> *He sickened, and he dieded.*

The 19th century children's writer **George Macdonald** composed the ultimate plea for mutual tolerance:

> *Here lie I, Martin Elginbrodde:*
> *Hae mercy o' my soul, Lord God;*
> *As I wad do, were I Lord God,*
> *And ye were Martin Elginbrodde.*

DEFINITIVELY SPEAKING

ALTERNATIVE DICTIONARY FOR DEVIOUS MINDS

**Extraordinary and ingenious definitions
of familiar words.**

DICTIONARY

OF

ALTERNATIVE MEANINGS

Giving the Sources and Originators
of Definitions
in Uncommon Use

by

Nick Harris

Acquaintance A person whom we know well enough to borrow from but not well enough to lend to.
(Ambrose Bierce, US author, 1842-1914?)

Actor An actor's a guy who if you ain't talking about him, he ain't listening. *(Marlon Brando)*

Armour The kind of clothing worn by a man whose tailor is a blacksmith. *(Ambrose Bierce)*

Atheist An atheist is a man who has no invisible means of support. *(John Buchan)*

Baby A loud noise at one end and no sense of responsibility at the other.
(Father Ronald Knox, English author and translator, 1888-1957)

Bachelor A man who never makes the same mistake once.
(Ed Wynn, 20th century US comedian)

Bank A bank is a place where they lend you an umbrella in fair weather and ask for it back when it begins to rain.
(Robert Frost, US poet, 1874-1963)

A bank is a place that will lend you money if you can prove that you don't need it. *(Bob Hope)*

Bigamist A man who marries a beautiful girl and a good cook.
(Chicago Herald-American)

Bore A bore is a man who, when you ask him how he is, tells you.
(Bert Leston Taylor, 20th century US writer)

A person who talks when you wish him to listen. *(Ambrose Bierce)*

Brain The apparatus with which we think we think.
(Ambrose Bierce)

Breeding Good breeding consists in concealing how much we think of ourselves and how little we think of the other person.
(Mark Twain)

Calamity Calamities are of two kinds: misfortune to ourselves, and good fortune to others. *(Ambrose Bierce)*

Cannibal A guy who goes into a restaurant and orders the waiter. *(Jack Benny)*

Caricature Caricature is the tribute mediocrity pays to genius.
(Oscar Wilde)

Celebrity A celebrity is a person who works hard all his life to become known, then wears dark glasses to avoid being recognized. *(Fred Allen, 20th century US comedian)*

Classic A classic is something that everybody wants to have read and nobody wants to read. *(Mark Twain)*

Committee A committee is a group that keeps the minutes and loses hours. *(Milton Berle, 20th century US comedian)*

Conclusion A conclusion is the place where you get tired of thinking. *(Arthur Bloch, 20th century US writer)*

Conference A conference is a gathering of important people who singly can do nothing, but together can decide that nothing can be done. *(Fred Allen)*

Confidence Confidence is simply that quiet assured feeling you have before you fall flat on your face.
                                    (Dr L. Binder, 19th century US historian)

Conscience Conscience is the inner voice which warns us that someone might be looking.
                    (H. L. Mencken, 20th century US humorist and author)

Cult A cult is a religion with no political power.
                                    (Tom Wolfe, 20th century US author)
. . . It just means not enough people to make a minority.
                                    (Robert Altman, 20th century US film director)

Cynic A blackguard whose faulty vision sees things as they are, not as they ought to be. *(Ambrose Bierce)*

A man who knows the price of everything and the value of nothing. *(Oscar Wilde)*

Dancing Dancing is a perpendicular expression of a horizontal desire. *(Anonymous)*

Débâcle Defeat at cricket and tennis.
                    (J. B. Morton, alias 20th century humorist 'Beachcomber')

Democracy Democracy is a form of religion. It is the worship of jackals by jackasses. *(H. L. Mencken)*

Diagnosis The physician's art of determining the condition of the patient's purse in order to find out how sick to make him. *(Ambrose Bierce)*

Diplomat A diplomat is a man who always remembers a woman's birthday but never remembers her age. *(Robert Frost)*

Economy Cutting down other people's wages. *(J. B. Morton)*

Editor An editor is one who separates the wheat from the chaff and prints the chaff. *(Adlai Stevenson, US politician, 1900-1965)*

Egotist A person of low taste, more interested in himself than in me. *(Ambrose Bierce)*

Epigram Any sentence spoken by anybody who is in the public eye at the moment. *(J. B. Morton)*

Epitaph A belated advertisement for a line of goods that has been permanently discontinued. *(Irvin S. Cobb, 20th century US writer)*

A monumental inscription designed to remind the deceased of what he might have been if he had had the will and opportunity. *(Ambrose Bierce)*

Expert An expert is one who knows more and more about less and less. *(Nicholas Murray Butler, US educator, 1862-1947)*

An expert is a man who has made all the mistakes which can be made, in a narrow field. *(Niels Bohr, 20th century Danish physicist)*

Faith It was the schoolboy who said, 'Faith is believing what you know ain't so.' *(Mark Twain)*

Fiction The good end happily and the bad unhappily. That is what Fiction means. *(Oscar Wilde)*

Friends

Friends People who borrow books and set wet glasses on them.
(Edwin Arlington Robinson, 20th century US poet)

Friendship Friendship is like money, easier made than kept.
(Samuel Butler, English writer 1835-1902)

Friendship is more tragic than love. It lasts longer. *(Oscar Wilde)*

Future That period of time in which our affairs prosper, our friends are true and our happiness is assured. *(Ambrose Bierce)*

Gambling The sure way of getting nothing for something.
(Wilson Mizner, 20th century US wit)

Genius Genius is born, not paid. *(Oscar Wilde)*

A genius is one who can do anything except make a living.
(Joey Adams, 20th century US comedian)

Gesticulation Any movement made by a foreigner.
(J. B. Morton)

Gossip Gossip is the art of saying nothing in a way that leaves practically nothing unsaid.
(Walter Winchell, 20th century US columnist)

Grand Old Man That means on our continent [North America] anyone with snow-white hair who has kept out of jail till eighty.
(Stephen Leacock, Canadian humorist and author, 1869-1944)

Home Home is the place where, when you have to go there, they have to take you in. *(Robert Frost)*

Imitation Imitation is the sincerest form of flattery.
(Oscar Wilde)

Imitation is the sincerest form of television. *(Fred Allen)*

Jury A jury consists of twelve persons chosen to decide who has the better lawyer. *(Robert Frost)*

Liberal A liberal is a man too broad-minded to take his own side in a quarrel. *(Robert Frost)*

Liberty One of Imagination's most precious possessions.
(Ambrose Bierce)

Life Life is rather like a tin of sardines: we're all of us looking for the key. *(Alan Bennett,* Beyond the Fringe*)*

Life is not a spectacle or a feast; it is a predicament.
(George Santayana, Spanish-American philosopher, 1863-1952)

Life is an incurable disease. *(Abraham Cowley, poet, 1618-1667)*

Life is just one damned thing after another.
(Kin Hubbard, US humorist, 1859-1915)

Life is the art of drawing sufficient conclusions from insufficient premises. *(Samuel Butler)*

Life's a pudding full of plums.
(W. S. Gilbert, English lyricist and poet, 1836-1911)

Logic

Logic Logic is the art of going wrong with confidence.
(Joseph Wood Krutch, 20th century US scholar and critic)

Love A temporary insanity curable by marriage. *(Ambrose Bierce)*

An abject intercourse between tyrants and slaves.
(Oliver Goldsmith, poet, 1728-1774)

Love is like linen often changed, the sweeter.
(Phineas Fletcher, poet, 1582-1650)

Love is like the measles; we all have to go through it.
(Jerome K. Jerome)

Man A creature made at the end of a week's work when God was tired. *(Mark Twain)*

Marriage A community consisting of a master, a mistress and two slaves, making in all two. *(Ambrose Bierce)*

Marriage is a romance in which the hero dies in the first chapter.
(Anonymous)

Marriage is give and take. You'd better give it to her or she'll take it anyway. *(Joey Adams)*

Marriage is like a cage; one sees the birds outside desperate to get in, and those inside equally desperate to get out.
(Michel de Montaigne, French writer, 1533-1592)

Memoirs When you put down the good things you ought to have done, and leave out the bad ones you did do – that's Memoirs.
(Will Rogers, 20th century US comedian)

Monogamy An obsolete word meaning a fidelity complex.
(J. B. Morton)

Moral indignation Moral indignation is jealousy with a halo.
(H. G. Wells)

Nation A nation is a society united by a delusion about its ancestry and by a common hatred of its neighbours.
(Dean Inge, dean of St Paul's, London, 1911-34)

Opera Opera is when a guy gets stabbed in the back and instead of bleeding, he sings. *(Ed Gardner, 20th century US comedian)*

Optimist An optimist is a guy who has never had much experience. *(Don Marquis, 20th century US satirist)*

An optimist is always broke. *(Kin Hubbard)*

A man who gets treed by a lion but enjoys the scenery.
(Walter Winchell)

An optimist is a fellow who believes what's going to be will be postponed. *(Kin Hubbard)*

Originality Originality is the fine art of remembering what you hear but forgetting where you heard it.
(Laurence Peter, 20th century Canadian writer)

Patriotism The last refuge of the scoundrel. *(Dr Johnson)*

Patriotism is your conviction that this country is superior to all others because you were born in it. *(Bernard Shaw)*

Patron Commonly a wretch who supports with insolence, and is paid with flattery. *(Dr Johnson)*

Pessimist A pessimist is someone who, if he is in the bath, will not get out to answer the telephone. *(Quentin Crisp)*

A pessimist is a man who looks both ways when he's crossing the street. *(Laurence Peter)*

The optimist sees the doughnut, the pessimist sees the hole.
(Anonymous)

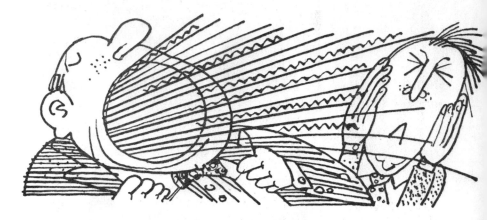

Politician A politician is a man who approaches every question with an open mouth. *(Adlai Stevenson)*

A politician is an animal which can sit on a fence and yet keep both ears to the ground. *(H. L. Mencken)*

The most successful politician is he who says what everybody is thinking most often and in the loudest voice.
(Theodore Roosevelt, US president 1901-9)

Prodigy A child who plays the piano when he ought to be in bed. *(J. B. Morton)*

A child who knows as much when it is a child as it does when it grows up. *(Will Rogers)*

Professor A professor is one who talks in someone else's sleep.
(W. H. Auden)

Psychiatrist A psychiatrist is a man who goes to the Folies-Bergère and looks at the audience.
(Mervyn Stockwood, Bishop of Southwark)

They say a psychiatrist is a fellow who asks you a lot of expensive questions your wife asks for nothing. *(Joey Adams)*

Punctuality Punctuality is something that if you have it, there's often no one around to share it with you.
(Hylda Baker, 20th century English comedienne)

Radical A radical is a man with both feet planted firmly in the air. *(Franklin D. Roosevelt)*

Religion The religion of one age is the literary entertainment of the next. *(Ralph Waldo Emerson, US writer)*

One's religion is whatever he is most interested in.
(J. M. Barrie, author of Peter Pan*)*

Revolution In politics, an abrupt change in the form of misgovernment. *(Ambrose Bierce)*

Robbery Any price charged for any article abroad.
(J. B. Morton)

Sex Sex is an emotion in motion. *(Mae West)*

Success The one unpardonable sin against one's fellows.
(Ambrose Bierce)

Teacher He who can, does. He who cannot, teaches.
(Bernard Shaw)

Television A medium. So called because it is neither rare nor well done. *(Ernie Kovacs, 20th century US film actor)*

A device that permits people who haven't anything to do to watch people who can't do anything. *(Fred Allen)*

Time That which man is always trying to kill, but which ends in killing him. *(Herbert Spencer, English philosopher, 1820-1903)*

Wickedness Wickedness is a myth invented by good people to account for the curious attractiveness of others. *(Oscar Wilde)*

Year A period of three hundred and sixty-five disappointments.
(Ambrose Bierce)

CRACKS OF DOOM

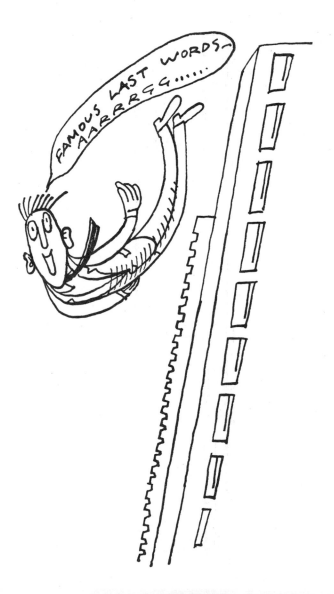

Last words of the great and famous.

CRACKS OF DOOM

We should all like to get in a good parting shot, and many well-known people have managed to do just that . . . or have had 'famous last words' invented for them.

King Charles II expired with exquisite politeness, saying:

> *'I have been a most unconscionable time a-dying, but I hope you will excuse it.'*

According to another account his last thoughts were of his mistress, Nell Gwynne:

> *'Let not poor Nellie starve!'*

Lord Palmerston, twice British prime minister, was witty to the last:

> *'Die, my dear doctor! That's the* last *thing I shall do!'*

When his nurse assured visitors that the patient was somewhat better, the Norwegian dramatist **Henrik Ibsen** growled:

> *'On the contrary.'*

He then proved himself right by promptly expiring.

George IV was evidently taken by surprise, calling to his page:

'Wally, what is this? It is death, my boy. They have deceived me.'

There are several versions of **George V**'s last words, including the solemn 'How is the Empire?' A less reverent story is that, when told he would soon be well enough to visit his favourite resort, the King answered:

'Bugger Bognor.'

When **Disraeli** was dying, he was asked whether he would like Queen Victoria to visit him. The ex-prime minister replied:

'No, it is better not. She would only ask me to take a message to Albert.'

Nero, Emperor of Rome in the first century AD, died as he had lived – with delusions of grandeur. Facing defeat and humiliation as revolt and insurrection raged around him, he committed suicide, exclaiming as he did so:

'What an artist the world is losing in me!'

The poet **Alexander Pope** wrote, towards the end of his final illness:

'Here am I, dying of a hundred good symptoms.'

Finding her family gathered round her bedside during her last illness, **Lady Astor** asked:

'Am I dying or is this my birthday?'

After their deaths, Roman emperors were officially recognized as divinities. But they were still reluctant to go. The **Emperor Vespasian** groaned:

'Dammit — I think I'm becoming a god.'

Lou Costello, the fat member of the Abbott and Costello comedy partnership, said:

'That was the best ice cream soda I ever tasted.'

Humphrey Bogart remained true to his tough-guy image. His last words are supposed to have been:

'I should never have switched from Scotch to Martinis.'

Dr Joseph Green, a 19th century surgeon, adopted a briskly scientific approach to his own case. He took his own pulse, uttered a single word:

'Stopped.'

Then he fell dead.

NICE ONE

John Philpot Curran, a famous Irish wit, was told by his doctor that he was coughing with more difficulty. Curran's answer was:

'That is surprising, since I have been practising all night.'

The French author **Paul Claudel** was one of those who suspected that Something He Had Eaten had hastened his end. He asked:

'Doctor, do you think it could have been the sausage?'

Richard Monckton Milnes, in his day a noted society man and diner-out, realized that the self-indulgence of a lifetime might have had something to do with his demise. He remarked:

'My exit is the result of too many entrées.'

Like many other patients, the world-conquering **Alexander the Great** blamed the medics:

'I am dying with the help of too many physicians.'

William Pitt the Younger was Britain's prime minister during the long wars against Napoleonic France. When he died, at a moment of crisis, he is said to have spoken these noble words: 'My country! My country! How I leave my country!'

But it was widely believed that this 'official' version was wrong, and that what Pitt actually said was:

'I think I could eat one of Bellamy's veal pies.'

Traditional last words on 'death row' in US prisons:

'Give me some bicarb, warden, I'm gonna have some gas.'

Anton Chekhov, Russian author of bittersweet stories and plays, emptied a sparkling glass, commented

'It's a long time since I have drunk champagne,'

and spoke no more.

The hell-raising Welsh poet **Dylan Thomas** boasted:

'I've had eighteen straight whiskies – I think that's the record.'

The witty and fantastic **Reverend Sydney Smith** died as a result of accidentally drinking some ink. His last words:

'Bring me all the blotting paper there is in the house!'

The wife of the German poet **Heinrich Heine** urged him to beg for God's forgiveness. Heine retorted loftily:

'God will forgive me: that's His trade.'

When a priest came in to see the American wit **Wilson Mizner**, the dying man revived long enough to make a last crack:

'Why should I talk to you? I've just been talking to your boss.'

William Palmer – 'Palmer the poisoner' – was caught, convicted and sentenced. About to step on to the scaffold, he enquired:

'Are you sure it's safe?'

American criminal **James W. Rodgers**, facing a firing squad, was asked whether he had a last request.

'Why yes – a bullet-proof vest.'

Jonathan Swift, author of *Gulliver's Travels*, lay dying when he heard that the composer Handel had come to visit him.
Swift called out:

'Ah, a German and a genius – a prodigy! Admit him!

The American poet **Kenneth Rexroth** remembered his father's last days:

> *'He said he was dying of fast women, slow horses, crooked cards and straight whisky.'*

According to the actor and comedian **Kenneth Williams**, this is a true story.

During a performance of a play, actor A was supposed to take out a gun and shoot actor B. When the moment came, A discovered that he had no gun.

In a state of panic, he could think of nothing better than to *kick* B.

In an inspired improvisation, B sank to the ground, gasping:

> *'The boot . . . was* poisoned *!'*

Gertrude Stein, American experimental writer, asked, 'What *is* the answer?'

Evidently none came, whereupon she laughed and said:

'In that case, what is the question?'

Then she died.

The actor **John Palmer** died on stage with superb timing, having just uttered the line

'There is another and a better world.'

Bing Crosby, Hollywood comedian and 'crooner' beloved of millions, collapsed and died after a friendly eighteen holes at his local club. His last words were happy:

'That was a great game of golf, fellers.'

The French writer **Bernard de Fontenelle** was a hundred years old when he died in 1757, as tranquilly as he had lived. He explained:

'I do not suffer at all, but I do experience a certain difficulty in continuing to exist.'

James Quin, 18th century actor, played the good trooper:

'I could wish this tragic scene were over, but I hope to go through it with becoming modesty.'

The novelist **W. Somerset Maugham**:

'Dying is a very dull, dreary affair. My advice to you is to have nothing to do with it.'

A dramatist proffered his latest work to the French critic **Nicolas Boileau**, presumably unaware of the seriousness of his current illness. Boileau's last words on earth were:

'Do you wish to hasten my last hour?'

American essayist **Logan Pearsall Smith**:

'Thank heaven, the sun has gone in, and I don't have to go out and enjoy it.' **GROAN!**

The great Scottish economist **Adam Smith**'s last words were unintentionally macabre. He told his colleagues:

'I believe we must adjourn the meeting to some other place.'

On his deathbed the American publisher **Andrew Bradford** was conscious of his failings. A newspaperman to the last, he cried:

'Lord, forgive the errata!'

During the American Civil War, Union **General John Sedgwick** peered over the parapet at the enemy lines, answering friendly warnings with the assertion:

'They couldn't hit an elephant at this dist--'

Lord Holland, expecting an acquaintance with rather morbid tastes, issued this final instruction:

'If Mr Selwyn calls, let him in. If I am alive I shall be very glad to see him, and if I am dead he will be very glad to see me.'

The Russian poet **Vladimir Mayakovsky** killed himself, but observed in his suicide note:

'I don't recommend it for others.'

During the French Revolution a condemned *aristo* was offered a last drink on the scaffold. He refused it, saying:

'I lose all sense of direction when I'm drunk.'

The fabulously rich **William H. Vanderbilt** died after remarking that

'I have had no real gratification or enjoyment of any sort more than my neighbour down the block who is worth only . . . half a million.'

At the end of his life **Oscar Wilde** was bankrupt. When told how expensive an operation would be, he remarked:

'Ah well, I suppose I shall have to die beyond my means.'

When the American Revolutionary soldier **Ethan Allen** was told that the angels were waiting for him, he snapped:

'Waiting, are they? Well, let 'em wait!'

Karl Marx:

'Get out! Last words are for fools who haven't already said enough!'

A TALENT TO ABUSE

A compendium of insult, scorn and criticism.

A TALENT TO ABUSE

It is perhaps a sad reflection on human nature, but certainly a happy truth for the collector of prize put-downs, that we are generally better at insulting than at praising our fellow man. Although some of the following were impromptu remarks, the insult is usually all the better for being long premeditated, for as the poet Byron explains:

Now hatred is by far the longest pleasure;
Men love in haste, but they detest at leisure.

PURELY PERSONAL

To begin with, a few brutal examples of crushing retorts by some real pro's:

W. S. Gilbert, writer of the Gilbert and Sullivan operettas, had this to say about some mercifully anonymous acquaintance:

'No one can have a higher opinion of him than I have; and I think he is a dirty little beast.'

Dorothy Parker in a (for her) mildly critical mood:

'She tells enough white lies to ice a cake.'

A TALENT TO ABUSE

Heinrich Heine, the author of exquisite lyrics, could be cruelly witty:

> *'She resembles the Venus de Milo: she is very old, has no teeth, and has white spots on her yellow skin.'*

The writer **Virginia Woolf** wrote with inverted snobbery of

> *'Those comfortably padded lunatic asylums which are known euphemistically as the stately homes of England.'*

A profound piece of observation quoted by the writer **C. S. Lewis**:

> *'She's the sort of woman who lives for others — you can tell the others by their hunted expressions.'*

An example of the unintentional insult: Dining with King George V, a cabinet minister declined the offer of a cigar, saying:

> *'No thank you, I only smoke on special occasions.'*

Voltaire, the wittiest of all French writers, sums up the rewards of a successful career as a literary scourge:

> *'My prayer to God is a very short one: "O Lord, make my enemies ridiculous." God has granted it.'*

A TALENT TO ABUSE

Sheer bitchiness from Hollywood star **Bette Davis**, describing a starlet:

'There goes the good time that was had by all.'

An interesting character trait, noted by **Dorothy Parker**:

> *'That woman can speak eighteen languages, and she can't say No in any of them.'*

When a woman told **Sir Winston Churchill** he was drunk, he retorted:

> *'Madame, you're ugly. Tomorrow morning, however, I shall be sober . . .'*

A TALENT TO ABUSE

When a flatterer laughed once too often at **Dr Johnson**'s sayings, the Sage crushed him with:

'What provokes you to risibility, Sir? Have I said anything that you understand? Then I ask the pardon of the rest of the company.'

A woman who was too complimentary to **Johnson** was told:

'Madam, before you flatter a man so grossly to his face, you should consider whether or not your flattery is worth his having.'

Johnson mauls an absent acquaintance:

'A fellow who makes no figure in company, and has a mind as narrow as the neck of a vinegar cruet.'

Dr Johnson on the actor Thomas Sheridan:

'Why, Sir, Sherry is dull, naturally dull; but it must have taken a great deal of pains to become what we now see him. Such an excess of stupidity, Sir, is not in Nature.'

As a practitioner of the art of the insult, New York poet and journalist **Dorothy Parker** was almost unrivalled. She particularly detested the socialite and the diplomat Clare Boothe Luce, and when told that Luce was invariably kind to her inferiors, asked:

'Where does she find them?'

When the two women happened to meet in front of a door, **Clare Boothe Luce** indicated that Dorothy Parker should go first, saying 'Age before beauty!' Parker swept through, retorting:

'Pearls before swine.'

Jumper-to-jumper followed by bumper-to-bumper? **Dorothy Parker** speculated:

'If all the girls attending the Yale Prom were laid end to end, I wouldn't be at all surprised.'

In a competition to decide the supreme master of the insult, Dr Johnson would probably emerge an easy winner. He admitted 'talking for victory', which meant that invective was his final resource in an argument, as **Oliver Goldsmith** ruefully observed:

'There's no arguing with Johnson; for when his pistol misses fire, he knocks you down with the butt end of it.'

NATIONAL LAMPOONS

What better target than the absurdities of nations and peoples?

Irish playwright **Bernard Shaw** on the maddening complacency of John Bull:

> *'The ordinary Britisher imagines that God is an Englishman.'*

The 'free-born Englishman' is a myth, according to **Bernard Shaw**:

> *'Englishmen never will be slaves; they are free to do whatever the Government and public opinion allow them to do.'*

English stolidity amused the American drama critic **Alexander Woollcott**:

> *'The English have an extraordinary ability for flying into a great calm.'*

Austin O'Malley on the impetuosity of his countrymen:

> *'An Englishman thinks seated; a Frenchman, standing; an American, pacing; an Irishman, afterwards.'*

A TALENT TO ABUSE

The English can be taciturn as well as stolid. In fact, the German poet **Heinrich Heine** simply notes:

'Silence: a conversation with an Englishman.'

Oscar Wilde, in his airy way, referred to

'One of those characteristic British faces that, once seen, are never remembered.'

TAKE THAT!

British insularity annoys their more cosmopolitan fellow-countrymen. Actor **Robert Morley**:

'The British tourist is always happy abroad so long as the natives are waiters.'

The American writer **Ralph Waldo Emerson** gives this crowning example of British wrong-headedness:

'An English lady on the Rhine hearing a German speaking of her party as foreigners, exclaimed, "No, we are not foreigners; we are English; it is you that are foreigners." '

Hungarian-born humorist **George Mikes'** view of the English seems unfairly dismissive:

'Continental people have sex life: the English have hot-water bottles.'

A TALENT TO ABUSE

A rather mild rejoinder to English insults came from the Scottish writer **John Wilson**:

> *'In all companies it gives me true pleasure to declare that, as a people, the English are very little indeed inferior to the Scotch.'*

Dr Johnson was strongly prejudiced against the Scots, and even included a sneer at their poverty in his famous dictionary:

> *'Oats. A grain which, in England is generally given to horses, but in Scotland supports the people.'*

Johnson, like many other Englishmen, resented the way in which able Scots left their own poor country to make careers across the Border. So, when a Scot defended his native land by saying it contained many 'noble wild prospects' (views), Johnson came back with

> *'Sir, the noblest prospect which a Scotchman ever sees is the high road that leads him to England!'*

Scots were believed to be humourless, and **Sydney Smith** declared that

'It requires a surgical operation to get a joke well into a Scotch understanding.'

At one time the Scots had a reputation for dubious financial transactions and insurance swindles. Hence the 19th century saying:

'Three failures and a fire make a Scotsman's fortune.'

Sacrilege – a calculated insult to a British national institution from politician-businessman **Lord Mancroft**:

'The British have never been spiritually minded people, so they invented cricket to give them some notion of eternity.'

A TALENT TO ABUSE

Oscar Wilde was born in Ireland and made his literary career in England . . . and found neither quite satisfactory:

> *'If one could only teach the English how to talk and the Irish how to listen, society would be quite civilized.'*

The poet **Samuel Taylor Coleridge** tries to explain away the military triumphs of the despised 'Frogs':

> *'Frenchmen are like grains of gunpowder – each by itself smutty and contemptible, but mass them together and they are terrible indeed.'*

Sir Henry Wotton, 17th century diplomat, had a love-hate relationship with Italy, which he described as

> *'A paradise inhabited with devils.'*

Dr Johnson exhibited one of his many national prejudices – here, inflamed by the successful American War of Independence against British rule:

> *'I am willing to love all mankind, except an American.'*

for

> *'They are a race of convicts, and ought to be thankful for any thing we allow them short of hanging.'*

More searchingly, **Johnson** asked:

> *'How is it that we hear the loudest yelps for liberty from the drivers of negroes?'*

A TALENT TO ABUSE

In one of his letters: **Bernard Shaw** made plain his feelings about visiting the USA:

'You are right in your impression that a number of persons are urging me to come to the United States. But why on earth do you call them my friends?'

Not all Americans have been fiercely patriotic. **Mark Twain** wrote:

'It was wonderful to find America, but it would have been more wonderful to miss it.'

Civil War leader **General Phil Sheridan** didn't love every part of the United States:

'If I owned Texas and Hell, I would rent out Texas and live in Hell.'

The American novelist **Henry James** settled in Europe – for good. He wrote to his sister:

'Dear Alice, I could come back to America (could be carried back on a stretcher) to die – but never, never to live.'

Dr Johnson's prejudices embraced the Irish as well as the Scots:

'The Irish are a fair people; they never speak well of one another.'

NICE ONE.

A TALENT TO ABUSE

In his play *A Woman of No Importance*, **Oscar Wilde** quotes the saying, 'When good Americans die, they go to Paris.'

> LADY HUNSTANTON: *Indeed? And when bad Americans die, where do they go to?*
> LORD ILLINGWORTH: *Oh, they go to America.*

Oscar Wilde's 'defence' of the United States:

> *'It is absurd to say that there are neither ruins nor curiosities in America when they have their mothers and their manners.'*

In his playful way, **Wilde** liked to pretend that America was a skeleton in the world's cupboard:

> *'Perhaps after all America has never been discovered? I myself would merely say that it has been detected!'*

> *'Of course America had often been discovered before Columbus, but it had always been hushed up.'*

This heartfelt cry of the weaker neighbour was uttered by Mexican leader **Porfirio Diaz**:

> *'Poor Mexico, so far from God and so near to the United States!'*

Insult or ignorance? Gangster Al Capone:

> *'I don't even know what street Canada is on.'*

GOVERNMENT CUTS

Politicians trade insults among themselves, and regularly receive them from outsiders.

A character in **Bernard Shaw**'s play *Major Barbara* says of a priggish young man:

> *'He knows nothing; and he thinks he knows everything. That points clearly to a political career.'*

Sir Winston Churchill on the equipment needed by a politician:

> *'It is the ability to foretell what is going to happen tomorrow, next week, next month, and next year. And to have the ability afterwards to explain why it didn't happen.'*

Prime Minister David Lloyd George was often accused of unfair tactics, especially by supporters of the prime minister he overthrew, H. H. Asquith. Naturally, the latter's daughter, woman of letters **Margot Asquith** felt the same way about Lloyd George. She said of him:

> *'He could not see a belt without hitting below it.'*

A TALENT TO ABUSE

Even in the 18th century the House of Lords was not known for its intellectual qualities. Debating whether the new peers for Westminster Bridge should be of stone or wood, **Lord Chesterfield** told the House:

> 'Of stone, to be sure, for we have too many wooden peers at Westminster already.'

Walter Bagehot, the greatest 19th century authority on the constitution, wrote;

> 'A severe though not unfriendly critic of our institutions has said that "the cure for admiring the House of Lords was to go and look at it".'

Lord Soper, Methodist minister and radical, on the present state of affairs:

> 'The House of Lords . . . is good evidence of life after death.'

A character in **Oscar Wilde**'s *A Woman of No Importance* on breeding and pedigree:

> 'You should study the Peerage, Gerald . . . It is the best thing in fiction the English have ever done.'

Only two cheers for democracy from **Bernard Shaw**:

> 'Democracy substitutes election by the incompetent many for appointment by the corrupt few.'

The elegant wit of the 18th century: when the Earl of Sandwich predicted that the radical **John Wilkes** would die either on the gallows or from the pox, Wilkes replied smoothly:

> *'That will depend, my Lord, on whether I embrace your principles or your mistress.'*

Sydney Smith was a diehard Tory. When he saw the Whig politician Lord Brougham arrive in the hall during a performance of Handel's *Messiah*, Smith remarked:

> *'Here comes counsel for the other side.'*

Victorian politicians tended to be a solemn lot, but **Benjamin Disraeli** was an exception. He first made himself felt by attacking the coldly correct Sir Robert Peel:

> *'The Right Honourable Gentleman's smile is like the silver fittings on a coffin.'*

> *'The Right Honourable Gentleman is reminiscent of a poker. The only difference is that a poker gives off occasional signs of warmth.'*

In the 1860s and '70s politics was dominated by the rivalry between Disraeli and Gladstone. No wonder **Disraeli**, when asked to distinguish between a misfortune and a calamity, said:

> *'If Gladstone fell into the Thames, that would be a misfortune, and if anybody pulled him out, that, I suppose, would be a calamity.'*

The quiet Labour leader Clement Attlee was one of **Sir Winston Churchill**'s victims:

> *'He's a sheep in sheep's clothing.'*

> *'Mr Attlee is a modest man. But then he has much to be modest about.'*

Quite early in his career **Sir Winston Churchill** had mastered the art of parliamentary abuse, which must be restrained but deadly:

> 'Lord Charles Beresford can best be described as one of those orators who, before they get up, do not know what they are going to say; when they are speaking, do not know what they are saying, and when they have sat down, do not know what they have said.'

When **Churchill** wanted to attack Prime Minister Ramsay MacDonald, he told the House of Commons how he had been taken to the circus as a child but had not been allowed to see an exhibit called The Boneless Wonder . . .

> 'My parents judged that this spectacle would be too revolting and demoralizing for my youthful eyes, and I have waited fifty years to see The Boneless Wonder sitting on the Treasury Bench.'

On another occasion **Churchill** mocked MacDonald's rather windy eloquence:

> 'We know that he has, more than any other man, the gift of compressing the largest amount of words into the smallest amount of thought.'

One of the few men to score off Disraeli was the Radical, **John Bright**. On being told that, whatever his faults, 'Dizzy' deserved credit for being a self-made man, Bright remarked:

> 'He is a self-made man and worships his creator.'

A TALENT TO ABUSE

Labour's **Aneurin Bevan** made fun of Winston Churchill's romantic Toryism and fondness for the sound of his own voice:

'He is a man suffering from petrified adolescence.'

'He never spares himself in conversation. He gives himself so generously that hardly anybody else is permitted to give anything in his presence.'

Aneurin Bevan, a fiery Welshman, found his leaders somewhat lacking in socialist fervour. Of Clement Attlee:

'He seems determined to make a trumpet sound like a tin whistle.'

Of Hugh Gaitskell:

'A desiccated calculating machine.' BOOM! BOOM!

Speaking in the House of Commons **Aneurin Bevan** said he would not bother to attack the Foreign Secretary, Selwyn Lloyd, when the Prime Minister, Harold Macmillan, was present. Implying that the relationship between the two was that of servant and master, Bevan quipped:

'There is no reason to attack the monkey when the organ-grinder is present.'

In 1962 Harold Macmillan dismissed a third of his Cabinet in an attempt to save his largely discredited government. Liberal MP Jeremy Thorpe commented:

'Greater love hath no man than this, that he lay down his friends for his life.'

A TALENT TO ABUSE

The two leading Conservatives of the early 1960s, Harold Macmillan and R. A. Butler, were colleagues but not necessarily the best of friends. Labour leader **Harold Wilson** professed to believe that

'Every time Mr Macmillan comes back from abroad, Mr Butler goes to the airport and grips him warmly by the throat.'

In the 1960s and '70s much was heard of Harold Wilson's poverty-stricken childhood. There were a number of sceptics, including MP **Ivor Bulwer-Thomas**:

'If Harold Wilson ever went to school without any boots it was merely because he was too big for them.'

Americans have, if anything, a lower opinion of politicians than the British do. Humorist **Artemus Ward**:

'I'm not a politician and my other habits are good.'

Presidential candidate **Adlai Stevenson** on the highest office:

'In America any boy may become President, and I suppose that's just the risk he takes.'

Gladstone was a good man . . . but . . . according to **Disraeli**:

'He has not a single redeeming defect.'

A TALENT TO ABUSE

Novelist **Gore Vidal** on Ronald Reagan, the oldest man ever to become US President:

'A triumph of the embalmer's art.'

Mark Twain delivers an eccentric judgement on George Washington:

'He was ignorant of the commonest accomplishments of youth. He could not even lie.'

Congressman **John Randolph** of Roanoak came face to face with his enemy Henry Clay.

CLAY: *I, sir, do not step aside for a scoundrel.*

RANDOLPH: *On the other hand* (stepping aside) *I always do.*

Coolidge was known as a man who did little and said even less. When the New York wit **Dorothy Parker** was told that he had died, she asked:

'How can they tell?'

Comedian **Mort Sahl**'s classic query about 'Tricky Dicky' – Richard Nixon:

'Would you buy a second-hand car from this man?'

A TALENT TO ABUSE

Mark Twain was sceptical about 'the American way':

'It is by the grace of God that in our country we have those three unspeakably precious things: freedom of speech, freedom of conscience, and the prudence never to practise either of them.'

Democrat **Adlai Stevenson** mocked the solemn style of his rival, General Dwight D. Eisenhower:

'The General has dedicated himself so many times, he must feel like the cornerstone of a public building.'

Thomas Dewey became Republican candidate for the presidency as a young man (by the standards of politics, anyway). Hence this comment by US Secretary of the Interior **Harold L. Ickes**:

'Dewey has thrown his diaper into the ring.'

Eisenhower's Secretary of State, Dulles, practised a belligerent 'brinkmanship' in his diplomacy. US trade union leader **Walter Reuther** called him

'Mr John Foster Dulles – the world's longest-range mis-guided missile.'

PROFESSIONALLY FOUL

The art of insult is perhaps most subtly practised among the learned professions. . . .

The famous advocate **F. E. Smith** often clashed with the Bench. When a judge declared that Smith's remarks had not left him much the wiser, Smith retorted:

> *'Not wiser, my Lord. But better informed.'*

> EXASPERATED JUDGE: *What do you suppose I am on the Bench for, Mr Smith?*

> F. E. SMITH: *It is not for me to fathom the inscrutable ways of Providence.*

The **Reverend Sydney Smith** did not spare other men of the cloth. When a proposal was made to surround St Paul's with a wooden pavement, he suggested:

> *'Let the Dean and Canons lay their heads together and the thing will be done.'*

Novelist **Arnold Bennett** finds a good reason for putting writers on the Honours List:

> *'Literature is always a good card to play for Honours. It makes people think that Cabinet ministers are educated.'*

A TALENT TO ABUSE

Alexander Pope's malicious portrait of the scholar:

> *The bookful blockhead, ignorantly read,*
> *With loads of learned lumber in his head.*

Army life – one of the less healthy professions, according to
H. G. Wells:

> *'The army ages men sooner than the law and philosophy; it*
> *exposes them more freely to germs, which undermine and*
> *destroy, and it shelters them more completely from thought,*
> *which stimulates and preserves.'*

Voltaire on the physician's skills:

> *'The art of medicine consists of amusing the patient while*
> *Nature cures the disease.'*

According to **Hilaire Belloc**, in the days before the inception of
the National Health Service it was only doctors who were certain
to benefit from medical care:

> *They answered as they took their fees*
> *'There is no cure for this disease.'*

Liberal leader **Lord Samuel** found that the civil servant was a
born obstructionist with

> *'A difficulty for every solution.'*

NICE ONE

SHOT DOWN IN FAME

The famous and the powerful have frequently borne the brunt of much witty invective. . . .

The historian Lord Macaulay maddened his contemporaries with his encyclopaedic knowledge and monopolizing of conversation:

THOMAS CARLYLE: *Macaulay is well for a while, but one wouldn't live under Niagara.*

Jim Fiske was the most notorious of the ruthless and crooked US financiers who flourished in the 'gilded age' after the American Civil War. One anonymous wit noticed him and said:

'There goes Jim Fiske, with his hands in his own pockets for a change.'

Randolph Churchill, Sir Winston's son and biographer, was a spiky character; and so was novelist **Evelyn Waugh**. When he heard that Randolph had had a non-malignant growth removed, Waugh wrote:

'A typical triumph of modern science to find the only part of Randolph that was not malignant – and remove it.'

A TALENT TO ABUSE

The writer Frank Harris was a powerful personality, but socially impossible. **Oscar Wilde** remarked on the result:

'Frank has been invited to every great house in England – once.'

Sir Winston Churchill on the most successful of his generals, Viscount Montgomery:

'In defeat unbeatable; in victory unbearable.'

Socialite **Margot Asquith** was introduced to film actress Jean Harlow, who irritated her by pronouncing the 't' in Margot – only to be told that

'The 't' is silent – as in Harlow.'

BOOM!
BOOM!

Kitty Muggeridge, wife of the celebrated writer and broadcaster, on the career of TV presenter David Frost:

'He rose without trace.'

Count Paul Waldersee on 'Kaiser Bill' (Wilhelm II of Germany):

'He can be most fascinating, and win hearts wherever he goes – and doesn't stay.'

SEXUAL ABUSE

The notorious 'battle of the sexes' has inspired some of the most sublime of all bitchy remarks. . . .

SAMUEL BUTLER (17th century satirical poet):

> *The souls of women are so small*
> *That some believe they've none at all.*

MADAME DE STAEL (18th century French woman of letters):

> *'The more I see of men, the more I like dogs.'*

Men have abused women so thoroughly and so often that it seems likely that they have been trying to compensate for something . . . **Max Beerbohm**:

> *'Most women are not so young as they are painted.'*

Oscar Wilde:

> *'Women give men the very gold of their lives. But they invariably want it back in small change.'*

A TALENT TO ABUSE

Good old **Anonymous**:

'Women's styles may change, but their designs remain the same.'

GROAN!

Heinrich Heine:

'As soon as Eve ate the apple of wisdom, she reached for the fig-leaf; when a woman begins to think, her first thought is of a new dress.'

Anonymous strikes again:

'A youthful figure is what you get when you ask a woman her age.'

Oscar Wilde:

'One should never trust a woman who tells one her real age. A woman who would tell one that would tell one anything.'

Sometimes women have joined the chorus condemning their own sex. **Diane de Poitiers**, the French king's mistress some 450 years ago, observed that

'The years that a woman subtracts from her age are not lost. They are added to the ages of other women.'

A TALENT TO ABUSE

American writer **H. L. Mencken** noted that

'When women kiss it always reminds me of prize-fighters shaking hands.'

Victorian novelist **George Meredith** writes with missionary assurance:

'I expect that Woman will be the last thing civilized by Man.'

Dr Johnson's famous put-down of a woman who did something she wasn't supposed to be capable of:

'Sir, a woman's preaching is like a dog's walking on his hind legs. It is not done well; but you are surprised to find it done at all.'

Women abuse men as a sex far less frequently than vice-versa. One exception was the American commentator **Helen Rowland**:

'The only original thing about some men is original sin.'

'Nowadays most women grow old gracefully; most men, disgracefully.'

One of the woman novelist **George Eliot**'s characters sums up the difference between women and men:

'I'm not denyin' the women are foolish: God Almighty made 'em to match the men.'

WEDDING SNAPS

The institution of marriage has taken a few hard verbal knocks in its time. . . .

Dramatist **William Congreve** on Before and After Wedlock:

'*Courtship to marriage, as a very witty prologue to a very dull play.*'

A TALENT TO ABUSE

An anonymous male (probably a cowardly husband) claims that:

'Bigamy is having one wife too many. Monogamy is the same thing.'

Lord Chesterfield's solution to marital troubles:

'The only solid and lasting peace between a man and his wife is doubtless a separation.'

Samuel Pepys observed that misery loves company:

'Strange to say what delight we married people have to see these poor fools decoyed into our condition.'

The last word is still **St Paul**'s:

'Better marry than burn!'

Helen Rowland's view of the morning after:

'There is a vast difference beween the savage and the civilized man, but it is never apparent to their wives until after breakfast.'

POISON PENS

Writers and writings have received (and inflicted) a wide variety of criticism and contempt. . . .

The born critic can work on any material — witness the American girl who was heard to complain about the Ten Commandments:

'They don't tell you what you ought *to do, and only put ideas into your head.'*

A critic, **Kenneth Tynan**, on his own trade:

> 'A critic is a man who knows the way but can't drive the car.'

The creative impotence of critics was expressed with maximum unkindness by the Irish playwright **Brendan Behan**:

> 'Critics are like eunuchs in a harem: they know how it's done, they've seen it done every day, but they're unable to do it themselves.'

Poet laureate **Lord Tennyson** strikes down critic John Churton Collins:

> 'A louse in the locks of literature.'

Relations between publishers and authors are often little better than those between authors and critics. A publisher's view, from **Michael Joseph**:

> 'Authors are easy enough to get on with – if you are fond of children.'

The subtlest rebuff to an author was probably **Disraeli**'s ambiguous acknowledgement:

> 'Many thanks for your book; I shall lose no time in reading it.'

A poet, **John Dryden**, on critics:

> They who write ill, and they who ne'r durst write,
> Turn critics out of mere revenge and spite.

A TALENT TO ABUSE

Same message, but in different style, from **Groucho Marx**:

'From the moment I picked up your book until I laid it down I was convulsed with laughter. Some day I intend reading it.'

As we might expect, **Dr Johnson** brought his mastery of insult to bear on contemporary literature. Asked whether Herrick or Smart was the better writer, he replied:

'Sir, there is no settling the precedency between a louse and a flea.'

On one occasion **Johnson** showed his opinion of a fellow-author by complaining:

'Sir, I never did the man an injury; yet he would read his tragedy to me.'

Dorothy Parker on a work of fiction:

'This is not a novel to be tossed aside lightly. It should be thrown with great force.'

TAKE THAT!

A. A. Milne's whimsical stories about Winnie the Pooh and Christopher Robin did not appeal to **Dorothy Parker**. Reviewing *The House at Pooh Corner* in her 'Constant Reader' column, she came to a point in the book at which:

'Tonstant Weader fwowed up.'

A TALENT TO ABUSE

Reviewing A. A. Milne's play *Give Me Yesterday*, **Dorothy Parker** wrote sarcastically:

'Its hero is caused, by a novel device, to fall asleep and a-dream; and thus he is given yesterday. Me, I should have given him twenty years to life.'

One of the books **Dorothy Parker** most disliked was *The Autobiography of Margot Asquith*. The tone of the autobiography can be gathered from **Dorothy Parker**'s comment that

'The affair between Margot Asquith and Margot Asquith will live as one of the prettiest love stories in all literature.'

Parker defined an optimist as

'One who thought that Margot Asquith wasn't going to write any more.'

Complaints about obscurity in literature are not new. **King James I** said of the poet John Donne:

'Dr Donne's verses are like the peace of God; they pass all understanding.'

In speaking, a pause makes all the difference. When the poet Southey fished for compliments to his epic *Madoc*, the classical scholar **Richard Porson** told him:

'Madoc will be remembered . . . when Homer and Virgil are forgotten.'

A TALENT TO ABUSE

While **Charles Dickens** was editing a magazine, a young poet submitted 'Orient Pearls at Random Strung' to him.
The novelist returned it with the comment:

'Too much string.'

Oscar Wilde on the pugnacious versifier W. E. Henley:

'He has fought a good fight and has had to face every difficulty except – popularity.'

Of a famous Victorian tear-jerker, Dickens's *Old Curiosity Shop*, **Oscar Wilde** remarked:

'One must have a heart of stone to read the death of little Nell without laughing.'

Oscar Wilde swats a novelist and a poet with a single blow:

'Meredith is a prose Browning, and so is Browning.'

Oscar Wilde's opinion of a ponderously portentous contemporary:

'Henry James writes fiction as if it were a painful duty.'

Novelist **Virginia Woolf** was not impressed when she read James Joyce's once-shocking *Ulysses*, dismissing it as

'The work of a queasy undergraduate scratching his pimples.'

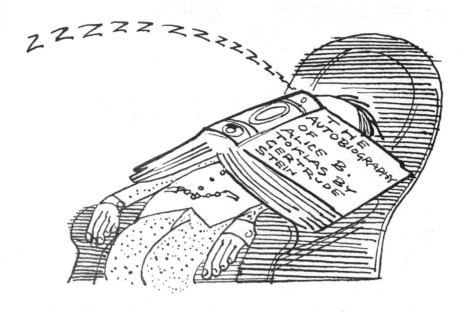

The American critic **Clifton Fadiman** on the experimental writing of Gertrude Stein:

> *'Miss Stein was a past master in making nothing happen very slowly.'*

When Gertrude Stein published *Everybody's Autobiography*, **Fadiman** wrote that

> *'I found nothing really wrong with this autobiography except poor choice of subject.'*

The poet **Philip Larkin** says of modern novels:

> *'Many have a beginning, a muddle, and an end.'*

A TALENT TO ABUSE

Logan Pearsall Smith on the rewards and punishments of popular fiction:

'A best-seller is the gilded tomb of a mediocre talent.'

American drama critic **Eugene Field** gave this classic verdict on an actor's nervous and understated performance as King Lear:

'Mr Clark played the King as though somebody else might be about to play the Ace.' ──── NICE ONE ────

A characteristic shaft from well-known New York critic **Walter Kerr**:

'Hook and Ladder is the sort of play that gives failures a bad name.'

The *Punch* writer **Douglas Jerrold**, when told that the actor Henry Holl had left the stage and set up as a wine merchant, commented:

'Oh yes, and I'm told that his wine off the stage is better than his whine on it.'

Irish dramatist Bernard Shaw dominated – and irritated – several generations with his talents . . . which included a gift for self-advertisement. The writer **'Saki'** satirized Shaw as

'Sherard Blaw, the dramatist who had discovered himself, and who had given so ungrudgingly of his discovery to the world.'

Israel Zangwill on Shaw:

> *'The way Bernard Shaw believes in himself is very refreshing in these atheistic days when so many people believe in no God at all.'*

Bernard Shaw combined universal benevolence with insufferable conceit. The result, according to **Oscar Wilde**, was that

> *'He hasn't an enemy in the world, and none of his friends like him.'*

The playwright **Henry Arthur Jones** developed an obsessive hatred of Bernard Shaw, whom he described as a b-----, or at any rate

> *'A freakish homunculus germinated outside lawful procreation.'*

After the first night of one of **Oscar Wilde**'s plays, an ill-wisher handed him – a cabbage. Unruffled, Wilde sniffed it appreciatively and said:

> *'Thank you, my dear fellow. Every time I smell it, I shall be reminded of you.'*

Writer **Rose Macaulay** describes a piece of over-light entertainment:

> *'It was a book to kill time for those who like it better dead.'*

153

MOVIE MOCKERY

The moguls and stars of the film business have refined the snide retort to a fine art. . . .

Even in the palmiest days of Hollywood, writers were not treated with much respect by the big producers. The famous novelist **Scott Fitzgerald** noted:

'You always knew where you stood with Sam Goldwyn: nowhere.'

Screenwriter **Herman Mankiewicz** had a poor opinion of screen-writers:

'I know lots of $75 a week writers, but they're all making $1,500 a week.'

The producer knows best: Hungarian-born **Joe Pasternak**:

'You call this a script? Give me a couple of $5,000 a week writers and I'll write it myself.'

Irish writer **St John Ervine**:

> 'American motion pictures are written by the half-educated for the half-witted.'

Humorist **Will Rogers** had much the same opinion:

> 'There is only one thing that can kill the movies; and that is education.'

Louis Sherwin on Hollywood standards:

> 'They know only one word of more than one syllable here, and that is fillum.'

GROAN!

Columnist **Walter Winchell** called Hollywood

> 'A place where they shoot too many pictures and not enough actors.'

Curiously enough, one of the greatest American directors, **D. W. Griffith**, was scornful of Hollywood's pretensions:

> 'The Academy of Motion Picture Arts and Sciences? What art? What science?'

Hollywood gossip columnist **Hedda Hopper** went to the cinema and

'For the first time in my life I envied my feet. They were asleep.'

Hollywood's men of power were not popular. **Herman Mankiewicz** on Louis B. Mayer:

'There, but for the grace of God, goes God.'

French writer and film director **Jean Cocteau** on a technical advance pioneered by Hollywood in the belief that 'Big is Beautiful':

'CinemaScope? The next time I write a poem I shall use a larger piece of paper.'

Harry Cohn was the legendarily unpleasant and colossally unpopular head of Colombia Pictures. Observing the throng at his funeral, actor **Red Skelton** remarked:

'It proves what they always say: give the public what they want, and they'll come out for it.'

Sid Grauman:

'I saw this empty taxicab drive up, and out stepped Sam Goldwyn.'

Film director **Billy Wilder** welcomed the arrival of television:

'I'm delighted with it, because it used to be that films were the lowest form of art. Now we've got something to look down on.'

Sam Goldwyn explained why there were crowds at Louis B. Mayer's funeral:

'The only reason so many people showed up was to make sure he was dead.'

ART ATTACKS

The creative fraternity are often the target of cruel and sarcastic wit. . . .

Basic music criticism from **Dr Johnson**, after hearing a violinist:

'Difficult do you call it, Sir? I wish it were impossible.'

Ludwig van Beethoven to a fellow-composer:

'I liked your opera. I think I will set it to music.'

Rossini's opinion of a younger competitor:

'Monsieur Wagner has lovely moments but some terrible quarters-of-an-hour.'

Oscar Wilde had nothing (well, almost nothing) but praise for the Teutonic thunder of Wagner's operas:

'I like Wagner's music better than any other music. It is so loud that one can talk the whole time without people hearing what one says. That is a great advantage.'

Mark Twain proffered a back-handed compliment to the German genius:

> *'Wagner's music is better than it sounds.'*

Hollywood columnist **Hedda Hopper** reviews:

> *'Her singing was mutiny on the High Cs.'*

Orson Welles's opinion of teenybopper idol Donny Osmond:

> *'He has Van Gogh's ear for music.'* — *TAKE THAT!*

Oscar Levant on the kidnapping of Frank Sinatra Jr:

> *'It must have been done by music critics.'*

Nancy Banks Smith voices a widely held view of 'modernism' and 'post-modernism':

> *'If you have to keep the lavatory door shut by extending your left leg, it's modern architecture.'*

Two cracks at the man with the camera, by American novelist **Gore Vidal**:

> *'Photography is the "art form" of the untalented.'*
> *'One word is worth a thousand pictures.'*

A TALENT TO ABUSE

Albert Wolff, an influential critic who attacked the
Impressionist painters, was also a singularly ugly man. Degas
dismissed Wolff's comments, saying:

> *'How could he understand? He came to Paris by way of the
> trees.'*

When the art critic **John Ruskin** dared to attack the painter
James McNeill Whistler he was sued. Yet all Ruskin said was:

> *'I have seen, and heard, much of cockney impudence before
> now; but never expected to hear a coxcomb ask two hundred
> guineas for flinging a pot of paint in the public's face.'*

As a young man, Oscar Wilde regarded himself as **Whistler**'s
disciple. When Whistler coined a particularly brilliant epigram,
Wilde sighed 'I wish I'd said that!'

> *'You will, Oscar. You will.'*

I DON'T BELIEVE IT!

ILLUSTRATED BY BILL TIDY

CONTENTS

Cops and Robbers

... or the long arm of the law ...

Keeping It in the Family

A woman in Mexico was caught red-handed stealing a juicy piece of meat from her local supermarket. She was marched off to the manager's office to be detained while the police were called. But there was much consternation amongst the staff when the policeman who arrived to arrest her turned out to be none other than her husband. . .

A Rash Porker

A sow and her six piglets were once tried in France on a charge of having killed a child. The defendants were found guilty, and the sow executed. But the defending lawyer managed to get the piglets off with a caution, on the grounds of their extreme youth and the fact that they had been influenced by the bad example of their mother.

Meanwhile, in Switzerland a cockerel was tried for the diabolical crime of laying an egg! Back in the fifteenth century it was believed that a cock's egg in the hands of a witch was evilly potent. The unfortunate rooster was found guilty, sentenced and burned at the stake – along with the egg.

DIY Organ Scholar

Hertfordshire church organists could never be certain that all would be well when they pulled out the stops for a special occasion. There was an outbreak of theft by what the police described as 'an organ nut'. The thief was taking out the pipes – and other bits and pieces – at an alarming rate.

The Rev. Keith Arnold, whose parishes suffered most, was convinced that it was not the work of a scrap thief, who would have taken larger quantities of lead pipes from each organ. He said, 'This can only mean that the parts are being taken by someone wanting to build their own organ.'

Small But Beautiful

In the Western world, more than five million people are engaged in law and its enforcement. (That is the equivalent of the whole population of Scotland.)

Will Rogers, an American noted for his wit and wisdom, said, 'When you read something you can't understand, you can almost be sure it was drawn up by a lawyer.'

In Andorra there is only one lawyer, and he is not allowed to appear in court. In that tiny country this decree was issued in 1864: 'The appearance in our courts of the learned gentlemen of the law, who can make black appear white and white appear black, is forbidden.'

. . . . . *An inventor in America worked night and day to develop a foolproof burglar alarm, and almost completed the first model. But then, unfortunately, his laboratory was burgled and the alarm stolen* . . . .

The Price of Red Tape

One evening in 1867, a poorly-clad man was shown into Lord Shaftesbury's study in London. The man warned that desperate Irishmen were planning to blow up Clerkenwell Prison.

Lord Shaftesbury believed him and hurried to Whitehall to warn the authorities. They demanded the informant's name and address, which Lord Shaftesbury admitted he was unable to give them.

The authorities then declared, 'There is nothing we can do. We have to disregard any information unless the name and address of the informant are given.'

Clerkenwell Prison was blown up within 24 hours. There were 37 dead and 120 injured.

The Right Place at the Right Time

A wife in Texas had had quite enough of her drunken husband, so she decided to teach him a lesson. She put in an emergency call to the police and requested that they come round immediately.

When the police arrived, she took them into the hall, pointed to her prostrate husband, and demanded that they arrest him. The officers pointed out that there was no law to prevent a man being drunk in his own home. But this failed to satisfy the infuriated wife. She dragged her husband into the street and insisted that the police arrest him there.

Set a Thief to Catch a Thief

The choice of guardians of the law in the 19th century left a lot to be desired.

At Chesham in Buckinghamshire, for example, the man appointed to be constable, thief-taker and peace-officer, was known to have been publicly flogged in Chesham, privately flogged at Aylesbury Gaol, once convicted of stealing lead and once committed to hard labour for assaulting and robbing a boy.

Bumper Hair Harvest

People in a small Oxfordshire village at the end of the last century were robbed of their crowning glory by a wigmaker who used a unique ploy to get his raw materials.

The man, wearing a badge with an authoritative look, called at each house in the village. He announced himself as a Government Barber from London, sent to cut the people's hair for free, as this was the most effective way of avoiding cholera.

So thorough was the trim given to the villagers that they were left almost bald.

Not So Well Read

Nothing went right for would-be robber David Morris. He was passing time before a date with his girlfriend when he wrote a note which said, 'I have got a gun in my pocket and I'll shoot it off unless you hand over the money.'

The amateur thief then went to three shops in London and passed the note over the counter – all with no success. In the first the girl assistant refused to accept the note, believing it contained an obscene suggestion, in the second an Asian assistant shook his head and said he couldn't read English and in the third the shopkeeper explained that he couldn't read the note without his glasses.

Priority for an Old Score

There was considerable excitement at an Irish murder trial when the 'corpse' made a sudden appearance in the court. As the hubbub died down, the judge told the jury to bring in the obvious verdict. The foreman immediately declared that the defendant was guilty.

The bewildered judge bellowed, 'But the murdered man is alive!'

Came the reply, 'Be that as it may. All I know is that the defendant stole my brown mare.'

. . . . . A thief who helped himself to both money and jewellery, told the judge, 'I believe that money alone does not ensure happiness.'. . . . .

Gotcha!

Lord Macaulay, the famous historian, was in Rome on holiday. One evening after dinner he decided to take a stroll to the Colosseum. On the way a dark figure in a cloak brushed against him. Soon after, Macaulay found that his watch was missing.

Being no weakling, Macaulay immediately gave chase and overtook his quarry. As communication proved impossible, neither being able to speak the other's language, the encounter ended in a struggle in the semi-darkness, during which the Italian was forced to hand over a watch. Feeling well satisfied with himself, Macaulay walked back to his lodgings.

There, he was greeted by his landlady who said, 'Excuse me, *signor*, I have put your watch on the dressing-table in your room. I found it in the dining-room after you'd gone.'

Tale of a Misspent Youth

Some citizens are so law-abiding that any slight misdemeanour hangs heavily on their conscience for the rest of their lives. One such was a defendant at a Southend court, who was asked if he had had any previous convictions.

The poor soul told the court that once during the war he had been unable to produce his identity card. He had been wearing a bathing costume at the time.

'Wild Bill's A-comin'!'

The last thing Wild Bill Hickock wanted was to be what he became – the greatest gunfighter in the West. It all began when he was accidentally involved in a gunfight in which he shot two roughnecks in self-defence.

Rumour spread quickly in the sensation-hungry West. One printed report stated that Hickock had stood at bay with a six-gun, an Indian knife and a rifle, and fought ten men. When the smoke cleared, all ten lay shot and slashed to death.

Bill tried to deny these stories but people thought he was just being modest. Wherever he went, folk murmured fearfully, 'Wild Bill's a-comin'!' As he became the target for every local killer who hoped to win fame by outgunning this hero, Bill realized that the length of his life depended on his becoming an expert with a gun. And that's what he became, by long hours of hard work and practice.

Bill learned to take other precautions too – like never sitting with his back to the door of a saloon. But one day in 1876 he forgot this golden rule. A roughneck with ambitions to be a famous gunfighter walked into the saloon, spotted his advantage, and pumped lead into Hickock. Wild Bill was dead before his body hit the sawdust-covered floor.

Sand in their Eyes

Twice a week a Belgian riding a bicycle crossed the German border and he always carried a suitcase filled with sand. Each time the customs officials searched the suitcase for contraband, but always in vain.

Sometimes they even emptied all the sand out, expecting to find jewellery, watches or even drugs. But always there was nothing but sand. They racked their brains – what was this Belgian smuggling? He must be selling something over the border!

It was many years later, long after the Belgian had vanished from the scene, that they learned the truth. He had been smuggling . . . bicycles!

170

On to the Millennium

A 76-year-old man appeared before magistrates in Leeds on his 500th charge of drunkenness. He was given an absolute discharge. But a few days later he turned up for the 501st time. His defence was that he had been celebrating the 500th anniversary.

He was fined 50p.

..... *When a golfing judge asked a boy in the witness-box if he understood the nature of an oath, the lad replied, 'Don't I! Aren't I your caddie?'* ....

One Bad Apple

When Pope Leo XII visited a jail, he insisted on asking every prisoner how he had come to be there. All the prisoners except one protested his innocence. Just one man admitted that he had been rightly convicted.

The Pope turned to the prison superintendent and said, 'Release this rascal at once. I do not wish that his presence should corrupt all these noble gentlemen here!'

If At First You Don't Succeed

A lawsuit in India dragged on for 761 years until it was finally settled in 1966.

The case was first lost in 1205 but the descendants of the plaintiff were a stubborn lot. They just refused to drop it until a judgement was given in their favour.

And their reward? The right to officiate at public functions and precedence at religious festivals.

Shot With His Own Gun

An Australian on an outing into the bush was bitten by a snake. He had no knife to open the wound and drain the poison, so he shot himself in order to bleed the area. Before passing out, he even managed to tie a tourniquet round his arm.

A short time later a group of walkers found him and hurried him off to hospital. He made a good recovery but the happy ending was spoiled when he was visited in hospital by a police detective. He was charged with carrying a firearm on a Sunday and fined £2.

One Law for the Law

A man in Teeside was taken to court for making a two-fingered gesture at a High Court judge in the street. He explained that the gesture had been intended for the mayor. He was acquitted.

An Arm for the Law

A lawyer was defending a man charged with housebreaking. The lawyer stated that his client had merely inserted his arm through a broken window and removed a few articles.

'As my client's arm is not himself,' the lawyer argued, 'I fail to see why the whole individual should be punished because of an offence by one of his limbs.'

The judge thought about this, and said, 'The sentence is one year in prison for the defendant's arm. The defendant can accompany his arm or not, as he chooses.'

The defendant detached his artificial arm, placed it on the desk, and walked from the court.

172

A Mugger Mugged

A attempted street robbery ended up with an intended victim being charged with the killing of the assailant.

The accused told the court that the deceased had ordered him to hand over his wife's purse. The purse was in a basket on the ground. So he bent down, put his hands up his wife's skirt, detached her wooden leg, and battered the assailant on the head with it.

173

Twelve Good Persons and True

A murder trial in America ended before it began, during the swearing in of the jury. One of the jurymen asked the judge to speak louder because he was very deaf.

Investigation of the jury revealed that another man, who was stone deaf, thought the trial had something to do with divorce; three could not understand English; and another had come to the court for a gun licence.

Shome Mishtake Surely?

Printed in the *Ely Standard*:

'We apologize for the error in last week's paper in which we stated that Mr Arnold Dogbody was a defective in the police force. This was a typographical error. We meant, of course, that Mr Dogbody is a detective in the police farce and we are sorry for any embarrassment caused.'

Indecent Exposure

It's not often that a burglar asks the police for help, especially when he's on a job. But sometimes there are extenuating circumstances . . .

In this particular case the wily villain had been trying to break through a skylight into a supermarket but found that either he was too big or it was too small. So he took off his clothes and tried again – throwing everything down into the shop below him. But finally he was forced to admit defeat – and was left standing stark naked on the roof of the store.

It was then that he shouted for help, and a passing policeman obliged. After all, at least it was warm in the cell!

Not So Horny

A thief who stole a rhino horn – believed in the Far East to be an aphrodisiac – from a Brighton museum failed to find his sex life pepped up much . . . it had been treated with a harmful chemical preservative.

Long Arm of the Law

From a US college magazine: 'The British legal system is the best in the world. Each case is tried with scrupulous fairness and justice is not only done, it is seen to be done. There are no inflexible rules: the law is elastic.' Which is why some people get longer stretches than others.

. . . . . *A British judge went to great pains to explain the rules of insanity to a jury. When the verdict on the case was returned, the foreman said, 'We are all of one mind – insane.'* . . . .

Enough's Enough

The jury had been out for hours, and the judge was growing impatient. A young man was charged with the savage murder of both parents, and it seemed obvious to everyone that he was guilty.

The judge recalled the jury and asked if he could give them any further guidance. The foreman declined, saying that they understood the evidence very clearly. The jury continued to deliberate.

Hours passed, and the jury finally returned with a verdict of 'Not guilty'. There was a gasp in the court and the judge almost exploded. Forgetting himself, he fumed, 'But we all know the prisoner's guilty and should hang!'

The foreman said, 'That's the trouble, My Lord. We don't doubt the prisoner's guilt, but don't you think there have been enough deaths in that family lately?'

A Sad Case of Self-Destruction

A man in Bangkok informed police that his watch had been stolen, and that he knew who had taken it. The informant believed that the thief had been on the wanted list for some months.

He told the police where the criminal could be found, and he even gave them a photograph to help with identification.

The police carried out a raid, shots were fired, and one man was killed. Alas, he turned out to be the informer. The police apologized to his family, but explained that he had sent them a photograph of himself by mistake.

. . . . . *A woman convicted of killing her husband with a kitchen knife applied for a widow's allowance. The application was refused* . . . .

Devil Women

In the Book of Exodus in the Bible, it says, 'Thou shalt not suffer a witch to live.' It was this sentence that inspired Pope Innocent VIII to create the Inquisition, an organization of men with the authority to imprison, convict and punish those guilty of witchcraft.

Ways of determining whether or not a woman was a witch were bizarre. Suspects were first examined by an experienced witchfinder. He searched the woman's body for a 'devil's bite'. This was any mark on the body that experienced no pain, or showed no blood when pricked with a needle or knife.

Another form of trial was to tie the woman's legs together, and throw her into deep water. If she floated, then she was considered guilty. If she sank, she was innocent.

During the three hundred years from 1484, the Christian Church put to death 300,000 women convicted of witchcraft.

176

That Guilty Feeling

A defendant in a closely contested case was unable to attend court because of illness. The verdict was in his favour, so his solicitor sent him a cable which read: 'Justice has triumphed!'

To which the client replied, 'We must appeal at once!'

Dummy

Magistrates ruled that a Scotsman acted in the public interest when he leapt into a shop front and wrestled with a tailor's dummy early one New Year's Day.

The Scot had been charged with housebreaking, but his defence was that he had heard a crash of glass from a shop and had seen two men running away. He also thought he saw a third man through the plate-glass window. There was a large hole in the glass, he explained, so he jumped through it and landed on the tailor's dummy.

It was at this point that the police arrested him.

The Law is an Ass

In 1819 the penalty for impersonating a Chelsea pensioner was death.

In Quebec, Canada, it is illegal to sell anti-freeze to Indians.

In Minnesota, USA, it is against the law to hang male and female underwear on the same line.

In Saskatchewan, USA, you must not drink water in a beer parlour.

In El Paso, Texas, all public buildings must be equipped with 'spittoons of a kind and number to efficiently contain expectorations into them . . .'

A transportation law in Texas: 'When two trains approach each other at a crossing, they should both stop, and neither shall start up until the other has gone.'

In Waterloo, Nebraska, it is illegal for a barber to eat onions between 7 a.m. and 7 p.m.

The Council of Widnes, Lancashire, introduced a fine of £5 for those who made a habit of falling asleep in the reading rooms of the libraries.

But good news from Ohio! 'A person assaulted or lynched by a mob may recover from the county in which the assault is made, a sum not exceeding five hundred dollars.'

. . . . . A police sergeant who found that the licence on his dog had expired took out a summons against himself . . . .

Out on a Spree

The richest bonus ever enjoyed by the criminal fraternity of London was the Great Smog of 1952. Under cover of the choking smog blanket which lasted for three weeks, thieves went on the spree of a lifetime. The looting of shops and other properties for rich pickings was so widespread that the police, unable to move speedily around the city, were almost helpless.

Lamb to the Slaughter

A handsome sheepskin coat hanging in the cloakroom of an hotel in Bognor Regis took the eye of a youth with few scruples. Wearing his booty, he hitched a lift from a passing coach.

He found to his horror that the passengers were all detective inspectors on their way home from a conference on crime. The thief made himself small and hoped for the best.

But his luck was out. One of the detectives began taking an interest in the coat, and finally identified it as his own.

The thief was dropped off at the nearest police station.

. . . . . One result of the prohibition of alcoholic drinks in the United States, 1920-1933, was that in one year the number of drinking places in New York doubled . . . .

Drinking and Driving Made Easy

A police car was patrolling the M1 late one evening, when the officers saw a Rolls Royce parked on the hard shoulder, with a man slumped against it on the far side.

They pulled over and asked the man if he had been drinking. When he admitted that he had, they immediately breathalysed him and found him well over the limit. After some disagreement as to which officer should drive the Rolls back to the station, one of them went across to the driver's seat – only to find that sitting patiently inside was the chauffeur.

. . . . . A drinks extension until midnight was granted by local magistrates to an Oxfordshire hotel, where there was a dinner-dance organized by Alcoholics Anonymous . . . .

There's Life in the Old Dog Yet

A notorious brothel in South Carolina was raided by the police, and dozens of clients were charged. The police were inundated with phone calls from men trying to get their names taken off the charge sheet.

But they also received a request from one elderly man who offered a bribe to have his name *added* to the list.

Way Out

... or there's nowt so strange as folk ...

Making a Meal of Communication

One problem with the first military tanks was communication between tank crews and the Infantry. The crude radio transmitters and receivers proved useless, because of the ear-shattering noise of the tank's engine.

So, two carrier pigeons were kept in each tank. Messages were to be written on rice paper and attached to the pigeon's leg. However, in the heat of battle, more than one tank commander forgot to send these messages and, rather than admit it, chose pigeon pie as a tasty way of destroying the evidence.

Old Habits Die Hard

Drawing attention to yourself when you're a fugitive on the run is not a good idea. Ignoring this simple rule cost the Marquis de Condonset his head during the French Revolution.

Disguised as a peasant, this foolish worthy strode into an inn full of half-starved (real) peasants, and called in a loud voice, 'Make me an omelette with a dozen eggs.'

General Chaos

Count Suverov was the greatest Russian general of the 18th century – and the oddest. Instead of mustering his troops with a bugle call, he summoned them personally by crowing like a cock.

His normal habit was to go to bed in the afternoon, and rise in the middle of the night. He slept on hay on the ground, rather than in a comfortable bed, and when he rode about on horseback, he wore only a shirt. And, most confusing of all to his loyal men, his orders were always issued in rhyme.

Means to an End

A blind man was standing at a crossroads in a town in Scotland, when a dog walked up to him and relieved himself down his trouser leg. To the astonishment of a passer-by, the blind man took out a biscuit from his pocket and offered it to the dog. This so impressed the passer-by that he congratulated the blind man on his kindness to animals.

The blind man replied, 'Not at all. I was only trying to find which end his mouth was, so that I could kick the other end.'

..... *Madame Tallien, who was a member of the French Court during the reign of Louis XIV, bathed in crushed strawberries when they were available* ....

183

Trumpets on the Wing

Latin tempers frayed and passengers were on the point of mutiny aboard a plane delayed for three hours at Madrid airport. Tough Civil Guards, armed with machine guns, were even summoned to quell the unrest.

It was then that Ray Simmonds, principal trumpet player of the Royal Philharmonic Orchestra from London decided a little light music was called for. So he took out his instrument and began to play – 'Viva Espana'.

Do Not Walk on the Grass

In the London suburb of Wimbledon in 1887, a fashionable entertainment was to pay a visit to Coleman's Circus – even though it consisted of only one man and his horse. The fascinating thing was that this horse wore rubber boots, and spent its time pulling rollers and mowers on grass tennis courts.

The rubber-booted horse was the brainchild of Thomas Coleman, the first full-time groundsman appointed by the All England Croquet and Lawn Tennis Club. Coleman took his job very seriously, and he didn't want the courts in his charge ruined by iron horseshoes.

Coleman remained with the famous club for forty years, and made the courts the finest in the world.

Management Tips

Lenten sermons at St Andrew-by-the-Wardrobe parish church in the City of London have been tailored to local tastes. They are being billed as: Start-up Schemes, Business Expansion, Profit and Loss and, finally, The Balance Sheet.

Noah's Ark on Mont Blanc

In 1960 an Italian doctor announced that the world would end at
3.00 p.m. on 14th July. He predicted earthquakes, floods and great
tidal waves. The good news was that survival was possible, but only
high on Mont Blanc in the Alps.

The doctor invited others to join him in building a house on the
mountain, and a total of 70 people joined the project, some of
them using all their life savings.

Soon after noon on the 14th, the doctor bought a one-way
ticket for the cable-car that ran up the mountain. He was joined on
the journey by his fellow-investors and a number of tourists,
curious to see what would happen. Three o'clock came and went –
and nothing happened. The tourists outside the house laughed and
jeered. At last the front door opened, and the doctor emerged.

He said, 'Anyone can make a mistake, and you should be
grateful that I have.'

Not in Front of the Children

A chief sugar boiler in a seaside rock factory pioneered a unique
form of protest. He was fed up with his working conditions and the
responsibility of making some 20,000 sticks of rock a day. So
instead of the usual 'Torbay', 'Bournemouth' or 'Brighton' running
all the way through, he turned out 1,000 sticks bearing a word that
has more to do with snooker than with the seaside . . .

The Biter Bit

What would Barbara Woodhouse say? A breeder of dogs has
been censured by the Kennel Club, of which she is a member, for
her unusual training methods. It seems that the lady believes that
the punishment should fit the crime, for when one of her dogs bit a
passer-by, she bit the dog.

Strictly for the Birds

The Rev. Favell Hopkins of Huntingdon was a rich man, but so miserly that he denied himself the basic necessities of life.

One Sunday morning, on his way to church, he noticed a scarecrow in a field. The Rev. Hopkins took off its hat, examined it carefully, and then compared it with his own. Deciding that the advantage lay with the scarecrow's hat, he placed it on his head, put his own on the scarecrow, and continued his journey.

. . . . . A café in Bridport, Dorset, displayed this notice in the window: 'Closed for lunch. Open 2.00 p.m.' . . . .

Nil All!

A small but select band of politicians in Britain share the doubtful honour of having scored no votes in an election.

The pioneer was Lord Garvagh, Liberal candidate for Reigate in 1832, who managed to avoid making himself popular with a single member of the electorate. Seven years later, another Liberal, L. Oliphant, repeated the achievement.

In 1841 the Liberal monopoly was broken by a notable double, in which two Chartist Party candidates scored zero. The Chartists went ahead in 1847 with a candidate for Tiverton. But their nil-vote supremacy heralded the end of the party, which went out of business a few years later.

This left the field open to the Conservative Party, which notched up a nought with Viscount Lascelles at Tewkesbury. Not to be outdone, the Liberals failed to score in the same constituency twelve years later. The last of this distinguished band, F. R. Lees, achieved total unpopularity in an 1860 by-election.

The list stops there – but only because candidates may now vote for themselves!

It's Never Too Late

Waldomiro da Silva was born in 1867 – 21 years before slavery was abolished in Brazil. In 1986 he married . . . at the age of 119. His sweetheart was a mere 65.

The elaborate ceremony was organized by the great grandson of da Silva's former slave master.

LOOKS LIKE THEY BROUGHT BACK SLAVERY

She Sells Sea-shells by the Seashore

But who was the 'she' in that well-known tongue-twister? She was Mary Anning, who lived at Lyme Regis on the coast of Dorset in the 19th century.

Mary and her father made a living by collecting and selling sea-shells and fossils. When Mary was only eleven, her father died, but the young girl carried on the business alone.

Then Mary found a giant fossil about 10 metres long. It was new to scientists, for it was the remains of a creature that lived a hundred million years ago. They called it Ichthyosaurus.

Further discoveries followed, so important that Mary was given a grant by the government – a rare event even in those days. She died aged 48. In a church in Lyme Regis there is a stained-glass window to her memory. And at the British Museum you can see a portrait of her, beside one of her greatest discoveries, the Plesiosaur.

Under False Pretences

A vicar gave a lady in his parish a birthday present of a Bible. She asked him to write his name in it. He did so, inscribing it as a gift 'from the author'.

Amazing Grace

Job opportunities for women were few and far between on the west coast of Ireland in the 16th century. But that didn't worry Grace O'Malley. She became a pirate chief of outstanding success. From Clew Bay she preyed on ships in the Atlantic.

Much of her youth was spent on pirate ships and when she became a captain, a small but fierce fleet was brought under her control. Though arrested a few times, Grace was never brought to trial and she retired happily in 1586 at fifty years of age to enjoy her loot.

The Result was a Draw

In 1808 two Frenchmen fought a duel half-a-mile above the gardens of the Tuileries. But instead of firing at each other, they used blunderbusses to blast away at the hot air balloon below which each was suspended.

Simultaneous hits occurred, and both balloons plummeted to earth, killing their occupants.

Stairs are Safer

Instructions abroad don't always tell the visitor exactly what they want to know. . .

A lift in a hotel in Madrid advised with confidence: 'To move the cabin, push button of wishing floor. If the cabin should enter more persons, each one should press number of wishing floor. Driving is then going alphabetically by natural order. Button retaining pressed position shows received command for visiting station.' *Olé.*

Budget Day Thoughts

' . . . the rapacity and greed of the Government go beyond all limits. It is now actually proposing to place a tax on incomes.

'Those with £100 to £105 a year are to pay a 1/40th part, and above £200, 1/10th. This is a vile Jacobin jumped-up jack-in-the-box office impertinence. Is a true Briton to have no privacy? Are the fruits of his labour and toil to be picked over, farthing by farthing, by pimply minions of bureaucracy?'

A familiar complaint – except this one was written by John Knyveton, a naval surgeon at the time of Nelson, dated 12 January 1799.

190

Sweet Smell of Success

Dudley Taw, of Cleveland, Ohio, recently concocted a cologne for men designed to promote its user to a position of great wealth and power.

The cologne is called 'CEO', which stands for Chief Executive Officer. For the man who wants to smell like the boss. . .

. . . . . Printed on the inside cover of a theological work: 'Spread the word of the Lord. No part of this book may be reproduced without permission from the publishers.' . . . .

Measure for Measure

Sir Francis Galton, who lived in the later part of the 19th century, was addicted to measuring, counting and analysing statistics.

One of his numerous projects was to gather material for a Beauty Map of Great Britain. Every woman he saw he classified as beautiful, middling or ugly. His general conclusion was that London had the prettiest girls and Aberdeen the ugliest. Another finding was that the finest men came from Ballater in Scotland.

Galton extended his research to Africa, for he had great admiration for the figures of the native women. Some misunderstandings occurred when he tried to use a tape-measure on them. So he devised a way of measuring hips and busts using a sextant.

Other projects included 'The weights of British noblemen during the last three generations', and he wrote a fact-filled paper on 'Three generations of lunatic cats'. He even set out to measure the honesty of nations. Not surprisingly he concluded that the British were top of the league. He declared that Salonika in Greece was 'the centre of gravity of lying'.

In the end Galton tried to persuade people to breed selectively – like racehorses – and produce a super race. He failed completely – people just went on doing what came naturally. . .

Beyond Belief

In Europe, yogurt is yogurt, and it is not difficult to believe that it is yogurt because it tastes like it. In the USA, things are not so simple.

There, a company called This Can't Be Yogurt, which patently is a yogurt company because it sells frozen dollops of the stuff, announced that it was floating off 505,000 of its shares. It was promptly sued by another company entitled I Can't Believe It's Yogurt, which is equally involved in the trade, owning a number of frozen yogurt stores.

I Can't Believe It's Yogurt claimed that This Can't Be Yogurt was a trade mark which infringed its own – and it asked for at least $750,000 in compensatory and punitive damages.

The Sport of Wings

Airmen on both sides in World War One often behaved more like rival sportsmen than deadly enemies. When the greatest German air ace of the war, Baron von Richthofen, known as the 'Red Baron' was shot down, Allied airmen buried him with full military honours.

Hell's Bells! We'll Sue

Hell's Angels sued their next-door neighbours . . . for giving them a bad name! The bike gang hit the roof when the McSorley family accused the Angels of forcing them to flee their £75,000 house at Windsor, Berks. And they blew a gasket when the local valuation court cut Mrs Pat McSorley's rates from £337 a year to a nominal £1.

'We are not nightmare neighbours. Our solicitors are taking action over this family's claims, and we will do battle in the court,' said a Hell's Angel spokesman. Mrs McSorley, 42, told of week-long parties, sword and gun-toting bikers, noisy motorbikes . . . and of Angels exposing themselves to her. 'This woman lives in a dream world,' said the Angels.

You Can't Take It With You

An old Lancashire man knew he was dying. Not long before the end he told his wife that he wanted to change his will, and summoned his lawyer.

The solicitor arrived and sat by the old man's bed. The dying man said, 'In the last few years I have become convinced that when I die, I will be reborn on this earth. I now believe firmly in reincarnation. Please change my will – I wish to leave everything to myself.'

CONGRATULATIONS. YOU'VE JUST BECOME THE RICHEST FLY IN THE WORLD!

Which End Up?

Confused by modern art? Try standing on your head.

'Le Bateau' by Matisse was hung upside down in New York's Museum of Modern Art for forty-seven days – and nobody noticed!

For Richer, For Poorer

A rich New York tailor went to extraordinary lengths to make sure that his money was left to the poor of the city.

In his will he stipulated that over seventy pairs of old trousers should be auctioned off, and that the proceeds should go to the needy of the city. The sting in the tail, though, was a paragraph in the will which stated: 'I desire that these garments shall in no way be examined or meddled with, but be disposed of as they are found at the time of my death, and no purchaser to buy more than one pair.'

The trousers were duly sold off to those not too choosy about their choice of garment – all at knock-down prices. Much to their surprise, all the pockets were found to be stitched up. And when they opened them they found the real legacy of the will – each pair of trousers contained a thousand dollars in banknotes!

Tour de France

The celebrations for the fortieth anniversary of D-Day included a series of mini-trips of the battle zone. One of these involved overnight travel on the ferry to France and then a day spent whizzing to the invasion beaches, Pegasus, Gold, Sword, June and Arromanches, together with side trips to Honfleur and Bayeaux, before collapsing back on board.

That package was called The Longest Day.

..... In the parish of Chingford, Essex, is Friday-Hill House, in which King Charles knighted a loin of beef on an oak table ....

Where There's a Will . . .

Here are some unusual clauses from a selection of eccentric wills:

'The undertaker's fees come to nothing, as I won them from him at a game of billiards.'

'I leave my lawyer, Hubert Lewis, the task of explaining to my relatives why they didn't get a million dollars apiece.'

'To my wife Anna (who is no damn good) I leave one dollar.'

'I direct that all my creditors be paid, except my landlord.'

'To my wife I leave her lover, and the knowledge that I wasn't the fool she thought I was.'

'To my chauffeur, I leave my cars. He almost ruined them, and I want him to have the satisfaction of finishing the job.'

Candidate for the Green Party?

Lord Rokeby, who was born in 1713, was way ahead of his time when he constructed a solar-heated bath-house on his estate near Hythe in Kent. He bathed several times a day, refused to drink anything but water, substituted honey for sugar, and would not eat products based on wheat.

When he inherited his estate, the land was fertile and well-cultivated. Lord Rokeby put a stop to all that. He ordered that the fields should be allowed to go back to wilderness, and that no tree or hedge should be chopped or even pruned. All the grounds, including the walled ornamental gardens, were opened up, so that the horses, sheep and cattle could wander at will.

In the decaying coach-house, the family carriages were left to rot, for Lord Rokeby walked almost everywhere. When he walked to the beach for a swim, a carriage followed him – not for himself, but in case the servants got tired.

For a time he was MP for Canterbury. But the party politics of the House of Commons so disgusted him that he told his constituents that he no longer felt able to represent them.

At the age of 87, feeling that death was near, he summoned his nephew, who was to inherit his fortune. When the nephew wanted to call a doctor, the old man warned him that if he did, and the doctor failed to kill him, he would use his last strength to cut the young man out of his will.

And when he died, his wild estates were prospering.

Shalom way To Go

The inflation in Israel is running at 60%, so when a tourist decided to go there for his holiday, he rang first to enquire about hotel prices. When he asked about the nightly cost of a room, the receptionist replied, 'It depends how soon you get here.'

Gold Bricks

Australia's latest gold strike is right in the city of Perth. At the State Mint to be precise.

Officials say that about 1,000 ounces of gold, which vaporized during the mint's 86-year history of refining, has impregnated the building and is to be recovered.

Mind you, to get the gold – worth A$500,000 – the buildings of the mint will have to be demolished and the walls and ceilings smelted. But the mint's processes are to be moved to a new site anyway. The golden windfall will go towards the cost.

The Very Conservative MP

The most conservative MP who ever lived was a Colonel Sibthorp, member for Lincoln from 1826. He was opposed to all changes, all innovations and all foreigners.

Indeed Sibthorp accused Queen Victoria of making a ghastly mistake in marrying a foreigner, declaring that Prince Albert's character was permanently damaged by his foreign birth. So while Sibthorp was MP for Lincoln, Queen Victoria refused to visit the city.

The Great Exhibition of 1851 was inspired by Prince Albert. The Colonel denounced it as 'one of the greatest humbugs, one of the greatest frauds, one of the greatest absurdities ever known!'

He believed it was designed to bring waves of foreigners to England's shores and warned the locals: 'Take care of your wives and daughters, take care of your property and your lives!'

But in one respect Colonel Sibthorp was way ahead of his time. He cunningly suggested that foreign travel should be curtailed by limiting the amount of currency that could be taken abroad.

Bookworm

Richard Heber ended his life as a recluse gloating over his treasures behind the shutters of his house in Pimlico. The treasures were – books!

As a child of eight Richard catalogued the vast library he had already accumulated in his father's house. When his father, a rich clergyman, died and left his fortune to Richard, the book-buying exploits became fantastic.

Rooms, cupboards, passages and corridors of his house became choked with books. Books were piled up to the very ceiling. When one house was stuffed with them, he bought another and began stuffing that. Once he took time off to propose marriage to a Miss Richardson Currer of Yorkshire, a well-known book-collector; it would have been a marriage of libraries but negotiations broke down.

When the Richard Heber estate was investigated after his death in 1883, trustees found one mansion in Cheshire, two houses in London, and houses in Paris, Brussels, Antwerp, Ghent and Germany – all crammed with books!

. . . . . A Turkish student in Japan demanded that the name of the communal hot bathing places be changed from 'toruko' (meaning Turkish bath), as the naughty goings on there demeaned the honour of his nation. They are now called 'soopurando' (soapland) instead . . . .

A Head for Business

Enterprising Gary Mason decided to get ahead in the world – by selling advertising space on his head. He shaved off all his hair, and offered companies the space – any message painted on for £30.

Said optimistic Gary, 'I'm surprised nobody thought of it before.'

Till Death Do Us Part

... or love and marriage ...

A Bride By Any Other Name

A couple of young farmers decided to get married on the same day. Before applying for the licences, however, they celebrated so thoroughly that by mistake they each gave the name of the other's intended bride.

As neither of them could read, it was left to the clergyman to discover the error on the day planned for the weddings. Rather than disappoint their friends, who were looking forward to the festivities, all four participants agreed to be paired as the licences decreed.

Like Father, Like Son

A teacher in Hull in Humberside sent a boy home because of his smell. When the lad returned to school the following day – no cleaner – he had a note from his mother.

It informed the teacher that Harold smelled the same as his father, and that his dad smelled just fine. As proof of this, the mother added that she had lived with Harold's dad for 25 years, and she should know.

Happiness Is A Waterworks Bill

Divorce has not always been the simple process it is today. One unhappy spouse went to the lengths of including provision for his own divorce in a special Act of Parliament.

He was a town clerk, and he sought his future happiness via a municipal Waterworks Bill. As he was in charge of drafting the bill, he wrote in a somewhat unusual clause.

The Royal Assent was granted to the bill, the town got its water supply, and the Town Clerk got his freedom. The extra clause stated, quite simply, ' . . . and the Town Clerk's marriage is hereby dissolved.'

Cornet Duet

A repentant wife admitted to her husband that she had committed adultery with the owner of an ice-cream cart. She agreed to write a farewell letter to her lover, and the husband insisted on delivering it in person.

When the two men met, they shook hands and had a friendly chat. Then the husband returned home to his wife with two free ice-cream cornets.

The Language of Love

A young Frenchman experienced a set-back and a slap in the face when he attempted to woo an English girl with words. His intentions were honourable, but his command of English was less than perfect. He meant to say, 'When I look at you, time stands still.' What he actually said was, 'Your face would stop a clock.'

Making the Most of It

These epitaphs appear on tombstones:

In loving memory of
SYDNEY WILLIAM SMYTHE
1898-1951
Cherished by his wife
Rest in Peace – until we meet again

In remembrance of
NICHOLAS TOKE
He married five wives whom he survived.
At the age of 93 he walked to London
to seek a sixth but died before he
found her.

Bedtime Stories

In his various palaces, Louis XIV of France had 413 beds. All were elaborately carved, gilded and hung with costly embroideries. His great joy was the magnificent bed in the Palace of Versailles, on which was woven in gold the words, 'The Triumph of Venus'. But when Louis married his second wife, who was a religious bigot, she had the pagan subject replaced by 'The Sacrifice of Abraham'.

Battered Wives Trek to Cheltenham

In the mid-1960s, a judge in Sheffield said that cruelty in marriage had to be assessed according to social background.

M'Lud's comments were made during a hearing on wife-beating. He argued that 'in some parts of England' a little thumping on a Saturday night might not amount to cruelty. On the other hand, his Lordship considered that the same carry-on in, for example, Cheltenham, would no doubt be an act of cruelty.

One . . . Two . . . Tree

Hindu men sometimes marry a tree – as a way of avoiding bad luck. They believe it is unlucky to marry three times, so, if a man wants to take a third bride, he marries a tree first. Then he burns it down, and this frees him to marry the woman of his choice.

All the Same in the Dark

When the love that Darsun Yilmaz of Damali on the Black Sea wanted to lavish on his neighbour's daughter was spurned, he opted for abduction. In August 1972, the yearning lover turned up in his beloved's garden at midnight with a ladder. He climbed into the bedroom, threw a blanket over her head, and bundled her into his car. Whispering endearments, he unwrapped the package, drooling at the thought of his first kiss.

But the wriggling female form was not what he expected. It was the girl's 91-year-old granny, who clouted him good and hard.

I DON'T THINK THIS IS YOUR CAR EITHER!

Third Time Lucky

During a case of bigamy in a Dublin court, a long tale of complicated relationships and deceptions was unfolded on the part of the defendant. The judge lectured the man, expressing his horror at what had been revealed.

But the defendant was unabashed. 'Sure, your lordship,' he said, 'wasn't I only tryin' hard to get a good one?'

A Lean Woman, Much Kissed . . .

If you want a slim, trim figure and are not too worried about your life span, then the recipe is kissing, and plenty of it.

Researchers in America claim that your heartbeat accelerates when you kiss, and that each kiss reduces the length of your life by three minutes. But the good news is that each kiss uses up three calories; to lose a stone, all you have to do is kiss 14,000 times.

Blind Love

Blind Jack of Knaresborough walked the 250 miles from London to his home in Yorkshire with just one thought in his mind – Dolly Benson. He wanted to get back to the love he had left behind when he had paid his once-in-a-lifetime visit to the capital.

But there was a shock for him on arrival. Dolly's parents had forced her to become engaged to a shoemaker, and the wedding was timed for the following morning. Blind though he was, Jack went into action.

Guided by a friend, Jack climbed a ladder to the window of Dolly's bedroom that night. Dolly was more than willing, and the pair eloped, while her parents snored peacefully. The happy couple were married the following morning, had four healthy children, and lived happily ever after.

Exit the Late Departed

The playground of a primary school in Liverpool is beside a cemetery, so that there were times when the children could watch and hear a funeral from a short distance.

One day the headmaster spotted a group of the younger children playing funerals. They had dug a hole, and one of them lowered a shoe box into it. As this was being done, another child said, in a sad voice, 'In the name of the Father, and of the Son, and into the hole he goes.'

. . . . . Lord Goddard, a former Lord Chancellor, ruled that divorce, not murder, was the correct way of getting rid of an unfaithful wife . . . .

A Problem for the Fish

The wife of a famous film star had numerous rows with her husband, mainly because he spent all his spare time fishing.

Soon after one of these domestic upheavals, one of her husband's cronies called at the house and asked where he was.

'Go down to the bridge,' said the wife, drily, 'and look around until you see a pole with a worm at each end of it.'

Staying Married the Hard Way

So desperate was one woman to get a divorce that she mobilized three male friends to drag her husband into bed with a strange woman. The plan was to photograph proof of 'adultery'.

The trap was sprung and the husband frog-marched into the bedroom. There a frantic struggle ensued, during which the husband smashed the camera and escaped. To prevent any replay of the incident, he joined the army.

Limited Bliss

Kathryn Sluckin changed her mind about marriage within an hour of being wed. She married Jerzy Sluckin at Kensington Register Office in November 1975 and the reception was in full swing when Kathryn decided that she wasn't sure the man was for her. She announced, 'It won't work!' and vanished.

Her husband later traced her to the Divine Light Meditation Commune in Finchley, where she was living happily without him.

'Loverly' Day

Why lovers send cards to each other on the feast day of St Valentine is something of a mystery. All we know about the saint is that he was a Roman dignitary who was clubbed to death for helping persecuted Christians.

Whatever the origins, the idea has caught on to the tune of between seven and eight million Valentine cards in Britain *alone*. It seems that more women buy cards, but the men who do spend fifty % more on a card.

One of the world's biggest spenders, Greek millionaire Aristotle Onassis, once lashed out £180,000 on a Valentine card for opera star, Maria Callas. The card was studded with diamonds and emeralds, and was delivered in no ordinary envelope – the wrapping was a black mink coat.

Marx Sparks

Chico Marx, one of the world-famous Marx brothers, was caught by his wife kissing a chorus girl. Tempers flared, and Mrs Marx demanded an explanation.

Unable to deny the evidence, the best Chico could do was, 'I wasn't kissing her. I was just whispering in her mouth.'

Woolly, Weedy, Weaky

Even Latin lovers have their wooing difficulties, and one such was Paco Vila, a student from Madrid. Paco was crazy about big English women, but they scorned his weedy frame, for he weighed-in at only seven stone.

So Paco made up his weight by wearing woolly jumpers beneath his shirt. Thus clad he sallied forth to a discotheque, where fortune smiled on his new-found bulk. An English girl who had abandoned her diet for the holiday consented to dance with him. Paco was in his seventh heaven, until a particularly energetic rumba began to weaken his overburdened body. The crisis came when, at the end of the dance, the English girl stroked his cheek. It was too much for poor Paco, who keeled over in a dead faint.

When they examined him at the hospital, he was wearing 17 woolly sweaters.

. . . . . Was Ethelred the Unready, one of England's least-loved kings, living up to his name on his wedding night? He was found in bed with both his bride and his mother-in-law! . . . .

A Flight on the Side

In the early days of flying, when people were wary of this new form of travel, a promotion man hit on the idea of giving free flights to the wives of businessmen who had booked seats.

The idea was welcomed, and the airline kept a record of the names of those who took advantage of the offer. Some time later, a letter was sent to the wives, asking if they had enjoyed the trip.

Unfortunately, a large percentage of them replied, 'What aeroplane trip?'

. . . . . *When Lord Chief Justice Russell was asked what the penalty was for bigamy, he replied, 'Two mothers-in-law.'* . . . .

Recorded Delivery

A German wife sacrificed her freedom as a result of last-minute weakness.

The day before the divorce hearing, she had gone to her husband's office to discuss the division of their property. Even at that late stage, her husband pleaded that the proceedings should be called off.

In court the wife was resolute – there would be no reconciliation as far as she was concerned. In backing her case she told the judge that she and her husband had not made love for eighteen months.

'It's a lie!' shouted the husband. 'We made love only yesterday in my office.'

The wife hotly denied it, but her husband replied, 'I can prove it. I managed to mark her bottom with the office date-stamp.'

And he had . . .

Just Listen, Darling!

In a bar in America, the most popular record on the juke-box was a novelty number in which the only sound to be heard was a typewriter. The record was played every time a drinker who was supposed to be working late at the office phoned home . . .

. . . . . A correction was necessary in a printing of the Bible which included the line: 'Greater love hath no man than this, that he lay down his wife for his friends.' . . . .

Love Is . . .

Just in case you are in any doubt about what love is, here is the definition according to the First International Conference of Love and Attraction:

'The cognitive-affective state characterized by intrusive and obsessive fantasizing concerning reciprocity of amorant feeling by the object of the amorance.'

. . . . . A defendant in a divorce case claimed ignorance of the true meaning of adultery. He said, 'I did not think it was adultery during the daytime.' . . . .

Long-Standing Engagement

A couple of lovers in Mexico City did not believe in making hasty decisions. Octavio Guillen and Adriana Martinez were engaged 67 years before finally getting married in 1969. On the big day they were both 82.

Encore

Getting married and staying married was not good enough for Jack and Edna Moran of Seattle, USA. Since the original and perfectly legal ceremony in 1937, they have renewed their vows no less than 40 times. Places in which they have been wed include Cairo, Egypt, and Westminster Abbey, London.

Sitting Pretty

Not content with its well-earned reputation for automobile engineering the German car-maker BMW is now trying its hand at a spot of social engineering.

Careful research by the company has decided them that few things irritate a driver more than to find that the driving seat has been moved from his or her favourite position by another driver. And wives are the parties most likely to be held guilty of that offence when the husband jumps into the family car in the morning – already late for work.

So BMW has started to offer with its more expensive models an electronically-controlled seat which 'remembers' the driver's usual seating position.

. . . . . A young Oxford couple married in the very same church where they were christened together 24 years before . . . .

Social Register

Eighteenth-century parish registers were just as keen on publishing 'human interest' stories as any of today's newspapers. This one is dated 1 June 1787.

'Anecdote – When the Rev. John Clark, late master of Charter-House in Hull, was curate at St Trinity there, four couples were married by him at the same time, and the following odd circumstances attended each:

With regard to the first couple, the bridegroom had forgot to bring a ring, in consequence of which he was obliged to borrow one; the bride of the second had lost that finger upon which the ring is commonly put.

A man shaking the iron gates leading into the choir, said aloud that the third bride already had a husband and with regard to the fourth, one of the bridesmaids begged the parson, for God's sake to be quick, as the bride was in labour.'

Manly Pursuit

The Canadians are finding that while good intentions about not offending any conceivable minority grouping sound fine and dandy they can prove difficult to put into practice.

A new and impressive museum was built across the Ottawa river from Parliament Hill. From the beginning the project had been given a working title: the National Museum of Man.

But the very idea of calling it anything like that in modern non-sexist Canada caused consternation, both in and out of parliament. A national search for a name acceptable to all Canadians, yet still describing the museum's proper function, was instituted.

The museum authorities came up with more than 50 names, including the Museum of Man and Woman, the Museum of Mankind, and the Museum of People. More original were some of the ideas from the public, who wrote in with nearly 2000 ideas. Proposals included the Museum of Herstory and History, the Museum of Men, Women and Gays, the Museum of Man and his Wife and the National Museum of Others.

. . . . . In his will a husband left his wife, 'One pair of trousers, free of duty and carriage paid, as a symbol of what she wanted to wear in my lifetime'. . . . .

Technical Tales

EMERGENCY STARTING BOOT

... or lies, damned lies and statistics ...

Repeats from Space?

In 1953, in the days before satellites bounced television signals round the world, viewers in Britain rubbed their eyes when the identification card and call letters of TV station KLEE in Texas, USA, appeared on their screens.

BBC engineers contacted KLEE, and were astonished to learn that the station had been off the air for three years! The picture seen in Britain must have originated in Texas, but where had it been meanwhile? And why was it seen only in Britain? Do TV signals hang about in space, waiting for the chance of yet another repeat?

Oil or Nothing

Despite all the modern aids provided by science, drilling for oil is still a gamble. Even with likely sites, the chances are less than 10% that oil will actually be found there. And even when oil is present, the chances are only 2% that it will be in commercially useful quantities.

..... The inventor who took the world's first photograph, in 1825, didn't dare ask anyone to pose for the shot. He photographed a building instead, which is hardly surprising, when you think that the exposure time was eight hours! ....

Downside-up

The following instruction is alleged to have originated from the Admiralty in London:

'It is necessary for technical reasons that these warheads should be stored upside-down. That is, with the top at the bottom and the bottom at the top. In order that there may be no doubt as to which is the bottom and which is the top, for storage purposes, it will be seen that the bottom of each warhead has been labelled with the word, 'TOP'.

Get to Work on That!

A fond grandfather in America sent for a hobby horse by mail order as a Christmas present for his granddaughter. The toy arrived packed in a large box, and it contained 189 pieces. The instructions stated that it could be put together in one hour.

Eventually, and just in time for Christmas, granddad managed to fit the bits together. When the time came to pay for the toy, he wrote a cheque, tore it into 189 pieces, and mailed it to the company.

Holding Your Breath for a Living

One way of earning a living in Ancient Greece was by salvaging valuable cargo from sunken ships. The going rate of pay was a tenth of the value of the goods in one metre of water, a third in four metres, and a half in eight metres.

Deeper than that? Without modern equipment, the diver didn't need to worry about getting paid – there was no chance that he'd survive at all.

Look, No Wheels

The Indians in America never invented the wheel, and didn't even see one until it was introduced with the arrival of the white man.

Their failure to reach this level of technology may be blamed on the fact that they had no horses or oxen, so they had few aids to carrying heavy loads. Sometimes they used dogs to pull a wooden frame along the ground, with the load placed on the frame.

To make up for this, though, the Indians were experts at making light bark canoes. As they travelled by water whenever they could, these craft ensured that they were just as mobile as their white invaders.

Kick Start

The human male has always had a weakness for measuring his strength. William Carter was trying to cash in on this when he invented the kick power meter in 1910.

For a small charge you could take a mighty swing at a dummy of a policeman. (Carter must have reckoned that the nature of the dummy acted as an incentive.) When your foot contacted the dummy's bottom, the head shot out on the end of an expanding neck. The neck was marked off with a scale, and this was the measure of your kick power.

WELL DONE, LADS. DID HE PUT UP MUCH OF A FIGHT?

Walkies?

If you get fed-up exercising your dog in all weathers, then it's a pity an invention of 1870 didn't catch on.

This was a vehicle with a large drum like a treadmill at the front. The driver sat behind on a comfortable seat, and steered with a wheel that controlled the direction of the drum. Dogs were placed inside the drum, and their job was to keep running, thus moving the drum forward.

Saddle Sore

Elijah Burgoyne thought that pedalling a bicycle was too much like hard work. So he invented a power unit known as the saddle pump.

The pump was fitted beneath the saddle and compressed air from the pump was fed into a cylinder under the crossbar. This was supposed to drive the turbine engine which turned the wheels of the bicycle.

And what worked the pump? Simple! The rider had to keep bouncing up and down on the saddle.

Spade Work

In 1921, William de Camp invented a counting spade. On the handle was a meter that recorded each dig.

What never became clear was why anyone would want to record the number of digs made. Perhaps the inventor had in mind the gardener who wished to prove something on a Saturday afternoon, but, not surprisingly, the device never became really popular.

. . . . . *Bertha Delugi invented a nappy for caged birds* . . . .

Don't Forget to Bend Your Knees

Benjamin Oppenheimer worried about what happened to people trapped by fire in skyscrapers. Evidently he was not impressed by the joke about the man who fell from the 60th storey and shouted, 'All right so far!' as he hurtled past the 30th.

So he invented an apparatus to deal with the situation. This was a parachute attached to a cap, which was strapped to the wearer's head. To absorb the impact of landing, the escaper was equipped with special shoes with thick soles and heels made of rubber.

Fortunately, the equipment was never used.

You Scratch My Back . . .

Does your dog spend all day trying to scratch those patches that he can't quite reach? The cure may lie in an invention of the early '70s.

This was an automatic animal scratcher, consisting of an electric-powered scratching arm mounted on a platform. First, the dog would have to be trained to step on to the platform, which would then switch on the motor and make the arm move up and down. Then, all the dog had to do was press the itching part of his body up against the end of the arm. Bliss!

However, the invention was not a success. Probably because most dogs are rather conservative creatures, and prefer to rub up against trees or fences.

. . . . . Almost 60% of the resources of this planet are consumed by only 6% of the world's population: the people of the United States . . . .

What Would Daisy Have Said?

The flying tandem would have been just the vehicle for honeymooners wanting to get away from it all – if it had worked.

It was the brainchild of an inventor named Gaunt. The 'aircraft' was made of an ordinary tandem with a pair of wings, a mast, and a large kite. Take-off would have been achieved by pedal power. Once airborne the riders would have turned two large propellers above them. But in the – likely – event of the propellers not providing enough lift, Gaunt thoughtfully included wings that flapped like those of a bird. These were also powered from the pedals.

The flying tandem never left the ground.

Whose Turn for the Rocker?

Many strange attempts were made to replace the ordinary sweeping brush before the coming of the electric vacuum cleaner. One such was the chair pump cleaner.

The cleaner required the labour of two people. One pushed the cleaner along, while the other sat and worked a rocking chair. The cleaner was joined by a flexible pipe to a bellows, which was operated by the rocking action of the chair. The bellows created a suction that picked up dirt and dust, and deposited it in the bellows. This was emptied later.

The big snag was that the rocking chair had to be carried from room to room – including upstairs!

A Zippy Idea!

It was a lady who invented a device to help zip up that awkward area between the small of the back and the base of the neck.

The equipment was attached to a wall. To dress or undress, the lady would have to back up to the invention and – somehow – hook the slide of her zipper over a catch fitted to the apparatus. This could then be moved up or down, as appropriate. The idea never caught on.

All for the Want of a Minus

The omission of one minus sign on a computer programme cost the US taxpayer more than $18 million.

It happened in 1962, when space probe Mariner I was being launched to take a close look at Venus. The lack of the minus sign made Mariner veer off course as the spacecraft separated from the booster rocket. NASA officials had to press a button to destroy both rocket and spacecraft.

Dam All Benefits

During the rainy season the Aswan High Dam in Egypt holds back the rising waters of the River Nile, which for thousands of years flooded farmland along the banks. Water collected by the dam was used to irrigate farmland during dry periods, and to generate electrical power.

But now the farmland which used to be fertilized by the silt in the floodwaters has to be enriched by expensive artificial fertilizers instead. And to produce these, the government has built fertilizer plants – powered by the electricity provided by the dam. In other words – they are almost back where they started.

A Cover-up Tail

In the days when transport was dominated by the horse, the state of the roads in cities was, to say the least, a mess – especially in wet weather.

One invention designed to clear things up was called the 'portable horse-bin'. This open-topped bag was suspended from the tail-strap of the horse's harness. Inside the bag was a little box full of disinfectant, which was opened automatically by the weight of the dung falling into the bag. The inventor pointed out that this was included 'in order to prevent any ill effects to drivers'.

He also suggested that bin boys should be employed at each cab stand and at the termini of omnibus and tram routes. The task of these lads was to empty the horse-bins into a larger bin in the middle of the road.

Give him his due, the inventor did see one objection to the widespread adoption of his invention. He admitted that many of the horses' tails were too short to hide the horse-bin to any great extent. But he suggested that this slight snag could be overcome by allowing the tails to grow longer.

220

WELL...WHAT D'YOU THINK OF STEPHENSON'S ROCKET LAUNCHED CUCUMBER?

Cool and Straight

In 1986 Chesterfield Council in Yorkshire bought a cucumber straightener for the local museum.

The straightener is, quite simply, a transparent glass tube open at one end. When a cucumber reached a certain size, it was placed in the tube, and continued to grow – straight. The device was invented by George Stephenson, the founder of railways in Britain, and the builder of the famous locomotive, *The Rocket*, in 1829.

221

Giving Up Arithmetic

The first personal computers to be made available to the public were the digital watch and the pocket calculator – in the late 1960s. Both had been made possible by research for the space programme.

In those early days the price of a pocket calculator didn't make it just the thing to help Johnny with his homework. It cost hundreds of pounds. But, unlike most things, the price has come down and down. By 1971 you could have one for £150. A year later it was £50. Now . . . well, most people can get one to satisfy their needs for less than £10.

Going for a Song?

One of the greatest technological boobs of all time was the original design for the famous Sydney Opera House. It was so way out that it had to be completely redesigned, giving Sydney the smallest opera house in the world.

Not only that, but the original budget of 7 million Australian dollars soared to 102 million. And still there wasn't room for a proper car park.

Bring on the Bridgesweepers

Four new minesweepers were built and ready in 1983 for the Italian Navy. All the latest technology had been incorporated, including glass-fibre hulls to prevent mines sticking to the vessels.

The manufacturers, Intermarine, had their shipyard a mile from the Mediterranean on the River Magra. All that remained was to launch the ships and sail them down to the sea.

Too late it was realized that there was a problem. The ships were too big to pass under a bridge at the head of the river. . .

222

What the Tramlines Left Behind

A dark, foggy night in 1933. Percy Shaw was driving to his home in Halifax, Yorkshire. Percy leaned forward, peering into the murk to take his bearings from the side of the road.

At last he reached the edge of the town – and the tramlines. There was a slight reflection from the shiny track. Percy breathed a sigh of relief and leaned back. That reflection made it possible to keep his car in a safe position on the road. What a pity there were no tramlines on the country roads!

It was then that Percy Shaw had the idea that made him a millionaire. Why not reflecting studs on the roads – like cat's-eyes? In 1936 the Ministry of Transport set up an experiment. Ten kinds of studs from different countries were put down on a busy road. After two years Percy's cat's-eyes were the only ones still in perfect condition and now millions of them are made every year for all parts of the world.

. . . . . *Some computers use a laser beam to read information from a laser disc. Each disc can hold about 80 million words (about the number of words in 1,500 novels)* . . . .

Foot and Mouth

In the days before trains were heated, passengers could emerge from a long journey feeling frozen stiff, despite muffs, furs and hipflasks. But where there's a need, there's bound to be an inventor.

One came up with the idea that something should be done with all the warm air being breathed out by the people in the compartment. So the invention consisted of a cup which was secured over the mouth, with two tubes running down and attached, one to each foot.

Thus the passenger would breathe in cold air through the nose, breath warm air out through the mouth, and this would go straight down to the feet. No waste!

Ready for the Ambulance

In 1932, Heinrich Karl invented a device intended to make being knocked down by a car a less hazardous experience. He mounted a folded blanket on a collapsible frame and placed it above the car radiator. If the car hit a pedestrian, the frame would unfold and spread the blanket beneath the stricken patient.

Mr Karl's theory was that the pedestrian would fall into the blanket, thus being protected from landing heavily on the road. Alas, the inventor failed to find volunteers for field trials.

ASK HIM, KARL.. HE LOOKS DAFT ENOUGH TO TRY ANYTHING!

..... Coding experts at the Pentagon in Washington are scratching their heads about what to do next. Their most complicated codes have been cracked by seven teenagers using ordinary computers ....

Going Up

When the Sears Tower in Chicago was 'topped-off' in May 1974, it became the tallest building in the world. Although it and the World Trade Center both have 110 storeys, the Sears Tower at 1,454 feet is 104 feet higher than its rival.

A Hair-raising Tale

Barbers who didn't want to join the ranks of the unemployed may be to blame for the failure of an automatic electric barber invented in 1951.

It was a mask that fitted over the head, but left the face free. When the machine was switched on, exhaust jets on the outside of the mask pulled up the hairs on the wearer's head. With the hairs positioned for action, the cutting took place. But it wasn't cutting as we know it – it was singeing.

Inside the mask were electric elements, and these singed the hairs to the desired length. There were to be different masks for different styles of haircuts, and the whole operation was meant to be completed in a matter of seconds.

Damp Squib

A firework designed to be the most spectacular on record was engineered by George Plumpton of New York in 1975. It weighed 720 pounds, was forty inches long, and was designed to reach a height of 3,000 feet.

Crowds watched in hushed expectation as the inventor himself set the trail. As Mr Plumpton stood back, the firework hissed a little, then whistled for a bit, and finally blasted a ten-foot crater in the earth.

A Matter of Punctuality

In 1976 Bill Hancock lodged a complaint with a bus company in Staffordshire that ran a route from Hanley to Bagnall. He was annoyed because buses on the outward journey failed to stop, even when up to thirty people were waiting in a queue.

Councillor Arthur Cholerton responded to the complaint. His defence was that if the buses stopped to pick up passengers, the time-table would be disrupted!

Half Measure

The house journal of the Semi-conductor Equipment Materials Institute – trade association of the U.S. microchip equipment industry – is entitled, with touching candour, 'Semi News'.

Computer on the Rampage

The behaviour of a computer installed by Avon County Council in 1975 almost led to a search for clerks with quill pens.

The computer began by raising a school caretaker's pay from 75p to £75 an hour. Having been found out, it sulked for a while, and didn't pay a canteen worker at all for seven weeks. Then, just to show it really was on the side of the workers, it began dishing out £2,600 a week to a janitor. This honest soul sent the cheque back, but the computer was reluctant to admit its error. So, by return of post, it sent him another cheque for the same amount.

This must have given the computer confidence, for it then paid a deputy headmistress her annual salary each month, and gave assistants more salary than their department heads.

Finally, almost 300 council employees attended a protest meeting. When they found that only eight of them had been paid the correct salary, they all went on strike.

Guarded Comments

Early morning commuters in a train pulling into Liverpool Street station in London were disconcerted to hear the guard apologize over the public address system that 'for technical reasons' the train had arrived three minutes early.

Another early arrival, this time at Waterloo, caused the guard to announce, 'Those ticket holders who feel they have not had their money's worth from British Rail are perfectly welcome to stay on in their carriages for the extra five minutes if they want to.'

. . . . . *A new company named Future Technology Ltd warned in its advertisements that the company's telephones were out of order* . . . .

Flying Imperial

Moves to bring down European air fares to something below piratical levels strike a chord in the 1926 Imperial Airways brochure of services between Croydon Aerodrome and the continent.

The return fare between London and Paris was £11.11 shillings that season – including a cabin trunk of luggage. And how reassuring the airlines were in those pioneer days.

'All pilots have brilliant records and long flying experience' and 'Each machine carries a highly trained and certified mechanic.'

Passenger comfort was given high priority. 'The passenger cabin is totally enclosed but well ventilated. And windows can be opened . . . ' 'Luncheon baskets can be provided on embarkation if ordered.'

Bank Note

Staff at the London branch of the Mitsui Bank have apparently not been as attuned as they should have been to Japanese working habits. They have been reminded in a memo from the management that though they can read magazines and newspapers during the lunch hour, 'after lunch hour you have to begin with your job.'

Food, drink, and personal phone calls, it is suggested, should not then be allowed to distract anyone from the job in hand. And the memo adds plaintively: 'Please don't sing a song during working hours.'

Unanimous

The legal profession prides itself on its ability to wrap a cutting insult within unexceptional language. But this exchange between a dissatisfied Englishman and a Scottish law firm is hard to beat.

'If this is an example of Scottish law,' wrote the outraged Englishman, 'thank God I'm not a Scotsman.' The law firm replied: 'Messrs . . . acknowledge Mr . . . 's letter and join with him in thanking God he is not a Scotsman.'

Legs, Legs, Legs

Scientists would dearly like to make a robot that could walk on two legs. Wheels are all very well on a smooth surface, and on some rough ground caterpillar tracks help. But as nature knows, there's nothing quite like legs for . . . well, climbing Mount Everest, for example.

Of course, it would be easier with four legs. But even then the robot could only move one leg at a time, which would be a very slow business, and not how four-legged animals move.

The US army tried to develop a four-legged truck for getting across very rough ground. The driver controlled it by movements of his legs and arms, which were linked to the four legs of the vehicle. The truck was so slow that it would have been a sitting target for enemy artillery and rockets, and the rocking motion made the driver seasick.

For Amusement Only

The first known steam engine was made more than 2,000 years ago in Alexandria, Egypt. The inventor was a scientist called Hero.

The engine was a hollow globe mounted on a pipe which ran to a kettle where water was boiled. Two L-shaped pipes were secured to opposite sides of the globe. The steam rushed out of the L-shaped pipes, causing the globe to whirl round.

The invention was looked on as an amusing toy and it occurred to no one that steam might be made to do useful work. Anyway, with plenty of cheap slaves available, why bother with engines? So the whole idea was forgotten, and 1,500 years passed before the first useful steam engine was developed in the 1600s.

Whoops!

. . . or accidents will happen . . .

Banking Figures

The latest annual report for the old-established banking firm of Grindlays caused a few city heads to turn – it contained a centre-spread of glamorous girls in, and not quite in, tight tee-shirts.

But this wasn't meant to be coverage of a growth industry for the company – instead it was what turned out to be a popular printing error. Some waste pages were temporarily stapled into copies of the report during printing to prevent smears from drying ink. All these should have been removed, but a few copies were overlooked. And the fates that govern this banana-skin type of situation ordained that the waste pages should be leaflets of an eye-catching nature for a tee-shirt maker.

So now we know what city gents read behind those pink pages of the *Financial Times.*

Mayday, Mayday

The lifeboat was called out to a yacht in trouble in dirty weather. The coastguard, trying to get the yacht's exact location, called it on the radio. 'What is your position? Repeat, what is your position?'

And the answer came, faint but determined, from the skipper: 'My position . . . well, I'm the marketing director of a medium-sized computer software firm in the East Midlands.'

When Upstairs Came Downstairs

Free TV advertising to an audience of millions was the happy prospect for a demolition company contracted to blow up a tower block in Hackney, London. So 'L.E. JONES' was painted in bold letters all over the doomed building.

The cameras rolled, the charges exploded, and all seemed to be going well for Mr Jones. But, when the dust cleared, the upper half of the block was still there – balanced, intact and almost vertical.

Rasher Than Need Be

A man was driving his friend along a country road when a car suddenly appeared round a corner, and on the wrong side of the road. Both drivers swerved and a collision was avoided. But the woman who was driving the car lowered the window and shouted, 'Pigs!'

Amazed by this unprovoked abuse, the man muttered, 'Women drivers,' turned the corner . . . and drove straight into a herd of pigs.

Audible Early Warning

Some aviation accident investigators think that the time to start worrying during a flight is when the pilot starts whistling. An air transportation consultant in the United States has said that of more than 260 cockpit voice-recorded tapes removed from aircraft involved in accidents, ranging from the minor to the catastrophic since 1966, over 80% have a recording of the pilot whistling during the last half-hour of the flight.

Out of the Mouths . . .

A high-sided lorry tried to go under a railway bridge that was just a few inches too low. There was a grinding crash, and the lorry was wedged firmly between the road and iron girders.

Tugging and hauling were to no avail. The suggestion that an acetylene torch should be used on the girders of the bridge brought howls of protest from railway officials. There was talk of dismantling the lorry, but this was vetoed by the driver.

Then a small boy, who had been watching with interest, approached one of the worried officials. 'Hey, Mister,' he said, 'why don't you let the tyres down?'

A few minutes later the lorry was on its way.

A Lot of Bottle

Her husband had gone off to work, so the young wife decided to have a leisurely bath. She undressed and then remembered that the gas was still burning in the kitchen. Wrapped in a towel, she tripped downstairs. She was about to switch off the gas when she heard footsteps. The milkman! The arrangement was that he brought it into the kitchen to save the cream from the tits.

So she dashed to the nearest door – the broom cupboard – making it just in time. The footsteps grew louder. The cupboard door was flung open. It was the man from the gas company, come to read the meter.

For a moment she was speechless. Then she said, 'Sorry. I was expecting the milkman.'

234

It Came Away In My Hand

When James Callaghan was Prime Minister, he was invited to open the new premises of the Anglo-Austrian Society. A plaque was to be unveiled to commemorate the occasion.

Evidently, Mr Callaghan didn't know his own strength. When he pulled the cord, the plaque was torn off the wall.

A New Way of Losing an Audience

Professors are often thought to talk to themselves, but this Swedish lecturer in a university in California found it a particularly disconcerting experience. It all began well enough in a fully automated lecture hall with a packed audience. The splendid desk in front of the speaker included an array of buttons. He had been shown how to use some of them to dim the lights, draw the blinds, change the slides, and so on.

Warming to his subject, he leaned forward – placing both forearms firmly on the row of buttons. With a grinding noise, the audience sank out of sight. At the same time a dance floor closed over their heads. Within seconds, the lecturer was quite alone . . .

The Major's Orderly Withdrawal

A tombstone inscription:

Sacred to the memory of
MAJOR JAMES BRUSH
who was killed by
the
accidental discharge
of a pistol by
his orderly
14th April 1831
'Well done thou good and
faithful servant'

From the Jaws of Victory

So appalling was the military defeat of troops led by General Burnside in the American Civil War, that President Lincoln said of him: 'Only he could wring spectacular defeat out of the jaws of victory.'

The general had ordered his troops to cross a river by a very narrow bridge. There was so little space that the soldiers moved slowly and two abreast. They became a sitting target for the enemy, and were all shot.

Had the general explored other possibilities, he would have found that the river was only two feet deep. The troops could easily have crossed almost unseen.

. . . . . *A Russian interpreter translated 'Out of sight, out of mind' into Russian, and then back again into English. It came out as 'invisible lunatic'* . . . .

Timber!

A police sergeant called to the scene of an accident found a car driven off the road into a wood. The driver was an RAF officer, obviously much the worse for drink.

Despite this, the officer said to the sergeant, with an air of authority, 'Shift the tree out of the way, so that I can press on.'

Stair-climbing Cow Floods Shop

In Inverness in 1954, some cows were waiting to be auctioned in a street where there were some shops. One of them broke out of the pen by way of an open gate. It ran into one of the shops and climbed a flight of stairs.

The floor above the shop gave way under the cow's weight. In trying to free itself from the debris, the animal turned on a tap and flooded the shop.

Reds Under the Chandeliers

A Dutch Foreign Minister was visiting Moscow for the first time. He had received a stern briefing about the possibility of electronic bugging in his hotel.

On arrival he set about a thorough examination of the room, scanning the walls, ceiling and floor for wires or tiny microphones. He was about to give up when he noticed a slight bulge in the carpet, leading from the wall to the centre of the room.

Lifting the carpet, he found a wire. With the cutters provided by his Intelligence Service, he snipped the wire. As he rose from his knees, there was a deafening crash from the room below as the chandelier fell from the ceiling.

Steady on the Pedals

The driver of a very old Mini was stopped by a policeman, who found that the car was not insured. The owner's excuse was that, having broken a leg jacking up the car, he had to drive it to get himself to hospital . . .

Toothless Pool Potter

Ken Richardson of Hemel Hempstead was enjoying his 32nd birthday celebration at the Oddfellows Arms. He played a game of pool and was about to make an easy pot when, unfortunately, his dentures fell out on the table. He potted them instead.

Ken's wife, seeing her husband's embarrassment, dashed to the pocket to bring the wayward teeth back into play. But it was not to be, for her hand jammed in the pocket, and stubbornly refused to emerge. Finally, firemen had to be summoned to get things back to normal with a power saw and washing-up liquid.

'Whoops!' Can Happen to Anyone

The Royal Society for the Prevention of Accidents was holding an exhibition. Special shelves were erected to display some of the exhibits. As people were walking round the display, the shelves collapsed, and one of the visitors was injured.

Vain Search for Peace

A 78-year-old grandmother living in Belfast felt that she wanted to spend the remaining years of her life away from the hate and violence. In 1970 she emigrated to New Zealand.

Two years later she was inadvertently caught up in an Irish civil rights march. She received a blow from a placard carried by one of the demonstrators, and died from head injuries.

What a sucker

Alfred Zuhl, aged 11, can claim the distinction of being sucked up whole by a vacuum cleaner. The lad was riding his bike when he skidded and fell in the path of a large street cleaner. Both Alfred and his bike vanished into the works.

The voracious machine was hastily dismantled, and Alfred emerged with little more than a few bruises.

Just Loosening Up!

Graham Smith, goalkeeper for Colchester, always carried out a pre-match routine. He kicked the base of one post, then ran across the goalmouth and kicked the base of the other. One Saturday it all went wrong when the crossbar descended with a crunch on his head.

But What Happened to the Burglar?

Soon after moving into a new house in Johannesburg, South Africa, the owner was awakened by the burglar alarm. He leaped out of bed, grabbed his revolver – and, the house being strange to him, walked through the glass partition between lounge and drawing-room. Suffering from cuts, he was taken to hospital.

Meanwhile, his wife set about cleaning up the mess. Water wouldn't shift the bloodstains, so she used petrol. On completing the job, she put the petrol into the lavatory, but forgot to pull the flush.

Then her bandaged husband returned. He relaxed on the lavatory, and lit a cigar. This mistake resulted in an explosion that threw him across the bathroom. The ambulance was again summoned, and he was carted off – this time on a stretcher.

To round off the night nicely, the ambulance men lost their way in the darkness of the garden. They stumbled over the rockery, tipping their patient on to the rocks. Added to his other injuries was a broken collarbone.

. . . . . *'I'm glad I'm not Brezhnev. Being the Russian leader in the Kremlin, you never know if someone tape-records what you say.'* *Richard Nixon* . . . .

A Waste of Good Priming Time

Crooks in a factory at Vang in Norway were working with quiet, well-planned efficiency. They found the company safe and set a small explosive charge, just large enough to blow off the door. Having set the fuse, they retreated to the safety of the next room and waited confidently.

When it came, the explosion was shattering. The entire factory descended on the unfortunate heads of the crouching criminals. The trouble was that the safe hadn't contained what they thought – it was packed with dynamite!

239

Natural Gas

When John Stratton's wife left him, he was so distraught that he decided to put an end to it all. So he placed his head in the gas oven and breathed deeply. But John had not taken into account that the oven had been converted to natural gas, which is non-toxic. By the time he had given up trying, a feeling of relief and gratitude to the gas board had swept over him.

He decided to relax and think things over. As he did so he also lit a cigarette. Alas, this wasn't the best thing to do. John Stratton and the house were blown sky high.

Sharp Practice

The fastest goal recorded in a soccer match was scored by Brazilian international Roberto Rivelino, representing his club side Corinthians against Rio Preto at the Bahia Stadium.

Receiving the ball directly from the kick-off, Rivelino launched a left-footed drive towards the goal. The opposition goalie, Isadore Irandir, who had yet to conclude his pre-match prayers, was unable to get off his knees in time to save the ball.

Before the match could be restarted, Irandir's brother rushed on to the pitch, pulled out a revolver and delivered six shots into the ball. The crowd cheered as he was led away.

Sadie Comes Back for More

Mrs Sadie Tuckey of Ontario was knocked off her bicycle by a bus and killed. As the coffin was being carried, the mourners were shaken to see the 'corpse' suddenly sit up and scream. Sadie was far from dead. She leapt out of the coffin, dashed off down the road – straight in front of a bus. She was killed outright.

It Works, Baby!

A policeman in New York was worried about his girlfriend being mugged or even raped. So he bought her a spray of knock-out gas, and looked forward to giving it to her that evening.

He had a good clean-up after duty, had a bath and reached for his can of deodorant. Next thing he knew was waking up in hospital the following morning. He had sprayed himself with knock-out gas.

..... An undertaker in Twickenham put £1250 in a coffin for safekeeping. Alas, it was cremated by mistake..................

Return to Sender

A bank in Reno, Nevada, was the scene of a hold-up that went badly wrong in 1983.

The crook walked casually up to a cashier and handed her a note. It instructed her to put all the money into a bag and hand it over. The frightened girl obeyed, and the crook made his escape through the crowded city streets.

But there was a nasty shock for him when he reached home. The police were waiting to pick him – and his loot – up. The note he had given to the cashier had been written on the back of an envelope. On the other side was his address!

. . . . . A strongman in Gloucester wanted to impress his friends after an evening at the local pub, so he went outside and lifted up the nearest car. Inside were two policemen, who arrested him . . . .

Fingerlickin' Good

Austrian Airlines tell us in a flight brochure: 'Our most demanding passengers have discovered that a top chef has a finger in our delicious menus.'

Bumps in
the Night

OOH!
OUCH!

. . . or ghosties and ghoulies and long-legged beasties . . .

Aunt Harriet Rules

A real Scottish castle rebuilt in the Mohawk Valley, New York State, is the abode of a ghost known as Aunt Harriet.

In life, Harriet Cruger was a woman with a mighty strong will. It was she, with her love of all things Scottish, who ordered the building of the castle, and she ruled her domain with an iron fist. Once, when she got annoyed with her husband, she had their double bed sawn in half.

In death, Aunt Harriet continues to rule the roost. If things are not done in the castle in the way Harriet would have liked, the living are informed in no uncertain manner. Pictures swing, doors bang and cups are smashed to the floor. Though these are never the cups chosen by Aunt Harriet herself. . .

Protest from the Grave

In 1941, the grass on a grave in Wales grew in the shape of a cross . . . without the help of a living soul.

The story goes back to 1821, when John Newton was hanged for a crime he swore he did not commit. In the court, on the day the death sentence was passed, he called out, 'I am innocent and to prove it, no grass will grow on my grave for a generation.'

Within days of his burial the grass on his grave turned brown and died. Not only that, but the bare earth was the shape of a coffin.

Many attempts were made to break the curse of John Newton: the topsoil was removed and fresh earth laid on; grass seed was planted but the earth remained bare.

After more than fifty years, the beginnings of a slow change took place. Grass started to appear in patches, almost like filling in a jig-saw puzzle. But it took 55 years for the patches to come together . . . in the form of a cross.

244

Knot to be Expected

Most poltergeists just throw things about, but some are specialists – like this one in the home of Frances Smyth in Montreal, Canada.

Over a period of six weeks, almost everything that could be tied in a knot, was. That included clothes in the wardrobes, curtains at the windows, bed covers ... One evening when the family returned home, they found that the arms of the overcoats of the five teenage boys had been done up in one huge complicated knot!

Extended Cover

'The most interesting 10 years of your life could start now,' promised Northern Rock Building Society in a circular addressed to 'R. M. de Berenguer, deceased,' and sent to the administrator of the estate.

Wash Out Your Mouth, Poltergeist

Many cases have been recorded of poltergeists using voices and speaking to the people they are tormenting. But almost always the voice used does not sound human. It is as if the poltergeist was having to master a new medium, the forming of sounds into words.

Very often the beginning of communication is just a series of grunts and moans. These gradually merge together, and become a gutteral voice. The words grow clearer as the poltergeist develops a sort of whisper.

The whisper progresses to a louder voice that is easy to understand – and then very often the bad language begins. Various researchers into the subject have used such words as 'foul', 'indecent', 'obscene' and 'disgusting' to describe the language used by poltergeists.

..... *In 99 per cent of poltergeist cases, there is present in the house a disturbed adolescent* ....

245

'She Liked Ike'

General Dwight D. Eisenhower struck lucky when he was given a furnished apartment for life in a Scottish mansion, Culzean Castle in Turnberry. The living accommodation was a gift in appreciation for his leadership of the Allied Forces in World War Two.

His ghost was a dark-haired young woman dressed in an evening gown, who was not only beautiful, but also very polite. A Mrs Margaret Penney met her one day in a narrow corridor. Mrs Penney, who was plump, squeezed herself against the wall to allow the young lady to go by.

The gorgeous apparition paused, and then remarked 'I do not require any room nowadays,' and passed gracefully through Mrs Penney's side.

. . . . . *Actress Olivia de Havilland once walked home from a party with a friend she hadn't seen for a long time. The next day she learned that he had died only hours before the party began . . . . . .*

What Was Carlos Up To?

Top of the league of haunted houses in Britain was Borley Rectory, which stood near Sudbury in Suffolk. It was haunted on a grand scale from 1875 until the middle of this century, when it was gutted by fire.

An earlier owner, the Reverend Henry Bull, who had a family of seventeen children, had added a new wing to the building. Every one of the thirty-five rooms was haunted.

Almost every kind of ghostly carryings-on happened there – a girl in white, a nun, a headless man, and Henry Bull's dead son. Noises heard included the galloping of horses, dogs barking, bell-ringing, rushing water, smashing crockery, breaking windows, and a woman's voice that repeated loudly, 'Don't, Carlos, don't!' It was never learned whether Carlos did.

After Hours Apparitions

Do the spirits of dead drinkers return to their favourite pubs? That was the question in the mind of Elizabeth Harding when she took over the 500-year-old 'Swan Inn' in Essex.

The ghosts were a noisy lot: as the landlady lay anxiously in her bed after 'Time, gentlemen, please', she could hear ornaments crashing to the floor, the saloon doors banging and chairs being dragged around the bar. And her dog, used to a lifetime of bar-room life, refused to sleep downstairs.

It was not unusual for the lights to be blazing and the saloon doors blocked with chairs on the following morning.

247

Unlucky Thirteen

Few people dared to spend a night, or an evening, at the old inn near Tisakurt in Hungary. Certainly local people stayed clear of the place, even during the day. But a few strangers, looking for a place to buy, had stayed there – though not for long! Always they left in terror, frightened away by the same ghastly apparition in the dining-room: thirteen phantom figures seated round the table, their lips curled back in the mirthless grin of death.

The old inn had been kept by Lazio Kronberg and his wife, Susi. There came a time when the couple had terrible problems. World War One had ruined their business, their daughter had run away to be a prostitute, and their son had left the house after being beaten by his father. The years ahead seemed hopeless. But they had a plan.

In the years 1919 to 1922, ten people ate their last meal in the old inn. The vintage wine after the meal was the killer – it was well-laced with strychnine. Each guest terminated his stay in a six-foot deep trench filled with quicklime in a nearby wood.

As the trench filled up, the wealth of the Kronbergs increased. The couple decided – just one more, and they would seal the trench for ever. The last guest was a jolly fat man, who carried a very heavy suitcase. It must contain something well worth while!

The meal was served, the vintage wine offered and sipped. The face of the jolly fat man convulsed as the others had done. He slumped in the remains of his meal. The Kronbergs searched the suitcase. There was a fortune in gold coins. But there was something else – a snapshot of the Kronbergs themselves! Horror dawned on the couple, and it gave way to a great grief. Their long-lost son had returned – returned with his fortune, and they had murdered him!

. . . . . *A Scottish sportsman was once curious about his eight Kaffirs who were on a hunting expedition two hundred miles away; a Zulu witch doctor was able to tell him exactly what was happening to them* . . . .

248

..... *The voice of James Cagney's dead father once warned him to slow down when he was driving very fast. He did. Around the next corner was a car towing a caravan that had stalled in the middle of the road ....*

Heart-stopper for a Heart-throb

People who are psychic are more likely to see ghosts than those who are not. Rudolph Valentino, heart-throb of the silent screen, was deeply psychic.

On his honeymoon in Europe, he took time off to see the ancient ruins of a castle. He was wandering through the gloomy dungeons and torture chambers when he had to stoop to enter a low doorway. Suddenly, he heard a scream of fear echo through the building.

About to beat a hasty retreat, he caught sight of large rusty hooks with chains dangling from the walls, and from one of the chains hung a skeleton, toes dangling just clear of the floor.

Intrigued, Valentino approached the skeleton and reached out to touch it. At that moment the terrible apparition disappeared.

There's a Corpse at the Door

A policeman's lot is not a happy one, especially, it seems, in Ghogte near Bombay. There, an unfortunate copper on duty outside a hospital mortuary opened the door one night only to be greeted by one of his charges – a 'corpse' with a slit throat.

The 'corpse' recovered nicely, but the astounded policeman went into deep shock ...

..... *According to those who study psychic phenomena, Britain has the highest density of ghosts in the world ....*

Your Turn, George

The ghost of Bessie Graves made sure that the man who made her a ghost got his just deserts. When living, Bessie had expected George Gaffney, who had made her pregnant, to marry her. But George had switched his affections to a more lucrative target, an elderly rich widow.

Then Bessie was found strangled with a silken cord embedded in the flesh of her neck. Scotland Yard detectives investigated, but there wasn't enough evidence to convict her lover.

Meanwhile, George was wooing in style. One evening he rolled up to the widow's house in a hansom cab. But as he neared his destination, he suddenly screamed. Sitting on the seat beside him was – Bessie! The ghost's eyes were glassy, and from the mouth lolled the swollen tongue.

A week later, George was entertained by the widow. During the evening she sent him to the cellar to fetch a bottle of wine, but George was only half-way down the steps when Bessie climbed out of the gloom. The silken cord swung from her neck, and the eyes stared even more glassily. George crashed headlong to the cellar floor.

After three weeks in hospital, George decided to leave England for Canada – widow or no widow – hoping to leave the shade of Bessie far behind him. Alas, on the evening before the journey he booked into a small hotel – and Bessie was there to greet him! The cord was no longer round her neck. It was in her hand, and she was holding it out to him.

George got the message. He sat down and wrote a full confession. Then he hanged himself.

. . . . . *Commander R. Jukes Hughes, serving in the Transkei, received a running commentary from local natives on a battle that was now taking place three hundred miles away – a commentary that proved to be accurate . . . .*

Sweet Dreams

Two stockbrokers were overheard drowning their sorrows in a City wine bar:

'All these changes in the share prices scare the life out of me,' said one. 'In fact, I worry so much, I either can't sleep, or have terrible nightmares.'

'I'm sleeping like a baby,' said the other. 'I wake every three hours and cry.'

Slay Ride

The headless ghost of Ormond Mallory rides its horse up the staircase of Castle Sheela in Ireland every Christmas night.

At the age of eighteen, Ormond was left a fortune by his father, and quickly began to squander it on every kind of indulgence. So disgusted was his mother with his behaviour that she returned to her native Hungary with the rest of her children – all daughters.

From then on, the domestic arrangements at the castle went to pieces. The only 'improvement' installed was a ramp by the main staircase, which allowed Ormond's dearly-loved horse to get to its master's bedroom, where it was allowed to sleep.

But one Yuletide, Ormond's mother returned, and arranged a huge party for Christmas night. During the day, Ormond went hunting, so the party was in full swing before he returned – in a most peculiar fashion.

The horse came to the castle door, and as it made for the ramp, the guests saw that tied to its back was the headless corpse of its owner – clearly grisly revenge for one of his worst misdeeds. The horse stumbled up the ramp, sank to the floor of the bedroom, and died.

Now, every Christmas night . . .

EEK
OOH
AHH
OUCH
OOF!

Phantom at the Opera

The old Metropolitan Opera House in America had a particularly unfriendly ghost. It was the wraith of former opera singer Mme Frances Alda.

Even in life, Mme Alda hated to see other singers being successful, and in death she did not change. Her ghost often rustled noisily into the audience, wriggled about in its seat, and crinkled its programme. When a soprano was on stage, it hissed, 'Flat! Flat!' and nudged its unfortunate neighbour. One opera-goer swears that her ribs were black and blue from the nudgings of the critical apparition.

Bloodstained Bandage Horror

Four men had been adrift in a dinghy in the Atlantic for 25 days, and they were crazed with hunger. Captain Rutt it was who made the suggestion that one of them would have to be eaten. Two of the shipwrecked sailors agreed, but 18-year-old Dick Tomlin said that he would never eat human flesh. So the obvious choice was to eat Dick.

The three survivors were picked up four days later. The captain of the rescue vessel was horrified to find Dick's remains under a tarpaulin. Back in England, the three were condemned to death for murder, but in view of the circumstances the Home Secretary commuted the sentences to six months.

After serving his time, one of the three, Josh Dudley, was employed as a drayman. Within a few weeks his team of horses saw something in the London fog that terrified them. They bolted, dashing Dudley to the road, where his skull was broken. Witnesses said that a figure swathed in bloodstained bandages appeared in the fog, and vanished after Dudley's death.

Badly shaken by this occurrence, Captain Rutt went looking for the third survivor, Will Hoon. He found the seaman, sodden with drink, in desperately bad health. Hoon was taken to the charity ward of a hospital. Within days he died screaming. Other patients in the ward said that a figure in bandages had held him down, and vanished when the seaman died.

Almost insane with terror, Rutt went to the police and begged to be locked up. In view of the man's mental state, they decided that it might be safer to put him in a cell for the night. That night at 3 a.m. screams of terror brought the police running to Rutt's locked cell. They unlocked the door and found Rutt on his bunk, his dead eyes staring. His hands were clenched, and locked in the fingers were shreds of bloodstained bandages!

Countdown

A five-year-old boy, Benjamin Blyth, was out walking with his father and asked him what time it was; his father said it was half-past seven. A few minutes later the child said: 'In that case, I have been alive . . . ' and named the exact number of seconds since his birth.

When they got home, his father took a sheet of paper and worked it out. 'You made a mistake – you were wrong by 172,800 seconds.' 'No I wasn't,' said the child, 'you forgot the two leap years in 1820 and 1824.'

Number Wonders

John and Michael are twins in a state mental hospital in America. Although they are mentally subnormal with an IQ of only 60, they can name the day of the week of any date in the past or future forty thousand years.

Asked, let us say, about 6 March 1877, they shout almost instantly: 'Tuesday.' And they have no more difficulty about a date long before the Great Pyramid was built.

Yet the twins have great difficulty with ordinary addition and subtraction and cannot even attempt multiplication and division.

From Beyond the Grave

A farmer named Michael Conley, of Ionia, Chicasaw County, was found dead in the outhouse of an old people's home, and his body was sent to the morgue in Dubuque, Iowa. Since the workclothes he was wearing were filthy, they were tossed outside the door of the morgue.

When the farmer's daughter was told that her father was dead, she fainted. And when she woke up, she insisted that her father had appeared to her and told her that he had sewed a roll of dollar bills in the lining of his grey shirt. She described precisely the clothes he was wearing – including slippers – and said that the money was wrapped in a piece of an old red dress that had belonged to herself.

No one took her dream seriously, assuming she was upset by her father's death. But the doctor advised them that it might set her mind at rest if they fetched the clothes. No one in the family had any idea of the clothes the farmer had been wearing at the time of his death. But the coroner confirmed that they were precisely as his daughter had described. And in the lining of the grey shirt, which still lay outside in the yard, they found a roll of money wrapped in a piece of red cloth and sewn into the bosom.

Home Grown

Daniel Dunglas Home was the most remarkable medium of the 19th century.

He performed his astonishing feats in broad daylight: he caused heavy articles of furniture to float up to the ceiling; he himself floated in at one window and out at another; he washed his face in blazing coals. He was tested dozens of times and never caught out in anything that looked like fraud.

And, in case you're thinking that someone as odd as this must have ended badly – he died at the age of 53, having spent his last years flitting between Russia and the French Riviera with his beautiful second wife. . .

The Sexy Spectre of Cannock

Some ghosts are, it seems, attracted by the 'emotional energy' of the living. Such was the case of the sexy ghost of Cannock in the Midlands. The ghost looked to be in his late thirties, and had black hair slicked back with some kind of astral hair dressing. It haunted the house of Denise Dyke and her mother, and had a way of leaping out of the wardrobe into the bed of the 17-year-old – when she was in it.

Even Ghosts Are Mortal

According to the experts, ghosts are not, as you might imagine, immortal. It seems that they begin to deteriorate after about 400 years. But there are exceptions to every rule, and one of these is a group of Roman soldiers that have been seen on three occasions marching in the cellars of the Treasurer's House of York Minster. Perhaps they are still looking for their back-pay!

The Grisly Hand of Tarrant Hinton

If you ever find yourself in the Dorset village of Tarrant Hinton, do not be worried if you see an unattached hand. The vision may have nothing to do with Hardy's Ale. The poor thing is simply looking for its arm.

It used to belong to Trumpet Major Blandford, a member of the dragoons, who did a little poaching on the side. He was surprised by gamekeepers in December 1880. There was an exchange of gunfire, during which Blandford's hand was severed. He escaped to London, but there he died. Villagers gave the hand a decent burial in the churchyard, but at times it does feel lonely. . .

Doctor! Doctor!

... or strong medicine ...

Cool-Aid

Researchers in Canada claim to have found a new way of easing toothache. It's a sort of do-it-yourself acupuncture – but without the needles. On the back of the hand is the 'Hoku' point, and it seems that rubbing ice on it works almost as well as needles.

So, in the small hours when it can be difficult to get hold of a dentist, visit the fridge instead!

No Respecter of Authority

When the plague known as the Black Death struck London in 1348, it was no respecter of persons. One of the first to flee the stricken city was the Abbot of Westminster. He was also one of the first to die.

In the space of one year, three successive Archbishops of Canterbury died.

New Teeth for New

So transplants are nothing new! Here is some advice from *The General Practice of Physic*, a publication of 1793:

> 'It is now become a Practice, especially in France, upon drawing a sound Tooth, to replace it in its Socket; where, with proper Precautions, it will fasten again. After the Extraction of the Tooth, have a Gargle of Honey, mixed with the Juice of the Herb Mercury, common Salt, and Spring-Water, and then put it in its former place; and it will become more useful than before.

> 'The French Operators have improved this Hint; and when the Tooth is rotten, or otherwise unfit to be replaced, they put another sound human Tooth in the Room of it, when it can be had; otherwise one of any other Animal, that is of a Size suitable for the purpose.'

But why draw a sound tooth in the first place? Odd!

Gardening with Tears

An eight-year-old boy in Cape Town, South Africa, was sent home from school one day with a swollen eye. The condition became worse, so his parents took him to a doctor. An examination showed a seed and sprout growing out of the left eye. It seems that his eyeball provided the essential conditions for germination: moisture, warmth, fresh air, and protection from strong light.

Microsurgery removed the growing plant from just under the surface of the eyeball, though it's likely the lad will never be keen on gardening.

Once Every Four Hours

Sufferers from arthritis who want a change from pain tablets might like to try an effective substitute . . . sex.

A director of the National Institute for Human Relationships in America says the sexual activity stimulates a release of additional cortisone into the blood, which reduces pain and swelling in inflamed joints. Arthritis patients were interviewed on the subject, and up to 70% of them confirmed that sex did help.

The soothing effect lasts from four to six hours. So the prescription is much the same as for pain tablets!

The Head of the Queue

The scene: a crowded doctor's waiting-room in Birmingham. There is an air of impatience.

Enter a Pakistani, who strides towards the surgery. A woman stands up, grabs him by the arm and says, slowly and deliberately, 'We are all before you. Do . . . you . . . understand?'

The Pakistani replies, equally slowly and deliberately, 'No, you are all after me. I . . . am . . . the . . . doctor.'

There's No Justice!

An inmate of Ohio State Penitentiary, Charles Justice, helped to design the jail's first electric chair. After his release, he committed a murder and was condemned to death. The place of execution was Ohio State Penitentiary. The instrument of execution was the electric chair.

Bandit on the Run

When the pop group Revolver were on holiday in Israel in 1969, their minibus was held up by a bandit. One of the group, Tony Price, found himself looking down the barrel of a sub-machine gun. 'Drive on,' said the bandit, 'or I'll blow your head off.'

Tony did drive on – fast – into a deep pile of sand. The bandit was flung forward and his gun went off, injuring his foot. Tony grabbed the gun and shoved the wounded crook out of the bus. The last they saw of him was a dejected figure, limping off into the dunes.

The police found him later, however, following his trail of blood.

. . . . . *Advertisement in the British Medical Journal: 'Surgical instruments: complete assortment of deceased surgeons.'* . . . .

Pin Money

In days gone by the Chinese used to pay their acupuncturists only if they remained healthy. A farmer who became too ill to work despite treatment would expect his acupuncturist to do his work for him.

Ruling-class families often kept an acupuncturist in their homes, and a severe illness or death in the family could result in the unfortunate man being beheaded.

260

Courtroom Crack

Court usher Jan Pearce, aged 64, of Plymouth, soon regretted his offer to be PC Brian Stable's guinea pig.

As the PC prepared to demonstrate an arm-hold necessary to detain a prisoner, a loud crack echoed through the court-room. At first the policeman thought he had torn the usher's shirt; in fact Mr Pearce's arm was broken.

The Constable was one of his most devoted visitors in hospital.

. . . . . *A hundred Spanish paratroopers had a special meal to celebrate an accident-free drop. Before they reached the coffee, they were all rushed off to hospital with food poisoning* . . . .

The Bump was a Drunk

Late one night in 1983, Mrs Sally Solomons was so fed up at having to wait for the return of her husband from a drinking session with the boys that she decided to go out and fetch him herself.

As she reversed the car by the front door, however, there was a nasty bump. Sally got out to look, and found she had driven over the prostrate form of her husband. Alas, he hadn't quite made it to the door!

Superman's Crash Landing

David Webb of Doncaster spent an evening watching videos of his hero, Superman. Later that night, in his dreams he *was* his hero, flying here and there on missions of mercy. But in the morning he woke up in the garden with broken ribs, a dislocated jaw and numerous bruises. It seems that he 'flew' out of the window in his sleep.

Knock-out Dinner

When the butler of the 19th century Scots physician James Simpson went into the dining room to clear away after a dinner party, he found all the guests stretched out across the table, fast asleep. But for once this wasn't because the conversation was exceptionally boring, or the food terrible. Instead, it was all in aid of an experiment.

Simpson was a pioneer in the use of chloroform as an anaesthetic, and after dinner he had asked his colleagues to take a whiff of the gas. They all agreed – and quickly found themselves falling asleep where they sat.

Despite this success, doctors were very slow to accept the idea of an anaesthetic for surgery. The person who really made the notion popular was Queen Victoria, who took chloroform to dull the pain of childbirth. And who can blame her – she had nine children in all!

Not Hear, Hear

A man in New York wore a hearing aid for almost 25 years despite a suspicion that it wasn't working as well as it ought. Then, during a visit to the local hospital, it was discovered that it had been fitted to the wrong ear. When it was switched over the man found he could hear normally again – for the first time in nearly a quarter of a century!

Stiff Task

American woman overheard in a Mayfair bar: 'Joe's not as limber as he used to be. These days, it's as much as he can do to touch his knees without bending his toes.'

Living by Numbers

Being ill at sea in an old sailing ship was a chancy business. The ships didn't carry a doctor, so the job was done by the ship's captain, who had no medical training.

But there was a system — of sorts! Each captain had a sea chest of medical remedies, and a copy of a manual entitled, *Cox's Companion to the Sea Medicine Chest.* This manual listed and numbered most of the known diseases, as well as their symptoms and remedies.

When a seaman was taken ill, the captain, with the manual handy, carried out a short inspection. He then boldly announced the disease and its number, and prescribed a remedy with the matching number.

Unfortunately, there were times when the supply of particular remedies ran out. At least one captain, when there was a shortage of remedy number 7, simply mixed the remedies for diseases 3 and 4, and used the result as a replacement.

Letting off Steam

A doctor in 1837 who was, naturally, interested in the effects of drugs, gave a friend some hemp – more familiar to us as marijuana. Having taken the stuff, the guinea pig sprang from his seat, shrieked with laughter, and shouted, 'Oh, ye gods! I'm a locomotive!'

For about three hours the happy man paced to and fro with measured stride, breathing out in violent gasps. When he spoke, he divided his words into jerked syllables, at the same time using his arms like the cranks of imaginary wheels.

The climax arrived when he was about to quench his thirst with a cup of water. He suddenly put it down without drinking, and exclaimed, 'How can I fill my boiler when I'm letting off steam?'

Just the Bare Bones

Human bodies for dissection were eagerly sought during the 18th century. A prize to be regarded with reverence was the body of one O'Brien, an Irish giant of seven feet seven inches. A famous dissector named Hunter determined to have it at all costs. But O'Brien had heard of Hunter's intentions, so he took special precautions to avoid the dreaded scalpel.

Before he died, O'Brien persuaded several of his countrymen to take his body to the sea, and sink it in deep water. Hunter, meanwhile, was in cahoots with the undertaker, and arranged to have the coffin locked in a barn while the mourners rested at an inn during their long progress to the coast. Just as Hunter had hoped, the mourners drank deeply and slept soundly. The coffin was opened and the huge corpse extracted. Then stones were placed in the coffin, and the lid secured.

Triumphantly, Hunter transported the magnificent specimen back to his surgery in Earl's Court, where O'Brien was soon reduced to one of the longest skeletons in the business.

All Wrapped Up in His Work

Doctors were set an unusual problem when a van rolled up to a casualty department at Southend in August, 1978. In the back of the vehicle was Janos, the Incredible Rubber Man, and he needed help – badly!

It seems that he was lowered to the floor of the circus, hanging from a trapeze. His legs were wrapped up behind his head. This was quite normal. What wasn't normal was that he stayed that way, despite the best efforts of himself and all his friends. It took doctors half-an-hour to sort out Janos. They then ordered him to lie flat on his back for a week.

The Good Old Days

According to one school of medical opinion in the 19th century, plunging children into cold water cured them of convulsions, coughs, inflammation of the ears, navel and mouth, rickets, pimples and scabs, suppression of urine, vomiting and a want of sleep.

Bathing in cold water was also recommended for a wide range of adult afflictions. It was suggested that, 'In winter, snow may be mixed with the water. With weaklings, warm water may be used at the beginning, then by and by, colder, and lastly quite cold water.'

Yellow For Go

Depressed? Need cheering up? Well, American doctor Elior Kinarthy says you don't need pills or drugs. Just look at something yellow. He has dozens of patients who simply carry a yellow card in their wallet and gaze at it for ten seconds when they're feeling down.

Wonder what colour his bills are. . .

265

The Surly Bonds of Earth

Jacques Lefèvre left nothing to chance when he decided to commit suicide. He tied a noose round his neck and fixed the end of the rope to a stake at the top of a cliff. Jacques then drank some poison, set fire to his clothes, and hurled himself over the cliff. At the last moment, he even tried to shoot himself – just to make sure.

By chance, the bullet missed Jacques, but cut the rope. Free of the threat of hanging, he plunged into the sea. The sudden ducking extinguished the flames, and made him vomit the poison.

A well-intentioned fisherman picked him up, and took him to hospital, where he died – of exposure!

Who Put That There?

A Great Surgeon, in whose presence lesser mortals trembled, was engaged in some difficult bowel surgery. His houseman, new to the job and very nervous, was keeping the patient's liver out of the Great Man's field of action.

After some time the Great Surgeon realized that the patient's arteries were not pulsating as they should, and he informed the anaesthetist of the fact. The anaesthetist confirmed that the heart had indeed stopped beating.

Cool as a cucumber, the Great Surgeon cut through the diaphragm, and began massaging the heart from inside the patient's chest. The houseman, functioning as he should, dashed off to get the emergency drugs suitable for the occasion. He primed a syringe with adrenalin, and fitted a long needle specially designed to inject the drug straight into the heart. Without hesitation he plunged the needle through the skin, between the ribs – and straight into the Great Surgeon's hand!

Night Shadows

A doctor not long qualified was in charge when a young girl was brought into hospital with fairly severe asthma. The time was 3 a.m. When the X-rays arrived, he saw that at the top of each lung there were vertical shadows of an unusual shape. He studied them, but could make nothing of them. Becoming alarmed, he rang up the consultant and called him out from his bed.

When the consultant arrived, he looked at the X-rays and at the girl. Then he turned to the doctor. 'You fool!' he grated between bared teeth. 'These are her pigtails!'

. . . . . A man in Stroud swallowed a pint of periwinkles, complete with shells. On request, he repeated the feat, and died . . . .

Campbell's Patent Poison Extractor

John Bunyan Campbell believed that the true secret of health was to get poison out of the body before it did any damage.

He reckoned that the body battles against three kinds of poison: animal, vegetable and mineral.

So he invented an electrical poison extractor. Patients suffering from one of these afflictions had to sit on a chair with their feet bared. Positioned below the feet was a poison receiver, which contained an appropriate object, such as a piece of raw meat, a lump of iron, or a vegetable. A positive electrode was attached to the patient's neck, with a negative electrode on one of the feet.

When all was in place, the electricity was switched on, and a current flowed through the patient's body. The idea was that the current would collect the poison *en route*, and at the end of its journey deposit it safely in the receptacle. A course of treatment was 6-8 sessions of thirty minutes each.

No records of results have been left to posterity, and readers are not advised to experiment with the idea.

A Gathering of Talent

While walking in Hove, a doctor noticed a crowd of people gathered round a prostrate figure on the pavement, so he decided to offer his professional skills. Bending over the patient as he approached was a man in tweeds. The doctor announced his qualifications, and was about to brush the fellow aside, when the tweedy character protested loudly, saying, 'I am a fully qualified instructor in First Aid with the St John Abulance Brigade.'

An argument ensued, during which the patient lay neglected on the pavement. But the vacuum was filled by a lad of eighteen, who pushed forward, declaring that he was a second-year medical student. The lad had hardly got to work when a lovely blonde appeared, knelt by the supine figure, and applied an ear to the chest.

Then she looked up and became aware of a certain tension in the air. She smiled sweetly and said, 'Oh, it's quite all right, I'm a social worker!'

. . . . . A Scotsman in court who was answering to a charge of poaching, said, 'I shot the pheasant because it was looking ill.' . . . .

Cough or Car Medicine?

Doctors in the old days often prescribed the drinking of tar-water for coughs, bronchitis and asthma. Patients were advised to pour a gallon of cold water on to a quart of tar, stir well and let stand for two days. When the tar had settled on the bottom, the water was bottled. Half a pint of the concoction was taken morning and night, and patients were advised that it was less unpleasant to drink the stuff if the nostrils were held at the same time.

The tar itself could also be used for 'greasing of coach or cart wheels'.

I DON'T BELIEVE IT!

..... *'We are sorry to announce that Mr Albert Brown has been quite unwell, owing to his recent death, and is taking a short holiday to recover.' Note in Parish Magazine* ....

What Doctors Are For

Konrad Adenauer, who was German Chancellor, developed a bad cold when he was in his late eighties. A doctor was summoned. After examining the old man, the doctor said, 'Please don't expect miracles. I can't make you any younger, you know.'

Adenauer responded, 'I don't expect you to make me younger. The main thing is that you should succeed in making me older.'

Under the Spotlight

MEMOIRS OF A WINDOW CLEANERS

... or tales of the famous and infamous ...

Bailing Out the Great

Herbert Sutcliffe's fame is legendary in the world of cricket. He was at the height of his powers when he consented to play in a charity match between two village teams in Yorkshire. Instead of the usual few dozen spectators on the day, thousands turned up.

Pleased by his pulling power, Herbert decided to thrill the faithful following with a six off the first ball. So he stepped out of the crease and opened his shoulders, determined to thrash the ball over the pavilion.

But the turf was not as smooth as at Lord's. The ball bounced well above the flailing bat, and into the hands of the wicketkeeper. In a flash, he whipped off the bails and yelled, 'Howzat!'

For a second there was a breathless hush. Then the umpire roared, 'Not out!' A sigh of relief went round the vast crowd.

In a voice low but full of menace, the umpire said to the wicket-keeper, 'Tha great blithering blockhead! Dost think these folk hez cum to watch *thee* stump?'

..... *The inventor of the modern lavatory system, Thomas Crapper, wrote an autobiography entitled 'Flushed With Pride'.* ....

Churchillian Modesty

A woman once said to Winston Churchill, 'Are you not thrilled to know, Mr Churchill, that every time you make a speech, the hall is packed to overflowing?'

The great man replied, 'Yes indeed, it is quite flattering. However, when I feel this way, I always try to remember that if, instead of making a speech, I was being hanged, the crowd would be twice as big.'

272

A Quick Starter

At four years of age, when most of us make 'music' by banging pan lids together, Wolfgang Amadeus Mozart was composing minuets and other pieces.

At the age of six he was playing before kings, and at seven he published violin and harpsichord sonatas. At eight he was performing the works of Bach and Handel before the English Court, and at ten writing his first oratorio. His first opera was written when he was fourteen.

Walking All Over Garbo

If you want to walk on the features of the great film actress, Greta Garbo, visit the National Gallery in London.

On the floor of the main centre landing of the entrance hall, her features are part of a mosaic representing the 'Awakening of the Muses'. The originals of the Muses are famous writers and other artists. Garbo lent her features to the Muse of Tragedy.

. . . . . The Welsh poet Dylan Thomas set his famous radio play in verse, 'Under Milk Wood', in an imaginary Welsh village, Llareggub. The name spelt backwards means just that . . . .

Royal Death

Charlemagne, King of the Franks and Holy Roman Emperor, did not allow even death to interfere with his royal dignity. In the year 1,000 his tomb was opened in Aachen Cathedral in Germany. His remains were revealed, seated on a throne, a crown on his head – well, skull – a globe in one hand, a sceptre in the other, and the imperial mantle on his shoulders.

273

Bacon and Chicken

Francis Bacon, 16th century philosopher and statesman, would have lived longer if he hadn't branched out and tried an early experiment in refrigeration.

Snow lay on the ground when Bacon and a friend were riding along in a coach. Bacon wondered if snow might not preserve flesh, as salt was used to do in those days.

The pair bought a hen from a woman in a nearby cottage, killed it and stuffed it with snow. Unfortunately, the snow so chilled Bacon that he caught a cold and died three days later.

Dewhiskered Hyena

Julius Jacob von Haynan, an Austrian general in the 19th century, was known as 'the hyena of Brescia'. He was notorious for the savage cruelty with which he suppressed revolutionary movements in Italy and Hungary. During a visit to a London brewery, he was set on by infuriated workmen who tore out his whiskers.

Job for Life

After conducting a concert in 1939, Sir Thomas Beecham returned to his hotel. He saw a lady sitting in the foyer whose face he knew well, but for the life of him he could not attach a name to it. But he greeted her, and said, 'I do hope you enjoyed the concert.'

There followed some small talk, and then Sir Thomas remembered that the lady had a brother. He said, 'How is your dear brother, and what is he up to at the moment?'

The penny dropped when the lady replied, 'Oh, he's still King, you know.'

Photographic Memory

The English historian Thomas Macaulay could read a page of print once, and immediately repeat it from memory. It is said that he could memorize rapidly the entire contents of a book, and later repeat them almost without a mistake.

Hanging On to Dear Life

Rasputin, sometimes known as the Mad Monk of Russia, proved hard to kill. In 1916, a group of high noblemen decided that the holy man's influence on the Czar was doing nobody any good. So they decided to assassinate him.

Rasputin became the victim of a series of attacks, all in one day. He was stabbed, shot and poisoned, but all to no avail. Finally, the assassins successfully completed the job by throwing him into the ice-cold waters of a river.

In fact, it was all a waste of time, because the Russian Revolution broke out within three months.

It's the Thought that Counts

Ecuador is not a rich country, but it was felt that the Ecuadorian poet, José Olmedo, deserved a statue in his honour. Instead of commissioning a sculptor to do the job however, it was decided to make do with an unwanted statue of the English poet, Lord Byron.

Cashing In

A boy at boarding school was broke, so he wrote to his grandmother, politely requesting a small funding. The response was a lecture on the evils of extravagance – but no money.

A few days later Granny received another letter. It read: 'Dearest Grandmamma, I received your letter, and hope you will not think I was disappointed because you could not send me any money. It was very good of you to give me good advice. I sold your letter for four pounds ten.'

The schoolboy became King George V. 'Granny' was Queen Victoria.

We Should Have Brought the Cat

If you're feeling out of your depth in grand company, the golden rule is to do exactly what your host or hostess does. Or is it?

Guests of President of the United States Calvin Coolidge followed this advice at a formal White House dinner. All through the meal they kept an eye on his every move and followed just moments behind. Then, when the coffee arrived, the President startled his guests by pouring half of it into his saucer. Unsure of the procedure, they followed suit. Then he added cream and sugar. So did they.

But they were completely disconcerted when he leaned down and placed the saucer on the floor. After all, there was only one cat!

..... As a way of warding off evil spirits, the legs of Disraeli's bed stood in bowls of salty water . . . .

The Second Coming

During a reception at Number 10, Downing Street, Mrs Mary Wilson was entertaining guests while her husband was completing some urgent paperwork upstairs. A group of the guests were discussing religion, and one of them said, 'At least we know there is one above who knows all the answers.'

Having heard only the last sentence of the discussion, Mrs Wilson said brightly, 'Yes, indeed. Harold will be down in a minute.'

Unsung Heroes

Sir Edmund Hillary and Sherpa Tensing will be for ever remembered as the men who first conquered Everest. What is often forgotten is that their triumph would have been impossible without the backing of twelve other expert climbers, 40 Sherpa guides and more than 700 porters.

Echo from the Past

When Humphrey Bogart, star of the film 'To Have and Have Not' was buried in 1957, a gold whistle was placed in the coffin with him.

The whistle was put there by his wife, Lauren Bacall, who appeared in the film with him. She had the whistle inscribed with this line from the film: 'If you need anything, just whistle.'

..... *The original 'Nosey' Parker was Matthew Parker, Archbishop of Canterbury from 1559, who had an unenviable reputation for not minding his own business. He also had an extremely long nose* ....

You Must Be Joking!

When two temperaments as different as General Eisenhower's and the actor, Michael Caine's, come into contact, sparks fly.

Michael Caine was doing his National Service in Germany, when his unit was visited by the General. Caine's platoon had been instructed to dig fox-holes, to give Eisenhower something to inspect.

While they waited for the arrival of the top brass, it rained heavily. For some hours Caine stood at the ready, up to his hips in water. When Eisenhower turned up at last, he asked Caine if he was thinking of staying in the army. The answer was a very positive, 'No thanks!'

Caine was confined to barracks for a month.

The Marriage of Heaven and Hell

The wife of the English poet William Blake used to complain that her husband spent so much time in heaven that he rarely spoke to her. According to Blake, he had long conversations with the bible prophets and other people famous in history.

With Spots On

The bandleader in a fashionable restaurant made the grave mistake of sending a note to the famous playwright, George Bernard Shaw, who was sitting at a table. The note asked Shaw if there was anything he would like the band to play.

Immediately the reply came back, 'Yes, dominoes.'

A Question of Parts

Lord Mountbatten once visited Malta to film scenes for a television series about his life. He was met at the airport by a young and rather over-eager reporter from the local radio station.

They talked about the series for a while, before the reporter asked seriously, 'And what part will you be playing in the series, Lord Mountbatten?'

But the Greatest of These is Charity

During a charity ball, George Bernard Shaw asked a dowager for a dance. The lady exclaimed, 'Oh, Mr Shaw, what made you ask poor little me to dance?'

To which Shaw replied, 'Well, this is a charity ball, isn't it?'

All Rounder

Most people think of the great W. G. Grace as one of the finest cricketers of all time. But few are aware of his prowess in a number of other sports. For example, during 1866, following a score of 224 not out over two days against Surrey, he went on to win the 440 yards hurdles at the National Olympian Association meeting at Crystal Palace.

Something To Be Grateful For

The famous author, Charles Lamb, was often mistaken for a clergyman, because of his habit of wearing a white cravat. Once at a dinner party he was asked to say grace. Lamb surveyed the company and said, 'Isn't there a clergyman present?'

When he was told there was not, he bowed his head and said, 'Let us thank the Lord.'

Giving Things a Lift

Derrick, the hangman, was so efficient at his job that, when he was condemned to death for a criminal offence, the Earl of Essex pardoned him. The sting in the tale for Essex was that when his turn came to be condemned to death for treason, it fell to Derrick to carry out the execution.

But Derrick's fame does not end there. So well known did he become during the fifty years of his grisly career, that the hangman's gibbet became known as a derrick. And then, when modern cranes were constructed, they were referred to as derricks, because of the similarity of the shapes.

In fact, the word *derrick* is now used for many devices involved in moving heavy weights, and even for the framework of an oil well.

. . . . . Denis Norden, the scriptwriter and broadcaster, once asked a lady at a party, 'What happened to that skinny blonde your husband used to be married to?' Came the reply, 'I dyed my hair.' . . . .

On Your Knees!

Tourists to Britain are often overawed by the archaic customs of our great institutions.

One day a party was being shown round the House of Commons. Down one of the corridors they saw approaching the Lord Chancellor's procession, led by Lord Hailsham. As he passed the excited group, the famous peer caught sight of an old friend walking just behind them. He raised an arm and called out, 'Neil!'

The tourists dropped to their knees.

. . . . . When Hitler's Central Bank Governor was told that Hitler was dead, he said, 'I wouldn't believe Hitler was dead, even if he told me so himself.' . . . .

What Service!

In the London Marathon of 9th May, 1982, Roger Bourban, a waiter from Beverly Hills, ran the full course in waiter's regalia. Not only that, but he carried a free-standing, open bottle of mineral water on a tray (weighing 3lb 2oz) all the way.

His time, which was 2hrs 47mins, was faster than those of the winners of the first four marathons of the modern Olympic Games.

Dead Wrong

Mayoral candidate Stanley Goldman, 69, died of a heart attack in Hollywood, minutes after a speech accusing his opponent of being too old for the job.

Death of a Legend

In 1860 an advertisement appeared in the *San Francisco Herald* which read:

'WANTED: Young, skinny, wiry fellows, not over eighteen, willing to risk death daily. Orphans preferred. Wages $25 per week. Apply Central Overland Pony Express.'

The cinema has made the Pony Express renowned throughout the world, but in fact it only lasted for 18 months and was a financial flop. The idea was to provide an express mail service from Missouri to California, by the fastest route – and that meant difficult country infested with hostile Indian tribesmen. Many of the young, skinny, wiry fellows ended their career with an arrow in the back.

The only people who used the service were those who needed to send urgent messages across the continent. But shortly after it had begun, the first telegraph wire across the country was completed. From then on, 'urgent' could mean 'instant'. It was the death of the Pony Express.

Jammed and Slammed

Renowned in the Royal Navy is the frigate HMS *Ulster*, which made the most remarkable manoeuvre in May 1966.

It was on training exercises in the Tamar estuary at Plymouth when the engine control jammed in the 'half astern' position. A frantic attempt to unjam it left it on 'full astern'. The ship picked up speed and sailed backwards towards a stone jetty.

The captain's attempt to telephone the engine-room having failed, he ordered an officer to go down and explain the situation. But the officer could make no headway down against the entire ship's company all heading up to emergency stations. When the frigate hit the jetty, the ship was instantly shortened by seven feet. This compressed the air inside the vessel to such an extent that a sailor was shot through a hatch and landed on the jetty – uninjured!

How's Your Banting?

If you are into slimming at the moment, then you are banting. It's not a word much used nowadays, but it's in the dictionary for all to see.

It goes back to a London cabinet-maker, William Banting, who was 66 years of age, short and very, very fat. He went on a diet, cutting out butter, sugar, milk, beer, soup, potatoes and beans. Banting ate only meat, fish and dry toast.

More than cold feet

Joanna the Mad really was crazy about her husband, Philip the Handsome of Spain. But perhaps she carried things a little too far when he died. Grief-stricken, Joanna refused to bury the corpse. Instead she kept it in her bed for over three years . . .

Cool Cuban

Fidel Castro of Cuba stands head and shoulders above other contenders for the honour of being the politician who has survived most assassination attempts. By 1984 he had notched up an estimated 24 not out.

He has been missed by poison pellets, shells exploded in Havana harbour and students wielding bazookas. Objects having failed so often, a beautiful blonde agent was sent in to try her luck. But she fell in love with her bearded target and so gave up her deadly mission.

..... Victor Hugo, the famous French author, found the discipline of writing each day very difficult. Sometimes he instructed his servants to steal his clothes in the morning, so that he could not go out ....

Auto Suggestion

Some noisy collisions between motoring buffs are soon to be expected. The wily French have started down what looks like being an accident-prone circuit, for their motor manufacturers have a plan to bolster national pride – and obtain some welcome international publicity for their marques – by proclaiming a Frenchman, Edouard Delamarre-Debouttevill, the true inventor of the motor car.

The French claim that this citizen of Rouen took to the road with a petrol-driven automobile in May 1883, and had his patent registered in 1884. While the Germans have not, so far, begun massing tanks on the Rhine to avenge what they see as a national insult, they have started a paper war to defend the name of their much-revered Gottlieb Daimler.

They assert that he, more than any other man, was responsible for the birth of the motor car through his development of lightweight, fast-running, internal combustion engines. Dr Bernd Gottschalk of Daimler-Benz, makers of Mercedes cars, says historians agree that the first functional automobile ran in 1886 and it was a joint production by Daimler and Karl Benz – co-founders of Daimler-Benz.

Lord Montagu, who runs the national motor museum at Beaulieu, has weighed in saying that the French invention 'staggered about 50 feet before collapsing and was never heard of again'. British sympathies are likely to lie with the Daimler claim. After all, the innovative spirit of the great man was fired by a visit to Britain during the industrial revolution in the 1860s, when he was a student engineer in Leeds and Manchester.

Animal Antics

... or all creatures great and small ...

It's Not the Same Without the Girls

Dinosaurs may have vanished from the Earth simply because the last batch of young were all the same sex.

The theory springs from a discovery made about reptile eggs. If alligator eggs are hatched at a temperature above 34°C the babies are all males. But when the hatching is carried out at less than 30°C the babies are all females. The same experiment on another reptile, the turtle, gave a similar result, but the other way round.

Man Friday

A race-card for the Prix de L'Indre-et-Loire at Enghien in France showed that one of the horses was named Robinson Crusoe. The jockey was listed as M. Friday.

Taken to the Cleaners

Skin-diving biologists have now identified forty species of what are called cleaner fish. They pick off lice and other parasites from the bodies of other fish.

Cleaner fish don't usually travel about with their hosts. Instead they have stations among the rocks to which the customers go when they feel in need of a clean-up. Queues of fish line up in the vicinity of a station and as one satisfied customer swims away, the next fish moves in for treatment.

Cleaner fish – no matter how small – have no fear of being eaten by their customers – no matter how big. The little Red Sea wrasse, which is rarely longer than five millimetres, serves as cleaner to one of the most ferocious of all fish, the moray eel. When the wrasse has completed work on the outside of the eel, the host opens its terrifying jaws, and the little fish swim in to deal with the interior. While the wrasse is at work, the eel keeps its mouth wide open until its tiny partner has emerged.

288

Gardener's Nightmare

One word guaranteed to give gardeners nightmares is – aphids. When greenfly and blackfly – both aphids – appear on the roses and the runner beans, we reach for our spray guns. But it's no use; though gardeners and farmers destroy them, and birds and other insects devour them by the billion, aphids are the world's greatest survivors.

If the offspring of one aphid could reproduce for a single season without any interference, the progeny would be so numerous that the whole Earth would be covered with a solid layer of aphids.

Jungle Juice

Things can get out of hand in the South African jungle when elephants gorge themselves on the fermented fruit of the marula tree. The huge revellers become involved in noisy, drunken brawls, reeling about and falling over in futile attempts to charge one another.

Too Many Pigeon Pies

In the United States during the last century, there were times when the sun was darkened by vast flocks of passenger pigeons. One flock, which took three days to pass, is believed to have had more than 2,000 *million* birds in it.

Unfortunately for the passenger pigeon, it was very good to eat, and easy to kill or capture. By the beginning of the twentieth century the great flocks had all but vanished, and vain attempts were made to save the species.

In a zoo in Cincinnati in 1914, the last passenger pigeon in the world, whose name was Martha, died of old age.

Aerial Surveillance

When a man in Halifax, Yorkshire, goes for a drive in his car, his pet pigeon goes with him. Not in the car . . . not on the car . . . but a few feet higher than the car, and to the right of it. It's the ideal spot for keeping an eye on its owner.

A Good Wash with a Skeleton

What is a sponge – animal, vegetable or mineral?

At one time it was thought that sponges were plants but, in fact, they are animals. When they are brought out of the sea they still have flesh on them so they are left out in the sun until the flesh decays. The dead flesh is then washed off, and we scrub ourselves with the skeleton that remains.

. . . . . *The insect population on 2.6 kilometres of land equals the total number of people on earth* . . . .

Monster Eats Monster

The giant squid is often portrayed as a ferocious wrecker of ships and eater of people. Yet the biggest of these creatures, with tentacles as long as telephone poles and eyes the size of footballs, are really quite shy.

They live 200 to 400 metres below the surface and usually come up only when dead or dying. Much of their time is spent hiding from whales, who eat them whole. One giant squid, 12 metres long, was found intact – but very, very dead – in the stomach of a 70-tonne sperm whale.

Gotta Glow

Deep in the sunless depths of the ocean live a whole range of glow-in-the-dark creatures. One is the flashlight fish, which has no worries about ever needing new batteries – it gets its light from hitch-hiking bacteria.

Fish and bacteria exchange benefits. The fish offers the bacteria a reasonably safe home and a source of nutrients; the glowing bacteria provide the fish with light for luring other fish within striking range, communicating with fellow fish, or avoiding other fish that want to make a meal of it.

A Very Rich Diet!

Zoos always have problems supplying their animals with balanced diets but one Swedish zoo found itself with an embarrassment of riches . . .

One of the resident seals suffering from stomach ache was found to have swallowed 256 coins thrown into its pool by visitors.

TAKE 1
ALKA SELTZER
EVERY 10 COINS
ZOO DIRECTOR.

Disposable Spectacles

Having no eyelids, snakes cannot close their eyes. And a life-style of crawling on the ground means a great deal of dirt and grit in the eyes.

But snakes don't have to worry. Each time they shed their skin, the new one comes complete with a fresh pair of clear eye covers.

292

Guard and Guide Gander

An aged, blind woman in the United States had a gander that led her to church by taking the hem of her dress in its bill. During the service, the gander waited in a nearby cemetery, where it spent its time clipping the grass.

In Dumbarton, Scotland, a flock of 70 geese mounts guard over a distillery, where 115 million litres of whisky are stored. Trespassers are greeted by hissing, honking and sharp bites.

..... The ribbon worm doesn't have to worry about food shortages. It can eat up to 95% of its own body and still survive ....

Antique Feast in a Deep Freeze

One day the peasants of a small town in Siberia in 1901 could not understand why their dogs were so excited. They followed them out of town – and made a fascinating discovery. The dogs had dug up a mammoth in perfect condition which though partly covered by the frozen earth was just close enough to the surface to let the dogs have a sniff of the meat.

Although the last mammoth died about 10,000 years ago in the frozen wastes of northern Russia, it is not uncommon to find parts of the creatures preserved in the ice. But to find a complete body was unique.

Experts were summoned to deal with the huge elephant-like monster. The thick skin was carefully cut off and mounted, and the contents of the stomach examined. There was evidence still of the animal's last meal – thirteen kilogrammes of cones, flowers, moss and pieces of tree.

Fortunately, the finders of the treasure received their reward. The still-fresh meat was given to the dogs, and they feasted on it for days.

Tail-end of the Story

A tadpole loses its tail as it turns into a frog – but where does the tail go? Part is absorbed into the body as tissue and the rest is absorbed into the bloodstream.

Unfortunately, the change does not do much for the creature's character – it stops being a vegetarian and becomes a greedy carnivore – sometimes even cannibal – instead!

Let Youth Take Its Turn

People are not the only mammals that exploit their own kind. During an experiment, rats were trained to press a key that delivered some food. Someone had the bright idea of putting a young, untrained rat in with an older, trained rat. Would the older rat show the younger rat the ropes?

Over a period of time the recording instrument indicated that the key was being pressed more frequently than usual. The scientists went to the observation window to see what was happening.

The old rat was reclining in comfort under the food spout, while the younger one was pressing the key with youthful enthusiasm.

Head Down for the Iron-eater

The giant panda, which lives in the wild only in China, is described in an ancient book as an 'iron-eater'. Proof of the truth of this was provided recently when a keeper gave a panda a meal in an iron basin. The panda ate the food . . . and then, to the keeper's horror, the basin as well!

. . . . . The giraffe can kill most other animals by using its neck and head as a club . . . .

Jilted Jumbo

For eighteen years Sandra, an Indian elephant, was looked after by her companion and trainer, Helmut Krone. But when the circus visited La Spezia, in Italy, Helmut fell in love with a pretty local girl. She did not care for the life of sawdust and so Helmut was forced to choose between her and the Big Top. The circus moved on without him.

Sandra protested by going on hunger strike. Vets from Paris to Milan did what they could, but even the honey they poured down her throat was rejected. Many attempts were made by the desperate circus owners to find Helmut, but he could not be traced. Broken-hearted, Sandra simply got thinner and thinner, and finally died.

HELMUT SAYS HE WISHES HIS OLD LADY WOULD GO ON HUNGER STRIKE!

Supreme Impression

The village hall committee at Wigginton in Yorkshire wanted a simple ceremony to open the rebuilt hall. The chairman of the committee insisted that they did not want lots of dignitaries.

So, the ceremony was performed by Mulgrove Supreme, a stud stallion owned by the Queen. He did the job by leaving an imprint of a hoof in the wet concrete.

Eat Dirt, Worm!

The solution to at least part of our rubbish problems may be – worms. In a test in Florida, 1.5 acres of worms consumed about 5 tonnes of waste – five times their own weight – in a single day.

Men Are All the Same

In the days of the Raj, a district officer in the Indian Civil Service was plagued with complaints from local farmers about bears damaging their crops. So he decided to shoot a bear to discourage the others.

Our hero took up a vantage point before dawn, but it was so cold that he could hardly feel the rifle. Then a large male bear appeared, followed by a female a few feet behind.

The officer tried to sight the quivering rifle, and fired. The bullet just nicked the male bear's backside. The animal stopped, sat down, and rubbed his rump. Then he gazed at his spouse, who was standing still, looking puzzled.

Arriving at the probable explanation, the male stood, cuffed the female firmly on the ear, and then continued on his way. The female, looking aggrieved, sat down and rubbed her head.

After a few moments, she ambled sadly after her mate, taking up her usual position a few feet behind him.

To Thine Own Dog Be True

A dog was put in kennels for a fortnight while husband and wife went on holiday. When they returned, the wife dropped off at the house to get on with the unpacking, while hubby drove over to the kennels.

The return journey home was something of a nightmare. The dog howled, yapped and barked, while the driver shouted, swore and threatened the animal with immediate extermination.

Back at the house, the husband complained bitterly: 'I can't imagine what they've done at those kennels! This dog's off its rocker! Perhaps he prefers it there. I don't know!'

'I do,' said his wife calmly. 'You see, you've got the wrong dog.'

Whose Side Are They On?

Laddie and Boy, two drug-detector dogs, just didn't have their hearts in their work. They were used by the drug squad in a raid in the Midlands in 1967. While a police officer was questioning two suspects, the offenders patted the dogs who responded by lying down and going to sleep.

But they woke up when the officer moved to arrest the suspects. One of the dogs growled at him, and the other leapt up and bit him. Laddie and Boy were given their cards.

Birdbrains

Do the animals we race for our amusement really want to race? The answer may lie in what happened in 1978 when 6,745 racing pigeons were released at Preston in Lancashire. A total of 5,545 were never seen again.

Experts have come up with two possible explanations. First, they flew over a grouse moor and were shot. But the secretary of the Ayrshire Federation of Homing Pigeons said, 'I can't believe they could have got all 5,545.' Second, the birds may simply have opted out, and gone to live by the seaside in Devon. And why not?

A Blessed Coupling

The Dean of Hereford Cathedral, a somewhat pompous cleric, decided to make his importance more public by riding a horse in front of a religious procession. So he mounted his mare, and opened his prayer book to show all and sundry the degree of his piety.

But a nearby stallion, unconcerned with the dean's dignity, had his own ideas. He broke loose, made for the mare and mounted her. The unfortunate dean was securely trapped while the stallion had his way.

It's a Dog's Life

TV personality Katie Boyle had a sticker on her car which read, 'Dogs Deserve Better People'.

While driving one day she noticed people pointing at the car and making agitated gestures. She stopped to investigate. Balanced precariously on top of the car roof was her Yorkshire terrier – sitting upright in its basket.

. . . . . Owls have a reputation for being wise. The truth is that they have very small brains, and are among the least intelligent of birds. Crows and blue jays are among the most intelligent . . . .

Elephants Won't Work Overtime

The Burmese working elephant is a stickler for routine. It goes like this:

5 a.m.   Its oozie picks it up from the jungle, where it has been free all night, eating and sleeping. The oozie takes it to the river for a bath. This lasts an hour.

7 a.m.   Breakfast – a dish of steaming rice, and sometimes lentils. Then off to work which may be miles away.

9 a.m.   Begins work, dragging cut-down trees to the nearest river.

Noon   Rest for an hour.

1 p.m.   Resumes work.

4 p.m.   Stops work, whether the oozie says so or not. An elephant just won't work overtime. Back to the river for another bath.

6 p.m.   Supper. Usually mashed oatmeal with some bananas and coconuts. After supper, back to the jungle, where it completes its eating for the day – usually about 600lbs.

Ten Hens on the Richter Scale!

Earthquakes are still taking us by storm, but for animals they come as no great surprise.

In August 1979, 200 instruments along the Calaveres Fault in California failed to predict an earthquake so powerful that it shook San Francisco, 80 miles away. But in 1974, before a massive quake in China, snakes abandoned hibernation and crawled out of the ground, pigs climbed walls, hens would not go to roost, and trained German Shepherd dogs refused to obey their owners. The Chinese heeded these warnings, evacuated the area, and hundreds of thousands of people were saved.

The Hunter Who Failed to Duck

A New Zealander who went duck shooting is wondering if he should wear a crash helmet next time. The hunter blasted his shotgun at a duck, missing with both barrels. The quarry decided to counter-attack, circled its target, and dive-bombed with deadly accuracy into the hunter's face.

Damage – a broken nose, glasses and one tooth.

..... *The horsefly has a cutting tool like a pointed rod that it drives up and down to drill into its victim's skin. Once the wound has been made, the horsefly plunges a tube into it and takes a long, warm drink* . . . .

Big Job

News of old boys in a Shropshire school magazine: 'After a spell at chicken farming Peter has been engaged by a carpet company to cover Lancashire and Cheshire.'

You Get Up My Nose, Darling!

The anglerfish is so named because of the way it catches its food. It uses a rod and line technique, the rods being spines on the back fins. As the anglerfish lives in the darkness of the deep seas, it has a light organ at the ends of the rods. To attract other fish, it waves the rods about, and then snaps up the prey when it comes within striking distance.

The female anglerfish weighs up to half a tonne. The male, which is only a few millimetres long, spends almost its entire life attached to its spouse's nose.

Put Down

A middle-aged woman on the train to Winchester had been trying for some time to quieten her small dog which was yapping and snarling at an elderly man opposite.

'Boysie usually has such a sweet nature,' she sighed. 'I just don't know what to make of him.'

The man peered over his glasses at the animal. 'Well,' he suggested, 'how about a nice rug?'

Beware of the Dog

Like most south coast towns, Budleigh Salterton, Devon, has a high proportion of the elderly and infirm among its population – animal, as well as human. But their needs are borne in mind. A holiday visitor reports seeing this sign in a narrow lane off the Exmouth road: 'Please drive slowly – dog is deaf.'

A museum whose stuffed exhibits include a lamb with four eyes and a pig with two faces was up for sale at Arundel, Sussex, price £340,000.

Ferreted Out

One of the biggest of the North Sea oil platforms in the deepest water had an intractable problem. It was necessary to link the underwater well-head to the platform above by an electric cable. The two were already connected by a pipe, but none of the experts could find a way of coaxing a cable through the pipe.

A ferret handler was called in and he arrived from Scotland with two ferrets and a dead rabbit. The rabbit was blown through the pipework by means of a compressor. Then the ferret was allowed after it, wearing a harness and pulling a thin line. The ferret followed the trail of the rabbit to the sea-bed and back and the cable was pulled through after it.

. . . . . *Millions of years ago, the plains of North America were inhabited by herds of camels, about the size of a sheep* . . . .

. . . . . *In a single day, a black widow spider has been known to devour twenty husbands* . . . .

Keeping Up with Consumer Demand

The only answer for a species that gets eaten in huge quantities is to produce enough young to keep ahead of the appetites of the carnivores.

This compensation by nature leads to some spectacular numbers in the undersea world where open, hungry mouths are the order of the day. The oyster keeps ahead of consumer demand by laying 60 million eggs a year, and the turbot between 8 and 14 million. The plaice manages 300,000, and the sole 130,000, while the herring manages to keep the species going with a mere 40,000.

Significantly, the elephant, which is rarely eaten, hardly ever even produces twins.

. . . . . Women are better than men when it comes to teaching a budgie to talk. The birds find it easier to imitate a high-pitched voice . . . .

A R.I.P.-off

The antics of most animals are as nothing compared with the antics of humans about their animal pets.

The Hartsdale Canine Cemetery in Westchester, USA, has more than just dogs interred there. The 40,000 laid-to-rest pets include goldfish, cats, parrots, monkeys, salamanders and even a lion.

One lady has lashed out for 58 top-pet funerals, including those for a piglet and a bantam rooster. One dog, said to be a war hero, is buried in a major's uniform.

On a fine Sunday, at least 100 people turn up, and spend the day visiting the graves of their departed pets. One woman, who turns up twice a week, takes off her shoes before entering the cemetery, as a tribute to her late dog.

Plots cost about $500.

. . . . . Each day, just to live, the shrew has to eat its own weight in food. If it eats nothing for two hours it dies . . . .

There's No Business

Business

DOUBLE YOLKS

. . . or the show must go on . . .

I DON'T BELIEVE IT!

Monopoly Money

Dynasty star George Hamilton surprised friends at his home when he played 'Monopoly' – using $10,000 in genuine $1, $5, $10, $20, $50 and $100 bills. He wanted to make the game more exciting. But when it was over, George made the winner hand the money back. Good game, eh!

Cheque-mate

Soul singer Gladys Knight couldn't get a Beverly Hills shop-girl to cash a cheque, even though she insisted she was a big star and good for the money. Finally to prove the point she broke into a rendition of her hit 'Midnight Train to Georgia'. That did the trick and the girl accepted her cheque.

..... When the TV serial 'Dynasty' was at the height of its popularity, Joan Collins was receiving 12,000 fan letters a week ....

Shall I Take Your Sausages, Sir?

When David Niven was a young officer in the Regular Army, he was invited to a fancy dress ball at a grand house in Leicestershire. Determined to impress, he went as a clown, complete with pompoms, a string of sausages, a long false nose and all the trimmings.

David arrived early, anxious to meet all the important people he knew would be there. There was just a flicker of surprise on the butler's face as he ushered him into the drawing-room. It was certainly full of smart people – but all of them were in full evening dress. David had got the date right but the month wrong.

And the host and hostess thought they were being kind and thoughtful when they invited him to stay for dinner.

Second to None

In a recent competition for choirs in Wales, there was only one entry, and even then it didn't manage to win. The adjudicators listened to the choir and announced their decision. The choir was placed second as a penalty for turning up late.

..... The longest kiss in cinema history was the marathon of 185 seconds by Regis Toomey and Jane Wyman – who later became Mrs Ronald Reagan! ....

Walkies in the Valley

Jayne Mansfield won the heart of the British public in 1967 when she tried to smuggle her two chihuahuas into the country under her fur coat. Clutching the two tiny dogs to her famous bosom, she appeared in the papers with the caption, 'I am animal crackers! I have had chihuahuas ever since I was a little girl. They are so dependent . . . they appeal to my mother instinct!'

Sing Something Simple

TV personality Dickie Henderson had a reputation for putting his foot in it. Sometimes he did even better than that. He put both feet in . . .

He was once at a big showbusiness party, during which a woman with an awful voice began to sing. Dickie turned to a man near him and told him what he thought of the turn.

Instead of agreeing, the man replied, 'I think I should tell you, the lady is my wife.'

Covering up desperately, Dickie said, 'Oh, it's not her fault. It's the song – it's dreadful!'

The man replied coldly, 'Do you think so? I wrote it.'

WE'LL GET A GOOD CROWD TOMORROW FOR THE BOTTOM HALF!

Not the Right Calibre?

The trouble with 'Rita Thunderbird' may have been that she didn't stick to her diet. Anyway, as cannon fodder she failed miserably on two occasions, getting firmly stuck in the weapon, instead of sailing gracefully out of its mouth in her gold lamé bikini.

One of these attempts was marginally successful. Although 'Rita' got stuck in the cannon, her bra didn't. It sailed, without 'Rita' in it, across the River Thames.

A Record Failure

The Norwegian entry for the 1978 Eurovision song contest was a number called 'Mile After Mile'. It was so unbelievably dreary that the voting from panels all over Europe was unanimous: 'Norway – no points'. This was a record that pushed even the winner, Izhar Cohen, out of the picture. Press photographers queued up to get a shot of the Norwegian pop star Jan Teigain. He was showered with offers of tours, TV appearances and radio interviews.

What a Choker

A pantomime Dick Whittington turned to an old showbiz remedy to cure a sore throat when Amanda Noar tried to restore her singing voice by gargling with port wine. But the croaky star swallowed some of the remedy – and later failed a breath test.

In court her lawyer explained, 'In addition to normal medication, Amanda resorted to something which is part of theatre folklore.' But the judge wasn't so sure, and fined her £200.

Bless This House

Harry Secombe's visit to Pentonville Prison may have been intended to provide a little innocent escapism for the inmates, but one song didn't go down as well as he'd hoped. It was 'Bless this house', which includes the lines: 'Bless these walls so firm and stout, Keeping strife and trouble out. . .'

. . . . . *A music critic wrote: 'An amateur string quartet played Brahms here last evening. Brahms lost.'* . . . .

Never To Be Repeated

At rehearsal, aerialist Tito Gaona had brought off the impossible: he had performed the first ever quadruple somersault from a flying trapeze 60 feet above the ground. When the circus came to New York in 1978, Tito was there as the star attraction. Confident publicity posters proclaimed: 'Can aerialist Tito Gaona – spinning at 75 miles an hour – accomplish the most difficult acrobatic feat of the twentieth century?'

The thousands who rolled up did not expect the answer to be 'No'. Every night for nine months poor Tito missed his catcher and plummeted into the safety net.

309

'Just Like That!'

The amateur magician was nervous when he made his first public appearance at the age of 17. From the beginning everything went wrong. For a start he forgot his patter. When he opened his mouth he couldn't think of anything to say, so he closed it again.

Then the tricks went haywire. He either made them obvious, or they didn't work at all. The audience watched spellbound. They'd never seen anything like it.

Then he came to his big finale. He produced a bottle of milk and placed paper over the top. In a shaking voice he told the audience, 'I shall turn the bottle upside down and take the paper away. The milk will stay in the bottle.'

The magician turned the bottle, paused, and took the paper away. The milk cascaded down his trousers. The magician felt that something needed to be said. He opened his mouth, but nothing came out. Sweating heavily and trembling, he tottered from the stage. He stood swaying in the wings, listening to the audience – cheering wildly.

Tommy Cooper's career had begun.

No Motion Replay

People in show business must have quite a job remembering who's married to who at any given moment. Billie Whitelaw, the actress, found herself in just that kind of trouble.

She was at a lunch given by the Variety Club of Great Britain. Billie was talking to a well-known actor who was recently divorced. Deciding he needed a lift, Billie said, 'There's a good friend of mine across the room. I'm sure you'll get on just fine. Come and meet her.'

A deathly silence greeted the introduction and only then did Billie realize that she'd introduced the actor to his ex-wife.

Critics Get the Bird

Never in the history of television entertainment has there been such a clash between critics and public as there was in 1984 over the blockbuster *Thorn Birds*.

The critics:

'I didn't realize it was a comedy show. Monday's episode was hilarious.' *Daily Star*

'The only things wrong with *Thorn Birds* are the story, the script, the acting, the settings and the pace. Apart from that, it's great.' *Daily Mirror*

'Tepid – another *Dallas*, only with more funerals.' *Daily Express*

The public:

One episode had more viewers than the Royal Wedding. So many people switched on – 22 million – that an extra power station had to be brought into operation.

..... Glasgow graffito: 'Listening to the bagpipes is a fate worse than deaf.' ....

Farce of a Festival

David Garrick, the famous 18th century actor-manager, was responsible for organizing a Shakespeare Centenary Festival. Unfortunately, everything seemed to go wrong.

First of all, he laid it on in 1769, which was five years late, and in the wrong month. Then on the appointed day it rained very heavily, causing all the fireworks to fail to light. And to crown it all, a wall collapsed, injuring an honoured guest.

Plus ça Change?

Do people who make TV documentaries really have their heart in their work? A BBC crew made a series in Sierra Leone, in Africa. A number of extras were employed, and the going rate for whites was five times that for blacks.

The series? 'The Fight Against Slavery.'

An Initials Error

Magnus Magnusson of *Mastermind* would have done well to say 'Pass' when he went to make a documentary programme with archaeological excavators in Dover.

He reported the discovery of evidence that Dover had been the headquarters of the Roman fleet (*Classis Britannicus*), and that the chief evidence for this was a slate with the Roman initials C.B. inscribed on it. The slate was handed with great care to Magnus, so that he could hold it up for the cameras. Instead – he dropped it.

The fracture went straight across the precious initials.

Softly, Softly, George

George Cole, the actor who made his name in television's *Minder*, was once appearing in a play with the famous character actor, Alastair Sim. On one disastrous evening George made a bad-tempered exit from the stage and took with him the door handle. Which left Alastair Sim stranded without any obvious way of making his own exit.

After the show, George was driving the irate Alastair home, and received a lecture on the desirability of acting properly and controlling his strength. Somewhat upset, George changed gear with unnecessary violence, only to find that the gear lever had come away in his hand.

He handed it to Alastair and they walked home.

Musical Pigs

Louis XI of France once ordered one of his abbots to invent a ridiculous musical instrument for the amusement of the court. The abbot met the challenge by assembling a line of pigs. The squeal of each pig had a distinctive pitch and by pricking each of them in a particular order, the abbot was able to play a tune.

The Bridle Path

When Peter Sellers was a young actor, he met a girl at a dance and asked if he might take her home. It was a beautiful evening and so he suggested that they should walk along the bridle path.

The young lady's response? 'Oh, Peter, don't you think it's a little early to think of getting married?'

..... The Decca recording company refused to contract the Beatles because they thought they were too old-fashioned ......

Better Late than Never

Juan Potomachi, a wealthy Argentinian businessman, revealed his secret ambition when his will was published in 1955. Part of it read:

'All my life I wanted to be on the stage. I leave 200,000 pesos to a fund from which talented young actors shall get yearly scholarships. My only condition is that my head be preserved and used as the skull in *Hamlet*.'

Pass the Porter

It's not often that an opera singer manages to knock back a pint of porter on stage when she's meant to be dying of thirst in a desert. Nevertheless, Maria Milbran managed it every night during the run of *The Maid of Artois* at Drury Lane.

In the last act, as she sank exhausted behind a pile of drifted sand in the desert, a pint of welcome refreshment was slipped through a small gap in the scenery.

Minutes later, fully fortified, Maria rose to electrify the audience with a final burst of song.

In Limbo

At a performance of Gounod's famous opera *Faust*, the trap-door leading to the nether regions stuck, allowing only the lower half of Mephistopheles to disappear.

There was an awkward pause on the stage, and then a voice rang out from the gallery, 'See that, lads, hell's full!'

A Right Royal Welcome

Usually the BBC can be relied upon to come up with just the right sound effect for any occasion. But the introduction provided for the broadcast by the King of Norway was . . . well . . . not absolutely on the right note.

The effects department had been asked for a fanfare, but someone read the order as 'funfair'. So, the King's speech was introduced by, 'Roll up! Roll up! All the fun of the fair', with a barrel organ playing, 'Over the waves'.

. . . . . John Barrymore holds the world record for the number of kisses delivered in a single film. In Don Juan *he kissed at the rate of one every 53 seconds, making a grand total of 191 kisses . . . . . .*

All Right, I'm Going

It happened during a performance of Shakespeare's immortal play *Antony and Cleopatra* at Stratford-upon-Avon. Defeated in battle, Antony began to disrobe in preparation for his suicide.

'Off, pluck off,' he says, giving a servant the cue to remove his cloak.

But on this night the actor playing the servant didn't respond. He was obviously miles away, oblivious of his surroundings. 'Pluck off,' Antony repeated but there was still no response.

Desperate, the anxious hero said the line once more, this time in a loud and firm voice. The servant came to, looked offended and stalked off the stage.

It is said that he has since changed his profession.

315

Why must the show go on . . .

Alan Devlin is one actor who does not believe that 'the show must go on'. The occasion was a performance of HMS *Pinafore* at Dublin's Gaiety Theatre. Mr Devlin was in the middle of 'I am the ruler of the King's navee', when he decided he had better things to do.

He shouted out, 'Blow this for a game of soldiers,' and announced that he was leaving. Then he simply walked off the stage – leaving the chorus dumbfounded.

. . . and on

That wasn't the first time Alan Devlin had gone AWOL on stage. Nor the second. Nor, indeed, the third. When asked why he did it, he said honestly: 'The world and his wife know why I do it. I do it because I'm drunk.'

. . . . . *On the tombstone of the film comedian, W. C. Fields, are the words: 'On the whole, I'd rather be in Philadelphia.'* . . . .

The Martians are Coming

One of the most notorious moments in radio broadcasting happened in America in 1938.

It occurred during an adaptation of *The War of the Worlds*, H. G. Wells's futuristic novel about an invasion from Mars. The presenter was Orson Welles, and before the programme began assurances were given that this was fiction not fact.

Nevertheless, so realistic was Welles's reading that the people who switched on once the broadcast had begun were convinced that a Martian invasion had indeed begun. Some families even fled their homes to the safety of the countryside.

WHAT A MISTAKE!

ILLUSTRATED BY LARRY

CONTENTS

Transports Of Delight

.... Errors concerning travel and transport ....

Home, James

Prince Andrew, fresh (if that is the word) from his holiday with the talented actress Koo Stark, was being driven home across London after an evening in similarly sociable company. The chauffeur swung the limo down the Mall and into the Royal Mews. He then garaged the car and locked up before strolling away in the direction of home, a mug of cocoa and bed.

He was well on his way before he realized that he had left the Prince in the car! The highly-embarrassed chauffeur raced back to the garage to find the Royal personage still sitting in the back, quietly awaiting release.

'I would be frightfully grateful if you could deliver me to the right address in future' was H.R.H.'s only comment.

The Sinking Sun

Japan's first nuclear-powered ship, the *Mutsu*, was launched proudly in 1969.

However, it failed to leave port.

Local fishermen, fearful that a nuclear accident might endanger the scallops on which their livelihood depended, picketed the harbour entrance.

The great ship spent the next four years in port.

In August 1974 the *Mutsu* made a bolt for it under cover of darkness. Only yards beyond the harbour wall, the ship developed a radiation leak. The enraged fishermen blockaded the bay and refused to allow the floating albatross to return to dock for repairs.

Similar lack of enthusiasm being displayed elsewhere, the ill-fated *Mutsu* hung around off-shore for forty-five days, until the scallop-fishermen finally relented.

Whereupon – after four years' rest – the ship limped southward to Sasebo for repairs.

Four years, £33 million later, the Japanese government announced an allocation of £120 million for the construction of a specialized servicing centre for the *Mutsu*. It will take – predictably perhaps – four years to build; during which time the floating nuclear showpiece will remain tied up in port like an overgrown bath toy.

We'll Take Less Care Of You

For an airline that was awarded the 1982 Airline of the Year title
and that blazons its caring nature across every television screen
in the land, it was perhaps surprising that the British Airways PR
boys did not take more care about the announcement of a new
'keep it clean' policy with regard to their passengers.

As it was, BA's medical chief, Dr Donald Mackenzie, was
heard to declare that 'the feelings of the *normal* travelling public
must be the airline's top priority' and that in future no special
care facilities would be provided for invalids, women more than
35 weeks pregnant or those with skin complaints that might look
'repulsive to others'. Such unfortunate expressions could cost the
troubled finances of BA a pretty penny, if every unfortunate
acne-sufferer were to think twice before 'flying the flag'.

Keeping An Eye Out For Lost Property

Users of public transport fairly often make that mundane yet
most annoying of mistakes – leaving behind their parcels,
handbags, umbrellas, etc. Many of these items find their way
eventually to the relevant lost property office. Nothing very
remarkable in this, you may say. But consider for a moment the
forgotten articles of those who travelled on the London Midland &
Scottish Railway in 1947...

These hapless creatures must have suffered not only
inconvenience but also some considerable discomfort as a result
of their absent-mindedness. For catalogued in the annual lost
property report for that year of this august body, in addition to the
usual 5,630 or so brollies, were a barrel organ, several sets of
false teeth, a cage containing a calf with two heads, a
three-legged cock, three artificial limbs and a glass eye!

★ ★ ★ ★

............*Lord Stokes, then chairman of British
Leyland, carved a place in the history of optimism in 1974
when he told the nation: 'The company is not lost. We are
merely in a cyclical decline.'*...........................

321

Howe's That!

Many citizens of Great Britain probably think that they have lost the shirts off their backs to our Chancellor of the Exchequer, Sir Geoffrey Howe.

So no doubt they were not unduly distressed to learn that Sir Geoffrey had gone one better by losing his dinner suit trousers on the Manchester sleeper train.

They were, in fact, stolen from his compartment, and reappeared some days later by the side of the tracks somewhere in Warwickshire. Missing, however, was the wad of notes – £100 in all – which the Chancellor had left in them. Symbolic, perhaps, of what happens to the 'Pound in Your Pocket'!

Sky Highway

Motorists on the four-lane highway at Joliet, Illinois, were surprised, and even alarmed, to see a parachutist land in the middle of the road.

The 26-year-old skydiver was seized by the ever-vigilant highway patrol, who gave the matter due consideration and then, with some originality, decided on the charge: not using an authorized entrance!

All Of A Quiver

Baggage handlers at Calgary Airport in Canada became alarmed when they heard a strange humming noise coming from a suitcase which was being transferred from one plane to another.

The local police bomb squad was summoned as a matter of some urgency. The baggage area was cleared and the bomb-hunters pumped the suitcase with air.

When this exercise did not produce even a puff of smoke, never mind an explosion, the police were emboldened to open the case.

They discovered a personal, and rather noisy, vibrator which had succeeded in turning itself on in the course of a flight from Vancouver.

Back-Up-Front

Passengers attempting to travel on the much-vaunted British Airways shuttle between Scotland and England were convinced they were living in a wrong-headed, back-to-front world....

They were told, on checking in, that the back-up flight would leave *before* the regular flight which it was supposed to be backing up.

If you see what I mean.

★   ★   ★   ★

.............US businessman Chauncey Depew warned his nephew not to invest $5,000 in an unknown young man named Henry Ford. He told him: 'Nothing has come along that can beat the horse and buggy.'......................

★   ★   ★   ★

Nicholas The First

Nicholas Cugnot was a man of great importance in the history of motoring and the motorist. A French artillery officer, he became the world's first motorist in 1769 when he invented and then drove a three-wheeled car powered by steam.

Within minutes he had notched up another first. He drove into a wall and became the first crash victim. He was not really hurt, apart from his feelings, and went back to work with a will. Soon he had improved the steering and, more important, the brakes, and was back on the road with an advanced model capable of whizzing along at two miles an hour.

Things were really looking up for Nicholas when he was contracted by the French Ministry of War to design and build a military carrier. However, it is a long road that has no turning, and Nicholas' problem was that he kept turning into trouble. After a string of crashes during road tests, he achieved his hat-trick of firsts.

He was the first motorist to be jailed for dangerous driving.

The Longest Day

Travelling hopefully but never seeming to arrive anywhere on schedule, Mr and Mrs Thomas Elham made a no-passport day trip to Boulogne, and wound up seeing a great deal of Europe.

Having finished their shopping, the couple set out for a stroll to see the sights of the town. Unfortunately, their grasp of the French language was insufficient to enable them to understand the street signs, and they became hopelessly lost. The French people they met were very kind and eventually they got a lift to the railway station.

As the last ferry had left, the Elhams decided to go to Paris and make their way back to Dover from there. Unfortunately, they caught the wrong train and found themselves the next morning – in Luxembourg! The local police put the confused travellers on a train for Paris and they slept most of the way – all too soundly in fact, for they missed their connection and woke up in Basel!

The obliging Swiss police gave the couple directions back to Boulogne but somehow the doomed travellers lost their way again, and ended up hitchhiking over sixty kilometres to Vesoul in central France. A long-distance lorry-driver gave the bemused couple a lift to Paris, but when they reached the Gare du Nord, their troubles were not over.

'We misread the signs,' Mrs Elham explained, 'and took the train to Bonn.'

From Germany the Elhams were conveyed post haste back to France. At the border, a sympathetic *gendarme* decided to make sure the Continent was freed of this dreadful new scourge and drove the couple all the way to Boulogne.

It took twenty-four hours to persuade the Customs that their unlikely tale of misadventure could possibly be true. But at last they were allowed on to a ferry and soon the familiar white cliffs of Dover welcomed the Elhams back to their native land – and a twenty-three mile stroll back to their own front door.

Leading By Example

Delegates attending the 1982 Confederation of British Industry Conference at Eastbourne would have aided their case against the creeping evil of increased car imports by not themselves advertising the appealing nature of the rival foreign product.

On the very day that Ray Horrocks, chief executive of beleaguered BL Cars, led the onslaught on the alien invader, hawk-eyed press men gleefully counted 17 assorted Mercedes, Citroens, Alfa Romeos and BMWs parked in the courtyard of the popular Grand Hotel awaiting the arrival of their owners, exhausted by many hours' patriotic cheering at the conference centre.

Xenophobia begins at home, gentlemen.

Why The Lagonda Was Lagging

Woburn Abbey, ancestral home of the Duke of Bedford, has
been the scene of some eccentric publicity stunts in its time.
Few, however, have turned out as disastrously as that scheduled
for the occasion of the 17th wedding anniversary of the Duke's
son, the Marquess of Tavistock.

The Marchioness had decided to present her husband with a
little 'keepsake' – a £32,000 Aston Martin Lagonda. The car had
taken the 1976 Motor Show by storm, so when the story was
leaked to the press, reporters and television cameras galore
were on hand to witness the ceremony. The Lagonda made its
appearance right on time. However, instead of the anticipated
roar of exhaust and crunch of flying gravel, there arrived a stately
procession of red-faced Aston Martin men pushing the mighty
machine up the long drive.

Apparently, the mini-computer specially developed to
revolutionize the car's controls system had blown up.

'Someone misconnected a black wire to a red one,' explained
shamefaced director, Peter Sprague.

326

Clocking In

Customs man Colin Fisher was approached at Heathrow Airport by an elderly American who had just flown in from Miami.

'Can you direct me to the airport Post Office?' enquired the Transatlantic voyager. 'My son is meeting me under the clock.'

Fisher was puzzled. There was a Post Office in the Terminal Three building, but certainly no clock under which people could meet in the time-honoured fashion.

Could the traveller have got it right? he wondered.

'Why certainly,' responded the American. 'Here, look, I'll show you the letter from my son.'

Sure enough, there was the instruction from the attentive offspring. The only problem was that the lad was expecting to meet his father thousands of miles away at Kennedy Airport, New York.

Somehow, the old gent had managed to get on a flight from Miami to London, instead of New York, and had also failed to notice either that he was crossing the Atlantic, or that the flight had lasted almost twice as long as the usual trip to New York.

'I guess I fell asleep and lost track of things,' he mused.

Common Cents

The New York City Transit Authority overlooked one thing when they approved the design for the new 75c ticket machines on the subway: the slot provided would accommodate with equal success the 17½c tokens used by commuters on the road toll machines in nearby Connecticut. A fairly expensive mistake for the near-bankrupt city at over 50c net loss per journey.

Following an embarrassing exposé in the papers, New York's flamboyant Mayor, Ed Koch, decided to intervene personally to pour oil on troubled underground water.

Unfortunately, his hastily called press conference was less than a roaring success. For in announcing an all-out police initiative to stop the 'outright thieving' of the fare cheats, the grandiloquent Mayor got carried away and described the naughty commuters as 'leprous'. Only to find himself at the centre of another row, this time caused by complainants from many national lepers' charities.

327

Whitehall Farce

This is quite clearly the age of the strain, if you happen to be a commuter.

Take the experience of Mr Bernard Whitehall. He was sitting on a train which he believed to be the 7.23 from Reading to Waterloo. It was not. He was actually sitting on the 7.09 from Reading to Guildford, which trundles via Ascot.

Mr Whitehall is a resourceful chap. Having discovered his mistake, he remained undaunted. When the train pulled in at Ascot, he jumped out and had it diverted to Waterloo. Just like that.

This was, of course, something of a surprise to the Guildford passengers, all of whom were obliged to put away their crosswords, get out and wait another 30 minutes for the next train to their destination.

A British Rail spokesperson commented: 'Very few people travel from Ascot to Guildford. It seemed to Mr Whitehall far more sensible that the train should be diverted to pick up the path of the 7.23, which had been cancelled.'

Perhaps I should add that Mr Whitehall is manager of BR Southern Region's south-west division.

Time Slips By

Passengers arriving at Weybridge Station in Surrey were baffled by an announcement scrawled in inimitable BR script on an official blackboard. It appeared to announce that:

> STATION CLOCKS ARE FIVE MINUTES
> FAST DUE TO A LANDSLIP BETWEEN
> FARNHAM AND ALTON

Apparently a stray raindrop, coat sleeve or vandal's finger had deleted the requisite full stop (work it out!) and obscured the remainder of the message concerning delays to that morning's trains, rendering the notice thus more worthy of H.G. Wells than BR Tales.

Defeated Victor

Victor Grant was a man with a simple goal in life. He wanted to buy a car and, to that end, he saved up for the happy day, a pound here and a fiver there.

Being a man who liked to give others a pleasant surprise, he did not tell his wife of his plan and kept the money he accumulated hidden in a bundle of old clothes. He had collected £500 when the dustmen called at his home in Wrexham, North Wales.

Mr Grant's wife, seeking to clear out unwanted old rubbish, unwittingly gave them the bundle.

Mr Grant was not best pleased with this news when he returned home from work. He hired a mechanical digger to plough through the local rubbish tip, but after two days' fruitless search he gave up.

He went home and started to save up all over again. But this time he put the money in a bank.

Change For The Worse At Crewe

Sir Peter Parker, chairman of British Rail, is no stranger to the experience of getting on the wrong train.

In July 1978 he was on his way from Crewe to Carlisle for an important meeting. He arrived at the station with seconds to spare before the train was due to leave.

Flashing his BR train pass, a harassed Sir Peter dashed on to the platform and jumped aboard. But instead of snuggling into his comfortable seat on the fast train to Carlisle, the Chairman found himself speeding in quite the opposite direction, first stop Euston.

He talked a highly dubious guard into throwing a note on to the platform at Tamworth, asking those concerned to 'phone Cumbria County Council and tell them he would not be able to attend their meeting, owing to circumstances which were now completely beyond his control.

When he got to London he decided to fly back to the north, sensible fellow that he is.

Press Gang

.... Errors concerning newspapers and media ....

Up The Wall Chart

Doctor is a weekly newspaper for general practitioners. As part of its excellent service to its readers, it produces a weekly vaccination chart which is inserted in the publication. The chart shows, on brightly coloured maps of the world, what jabs are required and where.

Doctors, and indeed *Doctor*, know a great deal about anatomy. Unhappily this knowledge does not stretch to geography or even the recent history of the African continent. The map still in use in 1982 had a distinctly imperial echo. It clearly showed Southern Rhodesia where Zimbabwe is (and plain old Rhodesia was before it). Even odder, half the map of the dark continent was given in French.

Perhaps, if there is a doctor in the house, a new atlas could be prescribed for *Doctor*.

★　　★　　★　　★

. . . . .A travel article in **Ulster Magazine** *reported: 'The nearest hotel was five miles away in one direction and practically 12 in the opposite direction.'. . . . .*

★　　★　　★　　★

Paper Chase

An irate woman reader telephoned the offices of the *Washington Star* to complain that her edition had not been delivered for a couple of days. She was told that this was hardly surprising, seeing that the *Star* had gone out of business more than a year before and only a few accountants were left in the place tidying up the few loose financial ends that remained. They suggested to the reader that she might be thinking of the illustrious rival newspaper, the *Washington Post*.

The woman was most indignant. 'Certainly not,' she insisted. 'I never read the *Post*. It's definitely the *Star*.'

With such loyalty, how did the paper ever go broke?

Bottom Of The Form

The Sun got little that was more revealing than a cold shoulder when it tried to enlist girl students as Page Three lovelies. The super soaraway scheme was called The Nudie-Varsity Challenge and executives of the paper (known to its staff as *The Beano*) sat back and waited for sexy snaps of 'blue-stocking beauties' to cascade on to their desks.

They were doomed to disappointment. The student magazine at Cambridge University stiffly refused to publicize the event. A student spokesman at Manchester University told *The Sun*: 'You'll get a violent reaction if you try it here.' The National Union of Students was similarly unhelpful. It sniffed: 'Page Three is grossly sexist, insulting to women and debasing.'

The Sun attacked them all for being stuck-up, but in the end the whole idea turned out to be just a boob.

Foggy Period

An issue of *Arab News* regretted:

We are unable to announce the weather. We depend on weather reports from the airport, which is closed, due to the weather. Whether we will be able to give you the weather tomorrow will depend on the weather.

All clear now?

. . . . .A glance through the pages of the **Prestwich Guide** *reveals the following planning application: 235 Hayward Road, Change of use. Aquarium to fish and chip takeaway. . . . .*

★　　★　　★　　★

Getting It Taped

When Canadian photographer Peter Duffy was sent along to cover the unveiling of a plaque at City Hall, St George, British Columbia, his blood did not exactly race in his veins. In short, the prospect bored Duffy stiffer than the cold.

He decided to brighten an otherwise dull afternoon by taping a nude picture over the plaque. He then replaced the drape and stepped back to await developments, as the official party advanced on to the rostrum.

Let the splendid Duffy himself tell the tale. 'The Mayor did not see the picture at first. Then he did and his mouth just hung open. Instead of the usual ripple of applause, there was absolute silence. Then I was sacked.'

You Ought To Be In Pictures

At the time of the De Lorean scandal, photographers of the *New York Daily Post* were ordered to proceed with some haste to the Manhattan home of Christine, dishy wife of the disgraced car-maker.

This was no easy task for the eager snappers. Not surprisingly, Mrs De Lorean had little or no desire to perform before the shutters and flashes, and remained doggedly out of sight.

Eventually, after many hours of waiting around, the Press gang espied a mysterious-looking woman, well wrapped up against the autumnal chill. She hared out of the building and leaped into a chauffeur-driven limo. A photographer broke from the pack and raced across the sidewalk after her, shooting rolls of film in her wake. The film was rushed back to the office, along with the photographer, who modestly awaited the acclaim to which he was entitled.

The executive could hardly contain their glee as the film was processed and the prints spread out on the editor's desk.

What they were looking at was an interesting selection of pictures of an obviously highly-miffed Mrs Rupert Murdoch, wife of their own employer, who lived in the same block as the De Loreans.

Sorry!

There is little that is more noble than the sight and sound of a gentleman admitting that he was wrong, particularly when he is a gentleman of the Press.

On July 5, 1982, the American magazine *People* displayed a correction which stated:

> *The June 28 issue carried a story on a new diet product called starch blockers. On rechecking his tapes, reporter David Sheff has found he misquoted Dr John Marshall. Dr Marshall did not say that the writer Cameron Stauth was a 'dirty rotten scum who got greedy'. What he said was: 'He's an unscrupulous little (pause) gentleman.'*

Nice to have got that one cleared up, Dave.

Name Of The Game

Gossip columnist Nigel Dempster was approached by racehorse trainer Alan Jarvis, who wished to name a yearling after the great man of the *Daily Mail*.

Colleagues advised Dempster to agree, citing a dreadful example of what could happen if he didn't.

Soccer manager Brian Clough was once asked by an owner for permission to give his horse his prestigious name. Permission was promptly refused.

The disappointed owner then dubbed the nag Blabbermouth instead and was last seen cantering away chuckling in a vengeful manner.

★ ★ ★ ★

. . . . Spanish police on duty guarding the honeymoon retreat of Angus Ogilvy and Princess Alexandra spotted a heavily perspiring British cameraman perched in a tree in a bid to obtain an exclusive. With total lack of Andalusian charm, they simply chopped down the tree . . . . . .

Eye, Eye

The satirical magazine *Private Eye* is fond of making others the butt of its humour, but it is not often to be found on the receiving end itself.

So, when a prankster sent out a pile of false invitations to the magazine's 21st birthday party ball at the Reform Club, editor Richard Ingrams did not laugh immoderately. In fact, the only guffaw to be heard among the staff emanated from the convulsed culprit, Mr Paul Halloran.

As is only right and proper, Mr Ingrams exacted his full measure of revenge on the hapless hack. He informed the assembled staff that the cost of entertaining those invited by the hoaxer would use up all the cash set aside for the staff Christmas bonus.

There was much grumbling over this cheerless prospect, and Mr Halloran was plunged into a negative paddle area. The poor fellow suffered untold agonies of the damned for one full week before a savagely gleeful Mr Ingrams informed him that it was all a joke.

Garden Fate

A free newspaper distributed in the Surrey area contained the following disconcerting advertisement placed by a local landscape gardening firm:

DON'T KILL YOURSELF IN YOUR GARDEN LET US DO IT FOR YOU

Angus Ogilvy, Ace Reporter

Jounalists are often frog-marched out of Royal establishments, but it is not often that royal personages are mistaken for hacks and dealt with accordingly. It happened to the Hon. Angus Ogilvy, whose regal association is by way of marriage to Princess Alexandra.

When in Spain with his wife, Angus arrived late for an engagement with King Juan Carlos and Queen Sophia. At the gates he asked the police: 'Is the English princess here?'

Much to his astonishment he was seized and dragged off to the nick, accused of being an interloping reporter.

And there he remained until Alexandra popped along to have him freed.

Palace Revolutions

They're changing guard at Buckingham Palace – and not before time, it would appear.

Only days after Michael Fagan dropped in unannounced in the Queen's bedroom to ask for a light, two dreadful cheeky fellows from the *Daily Mirror* set out to test the authorities' claim that no such breach of security would ever happen again.

After a few friendly pints in the palace local, reporter John Merritt and photographer Peter Stone obtained an official parking permit from a palace gateman.

Armed with this valuable document, the newsmen were able to go in and out of the Royal Mews entrance at will.

They were even invited to sit in a royal coach scheduled, only a couple of days later, to carry the Queen to Westminster for the State Opening of Parliament.

When challenged with this further slackness, a palace spokesman dismissed it as 'absolutely an administrative matter', saying, 'I do wish people would stop calling it a security thing.'

Probed by, inevitably, a *Mirror* reporter as to whether staff were being questioned about the episode, the official continued: 'With a security matter like this, *of course* we are investigating.'

First With The News

Don't believe everything you read in the newspapers is not a piece of advice you would need if you had happened to be in Chicago on Presidential election night, November 2, 1948.

Thomas Dewey was red-hot favourite to win and the *Chicago Tribune* was so confident that it printed its first edition story of his triumph before the results started to come through.

DEWEY DEFEATS TRUMAN

screamed their banner headline in enormous front page capital letters.

Maybe the *Trib* knew something the rest of the country didn't, but Harry S. Truman was later properly revealed as a landslide winner.

The editor needed the aid of a trowel, if not a shovel, to get the egg off his face before popping along to the proprietor's office to explain how it all came about.

Read Letter Daily

A letter was printed in the letters column of the Paris edition of the *New York Herald* on December 27, 1899.

Enquiring about the relative merits of the Fahrenheit and Centigrade temperature scales, the reader's query seemed innocuous enough.

Imagine his surprise, therefore, to see the same letter, word for word, on the next day's editorial page.

The *Herald's* proprietor, James Gordon Bennet, also spotted the slip-up and was so livid that he decreed that the letter should be published in every single issue of the paper for the rest of his lifetime.

6,700 issues later, the old curmudgeon died – and we still don't know if the writer ever received a satisfactory answer!

Bread Sales In The Sunset

The people of recession-hit Tyneside are on the breadline in a very big way. Or so the fraternal comrades in Russia are led to believe by Vladimir Skosyrev, London correspondent of *Izvestia*.

He reported to his horror-struck native land that youths in Newcastle upon Tyne and its capitalist-oppressed environs were made to slave for 60 hours a week, without even so much as a break for lunch. Not that they could have afforded lunch even if the opportunity had presented itself.

Vladimir really had tears as big as bumper plates rolling down Russian cheeks all the way across the vast steppes with his account of the old and unemployed queueing for hours on end outside a baker's shop in the city in the hope of coming away with a cut-price stale loaf, or even two if it was a really big day.

The shop involved in this outrage was Greggs, the classiest bread emporium in the area. Mr David Parker, the firm's managing director, thought the whole thing was hilarious.

He said: 'One of our 70 shops sells day-old bread or mis-shapen cakes at half price. I think most of our customers buy in bulk for their deep freezes. I think we'll have to open a shop in Moscow.'

Better Late...

In July 1969, the lofty *New York Times* apologized to Professor Robert Goddard for maligning him 49 years earlier. The newspaper had ridiculed the space pioneer for suggesting that a rocket could function in a vacuum.

Nearly half a century later Apollo 11 proved the prof. absolutely right.

Donning unaccustomed sackcloth and ashes, with a hair shirt on the side, the *Times* said:

> *It is now definitely established that a rocket can function in a vacuum.* The Times *regrets its error.*

Hackademics

A recently established postgraduate course in journalism was staunchly defended by university authorities when the idea for it was announced to a barrage of taunts and criticisms from academics ('not a subject which readily lends itself to this type of in-depth academic study') and those 'untrained' practitioners of the trade who constitute the British Press ('who do they think they are anyway?').

The university's enthusiasm and confidence proved somewhat misplaced, however, when in 1982 it was revealed that 24 out of the 25 graduates attending the course had fallen at the first hurdle.

They had failed to pass the preliminary shorthand test.

Bathload Of Boloney

Many journals, books, government publications and even some encyclopedias erroneously include a totally fictitious account of 'America's first bathtub'. The author of this farcical 'history' was the famous American humourist, H. L. Mencken.

The whole saga began with the December 28, 1917 issue of the *New York Evening Mail* in which Mencken detailed the supposed purchase and installation of the first tub in 1842 by one Adam Thompson of Cincinnati. Allowing his zany imagination free rein, he went on to describe the incredible adventures of the bath – how it was banned by law by the health department, permitted only on prescription in Boston and subjected to a horrendous tax levy in Virginia. All-in-all, the whole story was a veritable Colossus of nonsense.

However, to Mencken's utter astonishment and considerable glee, the great clean-living American public did not see it that way. They believed every word of the ridiculous piece – and apparently continue to do so, in spite of the fact that an immediate and full retraction of the fable was printed in the same newspaper the very next day.

Body Language

.... Errors concerning the world of medicine.....................................

Mind How You Blow!

Coal-mining is a job that can easily get up your nose. So thought young miner Ronald Cutler in 1942 when, having just finished a shift at the Oakdale Colliery in Monmouthshire, he blew his nose to get rid of the clogging coaldust. To his surprise and consternation, as he blew, his eye fell out! Ambulance men managed to replace the eye on the way to hospital and the young man was later able to go home none the worse for his strange experience.

Mum's The Word!

18-year-old Sharon Fox went to bed with a stomach ache one evening after gobbling a bag of crisps. The following day, however, was really crunch time, for the pains got worse until finally an ambulance was called. Half an hour later, Sharon gave birth to a 7lb daughter.

'I was amazed,' said the young mother. 'I'd no idea. I didn't have any morning sickness, cravings, or even a lump in my tummy. I spent the whole nine months in my usual size 10 clothes.'

Reader's Digestion

The strange eating habits of a Canadian woman proved medically unfortunate when she was diagnosed as suffering from poisoning caused by a specific type of mercury, used in paper-making.

Every day for the last twelve years, she told incredulous doctors, she had eaten a box of tissue paper, and a cigarette pack, a bland diet spiced up by the occasional paperback novel.

So beware – a *consuming* interest in anything may be a fatal mistake!

Taking Steps

Although doctors are not *always* right, it is undoubtedly true that it can be unwise to disregard their warnings – even from the most laudable of motives.

Take the remarkable case of Samuel Flecknoe.

For four years he had been paralysed and unable to walk. Then one Sunday in 1913, when 'something' told him to get up, he obeyed the impulse, and set out to make up for lost time.

On the Friday, 32-year-old Samuel walked down to a matinée at the local theatre, returning home with a full programme of fun mapped out for the following day.

Cautionary words from doctors were waved aside. Young Samuel was determined to take up his bed and hop, skip and jump.

Pride comes before a fall, they say, and it was when he refused his anxious brother's assistance in climbing the stairs that night with the words 'Leave me. I'll carry *you* if you like' that he made his big mistake.

For at the top of the stairs he stumbled and fell all the way down, landing unconscious at the bottom.

He was out cold for several days and, on coming to, decided to learn from his crash course in remedial therapy and remain in bed until his recovery was complete some weeks later.

The Flickering Lamp

Florence Nightingale, the fabled Lady With The Lamp, was convinced that her own flame of life was about to snuffed out. After returning from the Crimean conflict in 1856, she managed to get about for another year before taking to her bed to await the dread footfall of the Grim Reaper creeping up the main staircase. She was consumed with the notion that she had a terminal heart disease and that her life 'hung by a thread which could snap at any second'.

In the event, the 'thread' proved more like a cast iron chain and failed to snap until the old nurse was knocking 91, having spent her last 54 years as a self-imposed semi-invalid.

Ice Scream

A flood knocked out the power and damaged the emergency generators at the Smith Hospital in Fort Worth, Texas. The absence of power had put paid to the air conditioning and the entire hospital was becoming something of a hothouse. With confusion reigning all around, a young psychiatric patient took charge, passing himself off as a medical official.

He sent a team of highly-trained staff on a search for ice which lasted all through the night.

A hospital spokesperson admitted later: 'We finished up with 2,000lb of dry ice in the lobby.'

She added that no one had thought for a moment to question the authenticity of the young fellow at the helm because 'Well, he seemed to be doing such a good job'.

What A Corker!

A Somerset man had been deaf in one ear since the age of three. Many years later he was visiting a new doctor, who decided to have a look at the offending ear. To the GP's utter amazement, a cork suddenly popped out and hit him in the eye.

The patient explained calmly: 'I must have put it in there when I was a lad.'

Living Death

A contender for the Freakiest Funeral Of All Time must be the mournful event at the Rumanian town of Moinesti, when the bereaved became unnerved, not to mention hysterical, at the sight of the dear departed lady's anxious face peering down at them from the open coffin as it was carried across the road to the graveyard.

The whole thing became altogether too much for them when the 'corpse' leaped out of her box and legged it down the road – straight into the path of an oncoming car, which killed her.

Toxic Shock

Lonely widow Dora Ashbough carried poison in her purse for 20 years, in case the world became too much for her. That day came in 1930, when Dora was 71 and almost destitute. She swallowed her poison and lay on the steps of the University of San Francisco to await death. In her hand was a note saying:

I leave my body to the university for medical purposes.

The university was obliged to delay taking up her kind bequest, for Dora was not dead. The poison she had carried around for two decades had lost its lethal powers.

Well, Strike A Light!

A man was admitted to the Intensive Care Unit of a North London hospital, suffering from a serious chest ailment. He was placed in an oxygen tent and soon began to make a recovery.

However, as an inveterate cigarette smoker, the man soon became desperate for a fag. Nurses and doctors constantly warned him of what would happen, but the stubborn smoker erroneously thought he knew best.

One day he managed to smuggle in some matches and a packet of Silk Cut. He lit up – and with an ear-splitting bang, patient and oxygen tent exploded in the same instant.

Ears A Funny Thing

Retired tailor Harold Senby had never been happy with his hearing aid. For one thing, it had never seemed to work very well or do him much good. In the 20 years he had worn it, his hearing did not seem to have perked up at all.

He discovered the reason for its inefficiency when, at the age of 74, he went along to Leeds Hospital for a check-up. Incredulous doctors gently broke the news to their patient that for all those years he had been wearing the deaf aid in the wrong ear.

Hard Centre

Doctors responsible for the opening of a new phobia centre in Derby should perhaps have considered more carefully the nature of the condition they were seeking to treat before launching such an expensive venture. As it was, it did not take long for lack of attendance to draw attention to the error.

'The trouble is,' said the organizer, 'many phobia sufferers are frightened to come to the centre.'

Elementary, my dear doctor.

Unkind Cut

July 21, 1907 was definitely a day to remember for railway porter Johann Kovacs, valued employee at the station at Bihar, Hungary. Poor Johann collapsed at work as a result of humping a particularly difficult trunk. He was taken to the local hospital where the doctors pronounced him very dead indeed. They then decided to hold a post mortem. Johann's body was stripped and laid on the dissecting table, whereupon the pathologist turned to the assembled group of medical students and announced, 'I shall now make the first incision.'

So saying, he bent to his labours, but at the first prick of the scalpel, Johann woke up with a start. It took him a few seconds to become fully aware of the awfulness of his position, after which he made a heroic effort to assault the amazed surgeon. It took several doctors to restrain him.

First Sign Of Madness

A sign which was put up in a hospital corridor was taken down again after only four hours. It read:

DEPARTMENT OF PSYCHIATRY – ROUND THE BEND

Slim And Unhappy

Dieting was the undoing of garbage collector Ruffs Jackson. He was very fat indeed; so fat the refuse collection authorities in Chicago ordered him to lose a gargantuan 200lb or be fired.

Ruffs single-mindedly went on a crash diet, suffering the usual agonies of the damned until the target was reached. Unfortunately, his dieting endeavours left him so weak that he could no longer lift the garbage bins and he was fired for inefficiency.

The very same day, his wife left him because she could not stand her new-look husband.

Unlucky Break

Toddler Andrew Bewell fell down the stairs at his home in Hebden Bridge, Halifax and broke his right ankle.

He was whisked off to Halifax Royal Infirmary to have treatment.

But when he came home his *left* ankle was in plaster.

Not even his parents noticed the clanger until bed-time when the swollen, unplastered right ankle was obvious for all to see.

So the following morning a red-faced casualty department received another visit from the unfortunate youngster.

Splashing Out

The 11-year-old son of an East London family had an unusual medical problem. Not only was he a regular sleepwalker, but during his somnambulatory wanderings he often put the plug in the bath, started the taps running and then went back to bed, leaving the family in the flat below to discover what had happened when the water began to drip through their ceiling.

This soggy habit cost the boy's family hundreds of pounds in repairs over a period of time.

352

When, in desperation, they consulted their doctor, he prescribed the immediate confiscation and concealment of the plug – and considered the problem easily solved. But he was very wrong. The mistake revealed itself when a cascade of water descended into the flat below. Undefeated, the sleepwalker had used the plug from the basin and returned to his old trick!

The parents were so disappointed and so reluctant to face their downstairs neighbours, whom they had reassured would not be troubled in this way again, that they asked a local radio disc jockey to apologize for them.

This was duly done. For good measure – though perhaps a little unfortunately – the DJ chose to play some 'mood music' – a record of Bobby Darin's old hit, *Splish Splash*.

Wrong In The Tooth

The Greek philosopher Aristotle may have been a great thinker, but when it came to medical knowledge, he left much to be desired. He believed throughout his life that men have more teeth than women, whereas, in fact, there is no difference.

It is known that Aristotle was married twice, but nothing is known of his wives' dental status!

Nun Nicer

The cure for the common cold is home-made rhubarb wine, according to the nuns of the Poor Clare convent in York.

The nuns have been producing the rhubarb tipple for around 100 years, but they never realized its medicinal properties until they stopped making it in order to economize. Suddenly they all started coming down with colds and chills, but soon recovered when the wine-making was resumed. The magic tipple was on sale at £1.50 a bottle and news of its sniffle-fighting possibilities led to a run on the brew. This in turn excited the interest of the Revenue men, who warned the sisters that, although the proceeds went to charity, the whole thing was illegal.

Sounds like a lot of rhubarb.

Lost Leaders

.... Errors concerning politics
and politicians ....

A Whopper Of A Majority

When President Charles King of Liberia offered himself for re-election in 1928, the voters were so enthused by the prospect of another Kingly term that they gave him a thumping majority of 600,000 over his opponent, Thomas Faulkner.

The colossal nature of this defeat was something of a puzzle to Mr Faulkner. Not surprising, since the total electorate of Liberia numbered less than 15,000 at the time!

Taverne In The Town

On a walkabout during the 1982 by-election at Peckham in South East London, would-be SDP mould-breaker Dick Taverne stopped an old man in the street and asked if he recognized him. The voter perused the elegant, Chelsea-based QC for a few moments and then responded: 'Aren't you Dick Turpin?'

A few days later it was highway robbery all right as the Labour candidate, Harriet Harman, romped home ahead of the luckless Taverne.

The Wrong Arm Of The Law

The legendary Mayor of Chicago, Richard Daley, not exactly known for his liberal attitudes, went on record to defend the brutality of his police force during the infamous Democratic Convention in his city in 1968.

He declared: 'The police are not there to create disorder. The police are there to *maintain* disorder.'

★　　★　　★　　★

. . . . .Mario Procaccino, Democratic candidate for Mayor of New York, told a 1969 audience of black voters: 'My heart is as black as yours'. . . . .

★　　★　　★　　★

Classic Loser

Horatio Bottomley (1860-1933), one-time MP for the London constituency of South Hackney, was also a journalist, financier – and notorious swindler.

On one glorious occasion at Blankenberg racecourse in Belgium he tried to put one over on the bookies. Entering six of his own horses in a minor race, he gave the compliant jockeys detailed instructions on the order in which they were to pass the finishing post.

Having placed his bets, Bottomley retired complacently to the grandstand to watch a satisfyingly large bundle of banknotes gallop happily past.

In the event, however, neither he nor anyone else was able to watch much at all, as a thick swirling mist rolled in from the sea just as the race got under way. The bribed jockeys lost sight of one another and crossed the line in anything but the prescribed order.

Bottomley, in his usual fashion, lost a small fortune, adding another to his long line of 259 bankruptcy petitions.

Hail Hailsham!

The awesome majesty of the Palace of Westminster has been known to stir the soul of the most ripped-off tourist, but never more so than in the dank and dreary November of 1979.

Lord Hailsham, the Lord Chancellor himself, was strolling across the lobby of the House of Commons when he saw Neil Marten, a Tory MP and long-standing friend.

Hailsham, ever attentive to such details, recalled that it was Marten's birthday and gave an imperious wave to his friend, as he called out: 'Neil!'

A troupe of camera-clad tourists crashed to their knees as one.

★　　★　　★　　★

. . . .*The eager and enthusiastic police at Sabah, Indonesia, prevented 138 communist sympathizers and other potential trouble-makers from entering the country. They identified the radical hordes of aliens because, as they put it, they all looked suspicious and 'wore red ties'*. . . . .

By George

George Thomas, the former Labour Cabinet Minister who became one of the great Speakers of the House of Commons, was out canvassing on the doorsteps of his beloved Wales one day, when the door was opened by a lady clad in mourning.

Mr Thomas, who was once President of the Methodist Conference, uttered a few words of condolence and was then ushered into the parlour where he found the deceased laid out.

After a few moments of properly respectful silence, the lady in mourning told her famous visitor: 'Granny would really have appreciated this, you know. She was dead Labour.'

Grave Allegation

Gerald Ford, who often found great difficulty in walking around without hitting walls or falling over, was as good with words as he was with budget figures. He once delighted onlookers, not to mention the scribblers of the media, by declaring: 'I say that if Abe Lincoln was alive today, he'd turn over in his grave.'

Oh, Grattan

Irishman Henry Grattan (1750-1820) was a man who deserved to
have his name writ large in the annals of parliamentary debate
as the only man ever to lose a motion that enjoyed unanimous
support.

Addressing the House on his theme of the day – precisely
what it was is lost in the mists of time – Mr Grattan found to his
great pleasure nothing but approving nods and murmurs from his
fellow Members. It was when it came to formulating a written
motion to be nodded through that things began to go wrong for
poor Henry. He took so long to arrive at a form of words that the
House began to get restive.

Finally, an opposition Member suggested that, instead of a
formal motion, the Government Minister concerned should give a
verbal assurance of support. Henry, by this time covered with
confusion, agreed. The other MPs, however, did not and so, on a
technicality, the motion was lost.

Sung Of Praise

Kim Il Sung, President of North Korea, certainly has a way with
words. Blowing his own trumpet with whole page ads in all the
British national newspapers a few years ago, detailing the
potential of his beloved country, was obviously very exciting. But,
like all great men, the President also has to undertake less
blood-stirring engagements.

During a visit to China, Sung was invited to inspect the
methane-generating units of Sichuan Province. (The gas is
produced from fermenting human and pig dung and straw. This
yummy mixture is an excellent source of energy and can also be
used for cooking – a really mouth-watering prospect.) Sung was
terribly impressed by the whole thing.

'That's very good,' he enthused, going on to say, somewhat
(we hope) misleadingly: 'We in Korea have all the right
ingredients in great abundance.'

History does not relate what kind of reception awaited the
President when he returned home to the people of whom he
apparently held such a *high* opinion!

Bombing Out

One of the perils of attending the annual season of political conferences is the blizzard of leaflets, pleas and assorted battle cries from well-meaning groups. One such piece of paper, thrust upon delegates to the Labour conference at Blackpool, was from the Jobs Not Bombs youth marchers. It said: 'If the power of the Labour Party and trade unionists is fully mobilized then nuclear disarmament can be stopped.'

Now You Hear It, Now You Don't

Addressing an audience of GIs about to be shipped out to Vietnam in 1966, President Lyndon B. Johnson announced that his great-great-grand-daddy had perished at the Alamo. This was a nice line to hand those perhaps about to perish for their country. It was also a complete, copper-bottomed lie, as the world's Press, which was covering the event, would surely find out. LBJ'S aide pointed out that a scandal would follow the remark. Johnson gazed at him and replied: 'I never said that.'

The aide swallowed hard and told him that he and everyone else had heard him say it. Johnson snorted. 'I don't give a damn what you heard,' he said. 'I did not say it. I can state categorically that my great-great-grandfather did not die at the Alamo.'

There was no scandal.

Madam Chairperson

Anarchy was brewing at the headquarters of the Amalgamated Union of Engineering Workers in Peckham, South East London, as leaders brooded over ways to bring Mrs Thatcher's government to its knees.

They must have thought that Mrs T. numbered ESP among her many phenomenal attributes when they walked into their top secret meeting room to be confronted by... the Iron Lady herself, seated in the Chair, bearing a look of glacial disapproval.

Several of the brothers began to murmur vaguely apologetic

and self-exonerating words until one, less short-sighted than the rest, revealed to them their mistake. Some joker had placed a lifesize cardboard cutout of the PM in the chair.

Seizing probably the only chance they will ever have of overthrowing the premier, the brothers with one accord picked up the offending cardboard personage, and threw her unceremoniously from the room.

★   ★   ★   ★

. . . . .Josef Stalin, the infamous Soviet leader, not noted for his humanitarianism or uproarious humour, remarked in 1933: 'Gaiety is the most outstanding feature of the Soviet Union' . . . .

★   ★   ★   ★

Two Stars For Amazement

There's a small hotel in the historic town of Chester and if its owner, Bill Whitelaw, ever wished it was well and truly on the map, he must have thought his wildest dreams were about to come true when a letter arrived from the top men at the American Embassy in London.

Mr Whitelaw's quiet, away-from-it-all retreat, which boasts eight comfy bedrooms, costing a mere £13 a night all-in, was block-booked for a Mr Reagan and 19 heavies from the secret service... Could it be? Surely not *the* Mr Reagan...

Bill, aged 56, was further amazed when a letter confirming the arrangements dropped on his door mat. It also insisted on a command post and special security outside the Reagan bedroom.

However, the tingle of excitement Chez Bill was dimmed more than somewhat when the red-faced Americans admitted that they had erred. They had somehow managed to confuse Bill's humble but homely Gloster Hotel guest house with the Grosvenor Hotel, where the top people stay when they are in town. The Mr Reagan involved did not even turn out to be Ronnie, but only his 36-year-old son, Michael, who was on a European tour along with his wife and son. And the 19 bodyguards.

Individual Interpretation

When Mr S. Seymour, a State Department interpreter, accompanied ex-President Jimmy Carter on an official visit to Poland, he helped create a situation more reminiscent of Whitehall farce than the dignified behaviour associated with official East-West diplomatic relations.

The scene went as follows:

Carter: (to bored but polite gathering of 500 Poles) When I left the United States...

Seymour: (spontaneously 'translating') When I left the United States never to return...

Sudden interest among audience. Exchanged glances of disbelief.

Carter: (oblivious) I understand your hopes for the future...

Seymour: (relentless) I know your lusts for the future...

Dawning realization among Poles. Giggles.

Carter: (desperately worried) I have come to learn your opinions and understand your desires...

Seymour: (delightedly) I desire the Poles carnally...

The story is still told with some glee at embassy parties the world over.

Less gleeful was the response of the US Press Secretary, who remarked coldly of the event, 'It was not a good translation. There will be a new translator tomorrow.'

362

Thinking Ahead

Mr Arthur Lewis, Labour Member of Parliament for Newham North, stood up in the House of Commons on October 18, 1982 and made a ringing call for improved redundancy payments for MPs. This was unwittingly sensible of him, for, very shortly afterwards, his local constituency party shocked him by deciding not to reselect him as their candidate at the next General Election.

★ ★ ★ ★

.............The great Lloyd George made a fool of himself at the 1919 Versailles Peace Conference, when he told the Italians to boost their banana crop as a means of reviving their economy. He was rewarded with much Latin glowering and muttering, for, of course, Italy does not grow bananas.....................................-

Expert Timing

Sir John Hoskeyns, the former head of the Prime Minister's élite Policy Unit, was due to speak at a lunchtime fringe meeting at the 1982 Tory conference. Unfortunately, he failed to turn up. Shamefaced, he later admitted that he had got the dates all mixed up.

Sir John is the man who used to advise Mrs Thatcher on such momentous matters as the precise timing of elections.

★   ★   ★   ★

. . . . .One of the greatest gaffes in the history of diplomatic relations occurred at a grand dinner held at the White House in honour of the Egyptian Ambassador, when one of President Carter's aides turned to the ambassador's wife, grabbed at her bodice and informed her: 'I always wanted to see the Pyramids'. . . . .

★   ★   ★   ★

Follow My Leader

President Calvin Coolidge (of whom Dorothy Parker remarked on hearing of his death, 'Why, I never even knew that he was alive') invited a bunch of his hick friends to dine at the White House. It was one of his first social evenings after his election.

The friends, not having the remotest clue how to behave in high society, had an informal council of war beforehand and decided to copy Coolidge's actions down to the smallest detail.

All went well until dinner was over.

Then the President, who perhaps had more of a sense of humour than his friends suspected, solemnly tipped half his coffee into his saucer and added cream and sugar.

Following the prescribed formula, the friends duly followed suit.

They then froze in consternation and embarrassment as Coolidge calmly placed the saucer down on the carpet for his cat.

Coffee And A Dash

Conservative Member of Parliament Michael Brotherton was most anxious to get to Grimsby (stranger things have happened) to pay a surprise visit to a Dr Barnado coffee morning. But, as so often happens to those relying on British Rail, his train from London did not enable him to make the vital connection at Newark, Nottinghamshire.

Nothing daunted, a resolute Mr Brotherton, who sits for Louth, Lincs, called on the services of no less than three police forces.

First, police at Newark drove him to the Lincolnshire border, whence a second patrol car sped him onward to the outskirts of Grimsby, where a third police car waited to take him to the actual coffee morning venue.

Unfortunately, by the time he made his way through the door, the public, which included some of his constituents, had all gone. Mr Brotherton later insisted that the three-car journey was absolutely necessary and he added: 'People love to see their MP.'

★　★　★　★

. . . . .Nguyen Co Thach, the Foreign Minister of Vietnam, seems to be something of a whizz at economics. He was able to make this proud boast to an appreciative audience: 'We are not without accomplishment. We have managed to distribute poverty equally'. . . . .

★　★　★　★

Load of Rubbish

A crowd of 250,000 earnest demonstrators turned up in Washington in 1978. They were there to celebrate Sun Day, a happening designed to raise the national consciousness of non-polluting solar energy.

Their cause was not overwhelmingly aided by evidence of their own slightly less than outstanding pollution-consciousness in leaving behind them 10 acres of ankle-deep litter and garbage, gleaming and glittering in the non-polluting sunshine!

What's That You Say, Mr President?

In spite of his well-known experience as a film actor, President Ronald Reagan is still more than capable of fluffing his lines, with hilarious, and sometimes embarrassing, results:

Ronnie the Peacemaker
In 1975, while still riding that long trail which led from Hollywood to Washington, Reagan told a gathering: 'The United States has much to offer the Third World War.'

Assuming from the stunned and attentive silence this remark engendered that he was on to a winner, the White House hopeful repeated the line no fewer than nine times during his speech.

Ronnie the Broadcaster
Waiting to address the American people over the Polish Government's decision to ban the free trade union Solidarity, President Reagan obliged the sound engineer with a few well-chosen words. Not for him the 'testing, testing, one, two three, four' of lesser beings; he launched straight into what was uppermost in his great presidential brain: 'My fellow Americans, yesterday the Polish Government, a military dictatorship, a bunch of no-good lousy bums...'

Needless to say, due to 'human error', these admirable sentiments were heard on trannies from coast to coast.

Ronnie the Historian
One day President Reagan and his good lady were patiently awaiting the arrival of royal guests. America's leader had prepared a welcome address to greet King Olav and his queen. Fortunately, someone rather better schooled in recent European history was on hand to save the President from a disastrous gaffe: the Queen of Norway died in 1954.

RONNIE IN BLUNDERLAND

Truth, And Other Lies

George Smathers was a man who believed in the truth – in the broadest and most flexible sense of the word. A truly fearsome right-winger, Smathers was out to defeat and destroy his Liberal opponent, Claude Pepper, during the 1950 US Senate primary elections in Florida. To achieve this end, without swerving one iota from his guiding principle of honesty, he hit on a brilliant scheme.

Relying on the limited vocabulary and unlimited impressionability of the voters, he revealed to them that Pepper was 'a known extrovert, with a sister who is a thespian'.

As this bombshell sunk into the thick skulls of the populace, more shock horror revelations swiftly followed. Pepper's brother was mercilessly but quite accurately exposed as 'a practising *homo sapiens*' while Pepper himself could be proved to have 'matriculated' at college. The real clincher was the appalling news that the beastly Pepper went in for 'celibacy before marriage'.

The hick voters out in the sticks reacted just as Smather knew they would, mistaking this catalogue of unexceptional attributes for evidence of intolerable and disgusting debauchery, and the 'foul fellow' was soundly beaten at the polls.

And *that's* the truth.

For The Record

Those who heralded Reaganomics as the unerring road to renewed prosperity and balance for the ailing US economy may be beginning nervously to wonder where they went wrong, as it appears to be proving more of a twisting lane towards a dead end.

By the year ending 30 September 1982, overspending had risen to a colossal £65,294 million.

This was almost twice as much as that achieved under the previous record-holder (Gerald Ford) and is confidently expected to rise to a staggering £120,000 million before the end of Reagan's term of office.

King Arthur

The problem of naming streets is one that besets town councils the world over. The worthy citizens of Selby in Yorkshire are no exception. When they opted, among others, for 'Scargill Rise', they felt no sense of impending disaster. It sounded inoffensive enough.

However, they reckoned without the activities of the Yorkshire miners' leader, Arthur Scargill, whose elevation to national chief suddenly made the innocuous side road sound like an intentional tribute to the great man.

Sensing the danger of a press 'exposé' and aware that public opinion was not in favour of Mr S., councillors decided to retrieve their error, and the name was withdrawn.

But the spokesman who announced this compounded the mistake. Explaining that the council wished to do nothing that could be understood in any way as implying political bias in either direction, he went on to fall very heavily off his elected fence by stating that the name had been dropped in order 'to make miners moving to the area feel more welcome'!

★　　★　　★　　★

. . . . *Viscount Montgomery, speaking in the House of Lords, dismissed the aims of the 1965 Homosexuality Bill with the following remark: 'This sort of thing may be tolerated by the French, but we are British – thank God'.* . . . .

★　　★　　★　　★

Suckered

Herbert Hoover, whose very name implies a great ability to deal with hot air, told a waiting nation in 1928: 'We in America today are nearer the final triumph over poverty than ever in the history of the land.'

So near and yet so far. Within only one year the American Stock Market collapsed and the nation went bankrupt.

Plains Speaking

When President Reagan visited the vast farmlands of Illinois, his aide led him to anticipate a crowd of some 8,000 eager rural voters. When only a quarter of this number turned up, Ronnie turned an accusing eye on his over-confident aide.

Red-faced and blathering, the young man tried to cover his blunder, but only succeeded in achieving a further one by asserting that 'the farmers did not want to get their tractors muddy.'

He was unable to explain to the President how the farmers managed to preserve the pristine cleanliness of their machinery when ploughing the dirt soil from which they obtained their livelihood!

★　　★　　★　　★

. . . .*A Democrat running for Mayor of New York in 1968 delighted his rivals by describing his appeal in the following attractive terms: 'Frank O'Connor grows on you, like a cancer'*. . . . .

★　　★　　★　　★

Non-Stick Mud

During the American presidential election campaign of 1884, the Democratic candidate, Grover Cleveland, was the victim of a smear campaign.

Having discovered that the unmarried Democrat was the father of widow Maria Halpen's son, the Republican camp rushed out a series of leaflets. Beneath pictures of the illegitimate offspring was printed the caption: 'One more vote for Cleveland.'

But the whole dirty trick backfired with a satisfying crash.

Cleveland decided on the highly unusual political course of telling the truth. He admitted the dalliance, and its results, and threw himself on the mercy of the sensible and forgiving electorate.

Much to Blaine's chagrin, the voters decided that they quite liked a man with a naughty secret, particularly when he had the decency to admit it, and Cleveland was duly elected.

Hung Vote

Seven Members of Parliament who missed a vote on the Transport Bill in October 1982 explained later to their respective aggrieved Whips that, far from being a deliberate revolt, their non-appearance was all a ghastly mistake, ironically caused by a bit of trouble with their chosen method of transport: they were stuck in a malfunctioning lift at the Commons.

Out Of His Own Mouth

One of ex-President Richard Nixon's most memorable blunders (apart from getting found out!) during the notorious Watergate scandal, occurred during a nationwide TV broadcast. Attentive viewers were astonished to hear the confident assertion: 'this is a discredited President.'

The mistake was soon made clear. Rather than an accurate description of his own unenviable position, Nixon had actually intended to object against the use of unfair legal *precedent* in the case against him. At least this unwitting shaft of honesty caused some members of his audience more amusement than most such speeches were to do.

Looking Glass

The go-ahead PR men of the Labour Party decided to install a 'magic glass' prompt machine for Michael Foot's rallying speech to the 1982 Conference at Blackpool. This device is designed to enable a speaker to appear to be speaking off the cuff, while in fact reading a cunningly reflected version of his speech off a specially constructed disguised mirror that stands before him like an innocent piece of protective glass.

Just in time, party chieftains examined the contraption and stepped in to prevent what could have been a disastrous (though hilarious) mistake. They pointed out that Mr Foot's somewhat erratic freestyle of movement while on the platform would inevitably result in him knocking the whole thing over – to the imminent danger of those faithful seated in the first few rows.

True Blue Blush

A prospective Conservative Parliamentary candidate was out canvassing one evening. He became lost in the narrow back streets of the town and wound up in the red-light district.

Still in a state of blissful ignorance, the young hopeful rang the nearest door-bell, which happened to be that of a 'house of ill fame'.

When the door opened the confused canvasser realized his mistake and could only splutter that he was from the Tory party.

'Never mind, love,' was the encouraging reply, 'you're all the same to us. Come on in.'

Seeing Stars

.... *Errors concerning*
film and TV personalities ....

Crossed Wires

When Ken Hughes was directing 89-year-old Mae West in *Sextette*, he encountered a delicate technical problem. The ageing star was unable to keep up with the constant changes in the script, so, eventually, a bizarre solution was developed.

A small radio receiver was concealed in her wig and her lines were relayed to her by Hughes just before she was due to speak them.

As solutions go, this was not a great success. First, other actors were disturbed by hearing Hughes' voice emanating from the wig, giving answers to lines they had not yet delivered.

Then, by some radiophonic mischance, a police helicopter tuned in to the wig wavelength, and the entire company was brought up short when, during a passionate love scene, Miss West delivered the unforgettable line: 'Traffic on the Hollywood Freeway is bogged down.'

What's In A Name?

When actor Joel McCrea decided to go freelance after his MGM contract expired, Sam Goldwyn threw a lavish lunch party for him, with some of the greatest names in the business seated around the table. He rose to his feet to address the gathering.

'And so we say goodbye to my good friend Joe McCrail...'

An embarrassed aide leaned across, tugged his chief's sleeve and muttered: 'Sam, it's McCrea...'

Goldwyn glowered down on him and hissed: 'For seven years I've paid him $5,000 a week and you're trying to tell me his name?'

★   ★   ★   ★

. . . . *Actor George Raft was not perhaps a great judge of potential box office success. He refused the leads in* High Sierra *and* The Maltese Falcon, *in the latter case because he did not wish to work with an unknown and unsung director – John Huston!* . . . .

★   ★   ★   ★

You Must Remember This, Or

Maybe You'd Rather

Forget

The film *Casablanca* made Humphrey Bogart and Ingrid Bergman immortal, for when it is shown on late night TV it regularly keeps up more people than overspiced curry.

It would have been very different, however, if the producers had had their way.

First choices for the roles, Hedy Lamarr and George Raft, turned down the parts – and doubtless kicked themselves all the way to the bank.

Bird Brains

The 1939 movie *It Ain't No Sin* was to be a big money-spinner for Paramount Studios and they wanted to give it the full publicity treatment.

An eager, and definitely imaginative, publicity man hit on the bright idea of shutting a platoon of parrots in a room with a record that played the name of the film over and over again. Quite soon Paramount were the owners of a flock of feathered friends which could squawk 'It ain't no sin' to order.

By this time, however, the studio bosses had changed the name of the picture to *I'm No Angel*.

Novel Attitude

Hollywood story editor Jacob Wilk was given an advance look at the galley-proofs of a forthcoming novel, for which the publisher had high hopes. He was so impressed that he rushed right in to see his boss, studio chief Jack Warner, and urged him to take up a $50,000 exclusive option on the available film rights.

To Wilk's dismay, Warner refused, saying: 'I wouldn't pay 50,000 bucks for any damn book any damn time.'

The book so confidently dismissed was Margaret Mitchell's *Gone With The Wind*.

Way Out West

Mae West was a sex goddess of the silver screen for more years than most people would like to remember. By the time she made her last movie, the legend and the star were both coming apart at the seams.

She was 89 when shooting started and was hardly able to move or hear. But she was still surrounded by a team of hangers-on who tried to tell her all the things they thought she wanted to be told.

'Miss West, you are wonderful, just wonderful,' they drivelled. 'Your skin, your face, your hair are in a class beyond compare. You don't look a day older than 29.'

Mae West drew herself to her full height and treated them to the famous bedroom drawl: 'Thanks fellers, I'm supposed to be 26.'

Taylor-Made Gag

Laurie Taylor is Professor of Sociology at York University. He is also well known for his acerbic wit, as displayed on such programmes as BBC Radio 4's *Stop The Week*.

This should have been enough to alert the thoroughly nice and unsuspecting people concerned with the Thames Television afternoon programme *A-Plus*. But, perhaps working on the principle that no one does anything wicked before teatime, they allowed themselves to be taken for something of a ride by Prof. Taylor.

Luring the programme's researchers to York with tales of a remarkable band of Arab musicians called El Moruhci, Taylor proceeded, along with his six accomplices, to adorn himself in authentic Arab garb and create what he hoped was the genuine Arab sound. So impressed were the Thames TV minions that they roared back to London full of their exciting find.

The pranksters duly appeared on the show the following week and, with the aid of giggling convulsions from the venerable professor, gave presenter, Kay Avila, the runaround.

Nina Burr, the producer, putting a good face on it, later observed: 'They certainly fooled us – but it made a very funny item.'

Abandoned Hope

Bob Hope found himself in the unaccustomed role of being on the receiving end of the cold shoulder one evening at a grand reception at the US Embassy.

A senior British official, failing to recognize the world-famous comedian, displayed less than the requisite diplomatic grace when he turned his back on Mr Hope in mid-anecdote and strode purposefully away.

The celebrity was not surprisingly offended. It is not known whether he whispered something of his pique into the ear of his friend, Mr Reagan, who was also present, or whether embassy walls really do have ears.

But at any rate it is rumoured in diplomatic circles that the poor humourless Brit is paying for his *faux pas* – perhaps by playing an unenviable part in *The Road to Siberia*!

Calling The Tune

Frederick Loewe, composer of the music for such famous shows as *My Fair Lady*, *Brigadoon* and *Camelot,* threw a lunch party in Hollywood one day. When the food was delayed by a crisis in the kitchen, Leowe filled the waiting minutes by playing a selection of his best-known numbers on his grand piano.

Among the guests was Sam Goldwyn, who was most appreciative. Afterwards, he patted the composer on the back and told him: 'You know, Fritz, you've got a few possible hits there.'

Double Agent

In the far off days when Lord Grade was still plain Lew, a theatrical agent on his way to fame and fortune as a TV and movie tycoon, he made it a practice to visit London shows in search of bright new talent.

On one such occasion he was much excited by a double act which was clearly destined for greater things. After the show he rushed backstage, warmly congratulated the two and told them that he would make them big stars if they signed up with his organization. The performers agreed that it was time their career took a new and more lucrative turn. But, they told Grade, he would have to get things sorted out with their present agent.

'And who is that?' Grade asked.

'Lew Grade,' they replied.

Gloria In Transit

Gloria Swanson, star of many silent movies and later sensational in *Sunset Boulevard*, took unto her a husband, one Marquis de la Falaise. Miss Swanson's mother congratulated her daughter on the event and then phoned her lawyer to ask: 'What the hell is a markee?' The lawyer told her: 'It is one of those things that they hang up in front of a theatre. It is intended to keep the rain off the customers.'

This was too much for Mother. 'Christ,' she wailed. 'Gloria just married one of those things today.'

Ballou Ballyhoo

Kirk Douglas was originally offered the classic role of Kid Shelleen in *Cat Ballou*. His agent talked him out of it, on the grounds that he should not allow himself to appear as a comic drunken gunfighter. It is not known whether Mr Douglas sent a congratulatory telegram to Lee Marvin, who won an Oscar for the role. Or what he had to say to his hapless agent.

A Quiet Laugh

Conrad Nagel, heartthrob of the silent days, once observed that silent pictures were a great source of merriment for deaf people everywhere. As expert lip-readers they were, he pointed out, able to understand *exactly* what the actors were saying to each other, which often had very little to do with the story in hand.

Nagel always denied the oft-quoted tale of the film in which he picked up a girl, carried her to the bed and leered down at her, only to hear her say: 'If you drop me, you bastard, I'll kill you.' He maintained that it was another actor, who was slightly unwell by virtue of a massive hangover, who tried to lift the actress. She told him: 'Why don't you just use your breath? It's more than strong enough to do the job.'

All of which had the deaf rolling in the aisles, to the total bewilderment of everyone else in the house.

The Age Of The Cable

The impudent journalist who sent a telegram to Cary Grant's agent inquiring:

HOW OLD CARY GRANT?

was mistaken if he thought his cheek would go unnoticed, or unpunished, by the great star. Having opened the cable himself, Grant telegraphed back:

OLD CARY GRANT FINE. HOW YOU?

379

Harty Cheers

Russell Harty, of TV chat show fame, was not surprised to receive an invitation to present the prizes at the annual Mr Hardware contest. Mr Harty, who frequently gets similar approaches from all sorts of organizations, was at the time taking part in the Black Pudding of the Year Award ceremony in the same town, and so agreed readily enough.

Supposing it to be an Ironmonger of the Year event, or some such extravaganza, Mr Harty went along to the venue at a popular disco in the city expecting a dull but uncontroversial evening. To his surprise and growing discomfiture, he soon found he had made a ghastly mistake. Not only was there not a single ironmonger to be seen, but he found himself having to judge between five effete-looking young men, each of whom wore the teeniest pair of tiny briefs and one of whom sported for good measure a pair of authentic-looking handcuffs!

The title of the competition, it later transpired, had little or

nothing to do with hammers and nails, but was taken from the name of a '*potent* medicine' sold in shops of a certain rather dubious nature in the city's red light district.

Proper Charlie

One-time Hollywood comedian Jackie Vernon was a childhood fan of Charlie Chaplin. Like all good supporters, he wrote countless letters to his idol. Unlike most, he did not get a single reply.

Many years later Vernon was, by chance, in London at the same time as Chaplin, who had come out of retirement to direct Sophia Loren and Marlon Brando in *The Countess From Hong Kong*.

As fate would have it, Vernon happened to be in a restaurant on the same night as the ageing Chaplin.

He simply could not resist walking over to the great man's table.

'Please excuse me,' he said. 'You won't know me, but I am one of your greatest fans. My name is Jackie Vernon.'

Chaplin looked up and replied: 'Tell me, why did you stop writing?'

Spot The Insult

When Hollywood producer Arthur Hornblow Jr had a son, his colleague, the legendary Sam Goldwyn, called to congratulate him.

Hornblow thanked him and revealed that the new arrival was going to be christened Arthur Hornblow III.

Goldwyn pondered this with puckered brow.

'Why Arthur?' he asked. 'Every Tom, Dick and Harry is called Arthur.'

Common Interests

Groucho Marx, the fast-talking, cigar-chewing leader of the famous Marx Brothers comedy team, once confessed to an unfortunate mistake made during a prolonged courtship: 'Many years ago I chased a woman for almost two years, only to discover her tastes were exactly like mine: we were both crazy about girls.'

24 Carat Goldwyn

At the time when he was completing his 'great production of *The Best Years of Our Lives*, top Hollywood producer, Sam Goldwyn, was invited to make an appearance on Bob Hope's radio show.

He asked screenwriter Harry Tugend to give him a gag for the occasion. Tugend suggested that Bob Hope should say: 'How are things going since I left your studio, Mr Goldwyn?'

The producer was to reply: 'Since you left, Bob, we've had the best years of our lives.'

Goldwyn was delighted with the idea, and with the plug for the film. Sadly, where Goldwyn was concerned, there was many a slip twixt script and lip.

He was so pleased that he told his associates: 'That Harry Tugend is a very clever man. He wants to have Bob Hope ask me how things are since he left MGM. Then I've got to say, "Since you left things are better than ever".'

Into Cattle

Celebrated horror film producer Alfred Hitchcock was most upset to read himself misquoted as having said that 'Actors are like cattle'.

Hurrying to rectify the error, he rang the newspaper concerned. What he had actually said, he told them, was: 'Actors *should be treated* like cattle.'

He Never Said That

James Cagney, the famous gangster-movie actor, is one of the most impersonated of all stars of the big screen.

Yet even the President of the United States, in his own very creditable Cagney impression, uses the mistaken expression 'you dirty rat'.

In fact, in all his many gangster films, Cagney never once used this world-famous phrase.

383

Works Of Heart

.... *Errors concerning romance*
and marriage ....

Unlucky In Love

One of the unluckiest lonely hearts of all time must be the 22-year-old Los Angeles man who advertised through the personal columns of a magazine for a woman to accompany him on the vacation of a lifetime in South America.

His ad struck at least one responsive chord, for he received a quick reply. From his widowed mother.

Aisle Be Seeing You

Irishman Albert Muldoon was delighted and honoured and charmed to be best man for his dear pal Christopher at the tiny church in Kileter, County Tyrone.

Unfortunately, the beauty of the occasion was altogether too much for him and he stood on the groom's left instead of on his right. The priest, not knowing either of them from Adam, duly put the questions to Albert, who responded by taking the time-honoured vows.

The awful truth emerged, to be sure, but only when the happy triple were involved in signing the register. A second ceremony was immediately held and this time the bride managed to leave on the arm of the right man.

In this case, fortunately perhaps, the best man did not win.

Rib-Tickling Romance

Anna Mitlow, known for miles around Minneapolis for her beauty, did not mind having a kiss and a cuddle with her boy friend, but when his affectionate squeeze cracked two of her ribs, she felt things were going a bit too far.

The bonny Miss Mitlow took the unfortunate young man to court, asking for $30 damages, plus $1.50 for her doctor's bill. The judge told her: 'I'll give you judgement for the doctor's bill, but as regards the other $30 – well, a good squeeze like that is worth $30!'

I need hardly add that the case was brought back in 1930, long before the days when feminism would have made the old boy think twice.

Happy Landings

Vera Czermak, housewife of Prague, was bitterly unhappy and depressed, for she had discovered that her husband was having an affair. She decided that the only answer was to end it all, and hurled herself from the window of their second-floor apartment.

She landed on Mr Czermak, who chose that moment to arrive at the main entrance to the building.

He was killed, but Vera survived.

Fat And Happy

Linda Leiro put an ad in her local newspaper at Wimborne, in Dorset:

Wedding ring for sale. Hardly used.

Anxious relatives and friends beat a path to her door to see if anything was amiss. But 29-year-old Linda was happily able to tell them that her marriage was not on the rocks. Far from it.

She had been on a diet and had shed so much of her chubby old self that her gold band kept falling off her new slimline finger. Husband Alberto, with true Latin chivalry, dashed into town and bought her a new one.

Then Linda got fed up with her diet and began to nibble the odd biscuit, cream cake and plate of pasta again. The weight came rolling back, 20lb of it, and so did the old wedding ring. The new one was by now far too small. So she put it up for sale.

'I'm very happy,' she said.

The Very Odd Couple

Appearances can be deceptive, as the neighbours of an ordinary-seeming couple were to discover. When Mr and Mrs O. arrived in town, she was pregnant. The local council granted them a flat, and everyone was happy.

But all was not what it seemed. For, far from being just another ordinary working couple Mr and Mrs O. were, in fact, both women!

'Mr.' O, who dresses in men's clothing and likes to be called Ossie, has lived with her friend for more than four years. They wanted nothing to complete their happiness other than a family. When conventional adoption proved out of the question, they disliked the idea of artificial insemination and so they found 'a tall, handsome candidate with a nice personality', who duly obliged.

The couple's neighbours were astonished that they could have failed to notice when their mistake came to light some time later, but it did not materially affect their feelings towards 'such a nice young couple'.

388

In The Picture

In 1936, Lady Beddoe Rees enthralled a women's afternoon meeting at Romsey in Hampshire with the tale of a young couple who thumped on the front door of the local cinema manager in the middle of the night.

They told him they had left 'an article of great value' in the cinema. The manager opened up the cinema and the great search was on.

They found their precious treasure where they had left it. It was their baby, still fast asleep on the seat next to where they had been sitting.

Lady Rees assured the audience that the story was true and persons of title are not given to telling tall stories, are they?

Catty Response

A couple in the Michigan town of Ypsilanti were arguing so loudly and vehemently that the local police were called in by the neighbours.

The forces of law and order discovered that the couple had been fighting over possession of the cat.

Sadly, the said cat had expired somewhat abruptly, due to being pulled asunder in a tug-of-love between the two combatants.

Which Is Switch?

A double wedding was about to take place in Saudi Arabia in 1978.

Unfortunately, the Moslem father of the two brides mixed up the names of the grooms and sent his daughters on the journey into matrimony with the wrong partners.

For several days the unhappy man attempted to set matters right, but the two girls told him not to bother about it.

They declared that they were very happy with the way things had turned out.

Thirty Years' Solitary

After 30 years of marriage, a 60-year-old North London woman decided she had made a mistake, and sued for divorce. When the appeal was granted, her husband was devastated. He told the judge he thought the marriage had been 'fairly happy.'

I suppose it depends on how you look at it.. during all those years, the man had kept his wife a virtual prisoner in her own home, allowing her out for half an hour each day to do the shopping, locking up the telephone and only allowing her to see other people in his presence. Moral: do not confuse absence of complaint for presence of contentment.

On The House

A recently-published survey on marriage carried out by a women's magazine reveals a startling misconception among us enlightened 'liberated' males! While stating the apparently shocking statistics that only one in three husbands makes any sort of token effort at helping with the housework, while one cad in ten does absolutely nothing at all, the magazine also shows that most wives are quite happy with this state of affairs.

53% said they actually *enjoy* doing the household chores. So – all of you who cry loudly about exploitation and the downtrodden housewife – you're *wrong*!

Hell Hath No Fury...

An airline pilot who decided to jilt his longstanding girlfriend should have chosen a better time to do it. Announcing his intention just before a round-world flight, he asked the girl to return some of his belongings to his flat. When he returned to his flat, the pilot found his 'phone off the hook. Puzzled, he picked it up and listened. A tireless American voice chanted: 'At the tone it will be three twenty-six and ten seconds.' The jilted girlfriend had dialled the Transatlantic speaking clock, and notched up a bill running well into four figures!

Change Partners

If you look forward to an exciting wedding night and are a self-employed shop-keeper, do not arrange to marry during the run-up to Christmas. The bride of a couple who made this mistake found herself spending her five-night honeymoon with – her mother-in-law!

Admitting that the timing had been unfortunate, the young husband yet made his position abundantly clear: 'Business comes first. If you don't make money, you just can't live.'

Luckily for him, his young wife says she gets on very well with her mother-in-law and that they had 'a lovely time'. She did add, however, a little ruefully, that her new husband 'was rather unromantic'.

391

Only Human

.... ***Errors concerning misjudgment***
and foible ....

Dead Loss

Church treasurer Angus Duncan came up with a raffle prize that the lucky winner really could take with him when he went. In addition to such fripperies as a colour television and an electric toaster, Angus offered a free funeral.

His aim was to raise £500 for the Baptist Church in the Worcestershire parish of Feckenham. Tickets said that the booby prize was a 'non-transferable' voucher for the £9 church funeral fee. But the local people took a very grave view of Angus' little wheeze and sent the tickets back.

Pub landlord Brian Grub was one of those who refused to sell the 50p tickets. He said: 'There are many elderly people in this area. Just imagine if they had won the funeral voucher. We would have felt awful.' And Betty Leek, from the village Post Office, said: 'It was very tasteless and not at all the thing to do.'

A somewhat cowed Angus said: 'It was all meant to be a bit of a joke, but obviously people have not got my sense of humour. Luckily I had only sold 40 tickets and when all the trouble started I was able to make sure that people got their money back.'

★　　★　　★　　★

. . . .*In 1979 a Spanish Air Force ace managed to shoot himself down: his bullets ricocheted off the practice target in the Iberian hills, and then hit his jet, forcing him to eject to safety – and ridicule.* . . . .

★　　★　　★　　★

Mouse That Roared

Adolf Hitler was a man with a lot of ideas, and most of them bad. One of his dafter schemes, designed to assist the Nazi effort towards world domination, was Project Mouse. Mouse was intended to be a battleship that confined itself to the land.

It was 50 feet long, with a 1,500 horse power engine, armour plating thick enough to withstand attack from a tank, and enough fire power to be most unpleasant. As befits a battleship, it was watertight and could get across rivers underwater.

Dr Porsche, who worked for Volkswagen and later found his niche in life with sports cars, was the designer of this monstrosity. In 1944 he sent the Mouse forth on a series of road trials. The series was very short, for the 180-ton monster ploughed up and ruined the roads, damaged the foundations of buildings it passed and, when it left the roads, simply sank into the ground. Along with the whole project.

Start The Day With A Bang

Danny Arnold, the gun-toting sheriff of Bexar County, Texas, was not best pleased when he missed his breakfast because his alarm clock went off three hours late at his London hotel.

He dressed hurriedly in traditional style – frock coat, fancy waistcoat and gunbelt – and then strode purposefully into the reception room where 129 guests were enjoying morning coffee.

To announce his arrival, he pulled out his .38 Smith and Wesson and fired it at the ceiling. Although the gun was loaded with nothing more alarming than blanks, the smoke activated the fire alarm bells at the Heathrow Sheraton Skyline.

Sheriff Arnold shook his head later, as he mused: 'It only took a couple of minutes for the whole place to be surrounded by fire trucks and firemen. I immediately apologized to everyone for ruining their coffee break. I never guessed that firing a gun would cause so much trouble.'

Down To A Tee

When the great American baseball player, Babe Ruth, challenged champion golfer Walter Hagen to a sociable eighteen holes, he made a grave tactical error. For Ruth seemed able only to maintain his game for half that number.

The explanation was simple. It takes about the same length of time to play nine holes of golf as it does to get through a whole baseball game. So established was the timer in Ruth's mind that it clicked off after its normal span, and that was the end of his concentration – and his game of golf.

How The Royal Melbourne Drove

Into The Rough

The Royal Melbourne Golf Club is quite the snobbiest in Australia. But it very nearly bunkered itself forever and, with stunning timing, chose the week in which it staged the Australian PGA championship to do it.

At the time, well-intentioned officials were attempting to raise cash for improvements by disposing of an acre of wasteland to a local developer. Sadly, the committee worthies were far more adept at reading the run of the greens than maps and plans and suchlike. It was only when the builder, Mike Warson, applied for planning and development permission that he discovered that he was the owner of 60 acres, including the 8th, 9th, 10th and 11th fairways on which such stars as Ballesteros and Miller were playing.

The value of the land was $20 million, a hundred times the sum Warson had actually paid out.

He said: 'We all had a good laugh at the club's expense.'

But, a sportsman and certainly a gentleman, he got the Royal Melbourne out of a very nasty hole by returning the land.

Artistic Licence

The Metropolitan Museum of Art in New York has made a few expensive mistakes in its time.

In 1918, for example, it paid $40,000 for an ancient Etruscan statue. One arm was missing, and the thumb of one hand was gone.

It was not until 1960 that one Alfredo Fioravanti came forward to confess that he and five other men had actually made the statue 50 years before.

He produced the missing thumb to prove it – it was a perfect fit!

Damn Dam

The massive May Dam near Konya was intended by the Turkish Government as the incredibly expensive answer to local irrigation and other watery problems.

It looked really impressive, but the whole project turned out to be totally useless, for the engineers responsible seemed to know little about geology. The huge reservoir created by the dam sat inconveniently on extremely permeable alluvium and karstic limestone. More than 30 sink holes formed, thus allowing all the gathered water to drain away into the ground.

Chess Congestion

A commercial artist, seeking to fire the infant population of Britain with his own enthusiasm for the ancient game of chess, produced a nifty little book called *The Amazing Adventures of Dan the Pawn*.

Dan is depicted as the hero of the piece, picked by the White King as his champion in the battle with the 'Black Army'.

Sadly, the artist reckoned entirely without the vigilance of the National Union of Teachers' official organ, *Teacher*.

The journal lashed into the book, accusing it of 'subtle racism'. The reason for its ire was that the white pieces defeated the black.

Dishonesty Is A Real Drag

A teenager went with his mother to the county court at Blackburn, Lancashire. Once there he nipped into the ladies and changed into his sister's clothes, adding a touch of realism by stuffing his socks into the bra to look like breasts. His mother then duped court officials into handing over £931 held in trust for her 17-year-old daughter.

The disguised boy told officials that 'she' was emigrating. The town's magistrates, who later heard them admit obtaining the cash by deception, thought the whole thing was a drag and gave the pair suspended jail sentences.

The Computer Kid

Gilbert Bohuslav loved computers, chess and Western novels. He had already taught his brainy computer, the DEC 11/70, to play chess with him, and the next step was obvious.

Gilbert, who worked in the computer department at Brazosport College, Houston, Texas, fed DEC 11/70 with the most-used words in every Western he had seen or read.

Then he sat back, eagerly awaiting the outpouring of his electronic J. T. Edson. And this is what he got:

> *Tex Doe, the marshal of Harry City rode into town. He sat hungrily in the saddle, ready for trouble. He knew that his sexy enemy, Alphonse the Kid, was in town. The Kid was in love with Texas Horse Marion. Suddenly the Kid came out of the upended Nugget Saloon. 'Draw, Tex,' he yelled madly. Tex reached for his girl, but before he could get it out of his car, the Kid fired, hitting Tex in his elephant and the tundra. As Tex fell, he pulled out his own chess board and shot the Kid 35 times in the King. The Kid dropped in a pool of whisky. 'Aha,' said Tex, 'I hated to do it, but he was on the wrong side of the Queen.'*

Even making allowance for Gilbert's own sense of humour (elephant? tundra?) it was clearly time to go back, if not to the drawing board, at least to the chess board.

Dash It All

A hyphen is a little thing, not even paramount among punctuation marks. It hardly ranks with the lordly full stop, or even the comma.

But it once cost the United States taxpayers no less than $18.5 million.

The day when the cash registers went wild was July 22, 1962, when Mariner 1, the Venus-bound rocket, had to be blasted into pieces as it suddenly surged off its ordained course.

The reason for this costly malfunction was that a humble hyphen had been left out of the flight computer programme.

No Escape

The Fire Brigade at Barnsley in Yorkshire were proudly on full dress parade for the opening of their smart new headquarters.

The splendour of the occasion was somewhat diminished by the arrival of some factory inspectors, who had turned up to give the custom-built showpiece the once-over.

They immediately ordered one tiny little modification...to include a fire escape.

Call Of The Wild

Paul White was exceedingly fed up, not to mention sacked from his job as car park assistant at Cambridge, Massachusetts, following a row with a lady driver.The irate woman had cursed him something rotten and left him with his ears burning at the abuse.

As a result of this episode, he decided to help all those suffering from an addiction to the same foul language. To this end, he founded Curseholics Anonymous and set up a round-the-clock hotline.

Unfortunately, he was obliged to scrap the whole idea – because he was getting far too many obscene calls.

Just The Ticket

People duped into paying cash to a Birmingham con man for cars they were never destined to receive, little dreamed that their unjust mistake was designed, in the criminal's eyes, to further the course of justice. It appears that the man conducted the swindle in order to raise funds to pay for his appeal against a previous conviction to be heard at the European Court of Justice!

Yela Peril

British soccer clubs, wistfully watching the World Cup on the telly, have often thought that the answer to falling attendances and standards might be the introduction of some Brazilian-style flair. Clydebank, the somewhat unglamorous Scottish League club, would be only too happy to point out some of the pitfalls of this course of action.

In 1967 they were able to boast the not inconsiderable services of the Brazilian, Ayrton Ignaccio. The fans duly turned up, eager to witness a spot of samba soccer, at Forfar. They were doomed to disappointment, for Senhor Ignaccio had to be taken off, shivering, long before the end of the game. He could not stand the ravages of the Caledonian cold.

Great Scott

Animal-lover Scott Brant was, quite naturally, delighted when a puppy came loping over to him as he strolled in the pleasant night air near his home in Minnesota.

The friendly little four-legged fellow licked his hand and showed no inclination to leave, so Scott took his new friend home, gave it some milk, and even cooked up a hamburger. The cheerful little visitor finished its meal and, as pets will, went for an exploratory roam about the house. But Scott was most distressed when the bundle of fun began tearing up the furniture.

He telephoned a vet for advice. The vet immediately contacted the local zoo, which sent around two keepers to collect its missing four-month-old lion cub.

Quiet Goes The Don

Australian Don Bradman needed only four runs during the Oval test in 1948 to achieve an unequalled average Test score of 100. Marching down the pavilion steps with calm assurance, the Don misjudged a ball and was dismayed to find himself, only seconds later, walking back, bowled for 0. How is the mighty's wicket fallen, went up the cry – and Bradman's average remained at 99.94, still the best in history by a long way.

Better Red Than – No-One

The Russians' attempt to launch their own wine in Britain was beset by disaster. The wines, which are big sellers back in the USSR were vilified by British wine experts. 'Chateau KGB', a white sparkling vintage, was described succinctly as 'awful', while 'Ruby of Crimea' and the grim-sounding Krim were 'unbelievable'.

To make matters worse, Russian trade delegate Alexander Krivenko confessed (perhaps after a few too many of the perilous red) that the biggest motive for making the wine was to lure his comrades from their notorious addiction to their beloved vodka.

VICTIMS RUSSIAN WINE TASTING 4 MAR 1963

KARL MARX

Swan-Downing

When a body discovered in an Indiana lake was found to have bite marks on the left cheek, the local sheriff's deputies (exiles from Hazzard County perhaps?) put their none-too-well-endowed heads together. Their conclusion? The attack could only have been made by a large swan. Of course.

Looking through their files, they came upon a likely suspect. Described as 'big and tough', the 50lb swan was duly arrested by these gallant upholders of Law and Order. It was only when the case came to court that the lawmen realized they had goofed. Under US law it is not possible to indict a feathered suspect! Back to the drawing board, boys!

★　　★　　★　　★

. . . . .Absent-minded footballer Mark Wadsley was very surprised when he turned up for a match at Carterton, Oxfordshire, for instead of bringing his kitbag he found in his hand only a sack of potatoes! . . . .

★　　★　　★　　★

Having A Ball, Boyo

During a rugby international between England and Wales at Twickenham in 1960, the match ball was punted into the crowd. The ball was then caught, punctured and concealed about the not inconsiderable person of an avid Welsh supporter.

Play continued uninterrupted, using a substitute ball, and the dastardly Taffy returned to the valleys with his trophy.

It was soon on display at his place of work, but his moment of triumph was short-lived. For a vigilant local copper (who had himself once played on the wing for Llanelly and therefore knew right from wrong in these matters better than most) confiscated the ball and posted it back to the powers that be at Twickenham. He received a courteous thank you from the R.F.U. who were, however, they said, astonished to receive the ball back.

Match balls, it appears, always disappear and nobody questions their final destination. This was the first time that any international ball had survived for so long.

Air Blackmail

Police got a flying start in a strange case of blackmail in Germany back in 1929. A mysterious parcel had been delivered to General Franz Pattberg at his home at Homburg on the Rhine. It contained a box holding a carrier pigeon. A note instructed the general to attach £250 to the waiting bird and then set it free. The penalty for non-compliance would be death itself.

This crafty plot was foiled by the general, who immediately demonstrated just why he had risen to the top of his chosen profession. He informed the police, and then arranged for a plane to go up and follow the unsuspecting pigeon all the way home. Aerial photographs were taken of the house where the pigeon settled and soon afterwards the villain was amazed to see the police swoop on him and drag him off to jail.

Why The Ladies Blue Their Top

Porn movies, one of the weekly attractions staged by the management of a social club in Hexham, Northumberland, were the cause of a complaint from the members of the ladies' darts team which played at the club on the same night. It was not that the ladies objected to any sexist or exploitative element of the blue movies. They merely said that the appreciative reaction of the audience was putting them off their game in the bar next door.

Mind Your Language

When a used car dealer decided to advertise his latest shiny new model as on sale for a knock-down price of 1,395 'bananas' (a local slang expression for dollars), he reckoned without the literal-mindedness of his clientele. He was very taken aback when a woman arrived offered him a deposit of twenty-five bananas – of the yellow, edible variety. The proprietor was reluctant to agree to the deal. But the determined woman took him to court and won her case.

Then, having delivered the outstanding 1,370 pieces of fruit, she drove away in the car.

What you might call a banana split!

Prophet And Loss

Something for nothing is the lure that fills casinos and betting shops. Many punters are prepared to believe in anything, 'foolproof' systems, dreams, visions, the lot. Thousands of them came forward in Italy in 1926, eyes glittering with lire signs, when word got around that a crippled peasant named Torraca had foresight of the numbers that would be drawn in the national lottery.

Crowds besieged the home of the little limping prophet. He told reporters: 'My family, assisted by the hand of God, found the key to the lottery. The secret was divulged by my father on his deathbed. But he told me I must benefit only the people and must never enter the lottery myself.' Cables and express letters poured in from all over Europe and the United States, as emigré Italians begged for the numbers. Armed men stood guard outside Torraca's home to keep away the throngs.

At last the numbers were given and there was an immediate rush on the lottery ticket offices. One office manager was nearly lynched for keeping the anxious punters waiting. Many poor people sold their few possessions to raise money to buy tickets.

Come the day of the lottery, incredible to relate, not one of the miracle numbers came up. It was obvious why Torraca's dying father had told him not to buy his own tickets! The prophet was a complete dead loss. He was also missing, having wisely decided to leg it, crippled or not. The Italian Government, however, was naturally highly delighted. They had made millions on top of the usual lottery revenue.

Game, Set And Match

The sounds of dissension and derision addressed to line judges and referees are now as much a part of the Wimbledon Tennis Championships as strawberries and cream or Dan Maskell.

When McEnroe made his famous outburst in the 1981 Championships the press and public opinion were united in their conviction that he was – to put it mildly – mistaken. Thanks to scientific tests inaugurated in the US soon after this event, it is now possible to show the truth of this beyond doubt.

During the tests, twelve professional coaches played against each other, watched by an umpire, the full complement of line judges and twenty spectators seated at strategic angles in the public seats. The humans' eye view was then compared with electronic and computer analysis of the play.

The results showed that the players were the lousiest judges of all. Even the ice cream seller would have done better. The best of all – by a long puff of chalk – were the much-abused 'pits of the world' themselves, the line judges. So – Messrs McEnroe, Connors and Nastase, among many others, please note – any further such disputes would be a *definite* mistake.

★   ★   ★   ★

. . . . .It is obviously unwise to be too cheerful at work these days. An 18-year-old girl discovered the truth of this when her boss fired her – for laughing too much . . . . . .

★   ★   ★   ★

Rock Off, Alf!

The Locarno ballroom in Birmingham was one of Alf and Mary's favourite haunts. And when the old place was transformed into a mixture of flashing lights and 3,500 watts of sound called The Powerhouse disco still they remained loyal. At least, they would have done if they had been allowed in. Alf, who is 48, and Mary, three years his junior, were amazed to be told to rock on elsewhere because they were too old.

The Mecca organization, which owns the disco, admitted that they had refused admission to 400 people because they were over 25. An official said: 'Young people don't like old folk at their discos. They don't want to go out and meet their mum and dad. They've probably gone out to get away from them in the first place.'

Someone up in the Mecca public relations department must have turned an even more violent colour than the disco lights when the papers carried the story. To show they were sorry, they hastily invited Alf and Mary back to The Powerhouse for their very own session, after which they were treated to free cocktails.

But they weren't all that sorry, for the 'Darby and Joan' couple still won't be allowed in on Saturday nights.

Walkies!

An audacious burglar failed to effect illegal entry into a house at Darlaston, West Midlands. No doubt finding the garden shed too heavy to pick up, he nevertheless determined to steal something. Professional pride was satisfied, for he walked off with Laddie, the house's brilliantly alert guard dog.

For It Is Written

When ancient graffiti were found on the roof of the Church of Saint Nicholas at Agschurch, in Gloucestershire, the vicar was so proud of the discoveries that he decided to put on an exhibition.

But he hastily withdrew one prospective exhibit when he realized it described the author's sex life in amazingly explicit and intimate detail.

That's Dynamite

During the American Civil War, a certain high-ranking officer decided one day to blast a trench into the middle of a Confederate camp.

After the smoke had cleared, his men jumped cheerfully into the newly-created trench and, following their orders, careered along it towards the Rebel forces. They were brought up short, however, by the discovery that their esteemed leader had failed to think of providing a way out!

The Confederates were amazed suddenly to see their entire opposition presented to them on a plate – or rather in a 6-foot hole.

The commanding officer, it is said, went on to bigger and greater things, having followed the time-honoured custom of lighting the blue touch paper and standing well back.

A Big, Big Problem

When the powers-that-be at Central Park Zoo in New York City came up with a spectacular plan to rebuild and refurbish the zoo, they thought they would have no problem in finding temporary homes for the animals while the necessary work was carried out. But they were wrong – at least in the case of their four-ton elephant, Tina.

They failed to take into account Tina's widespread reputation for being more dangerous than the muggers and villains who reportedly lurk behind every scrub bush in the Park. The huge elephant has a pronounced predilection for crushing her keepers' arms and charging at strangers.

Not the ideal house guest! At the time of publication, the zoo's plans still remain in the 'pending' file owing to Terrible Tina.

Damp Squib

A History Museum in the North of England thought it would ring the changes and organize a different kind of Guy Fawkes celebration.

It advertised a special Victorian Bonfire Night. Tickets were sold and, come November, a large crowd gathered in the Museum grounds.

They lapped up all the authentic traditional goodies – faggots and peas, groaty puddings, real ale, etc.

But, as the evening wore on, the crowd began to get restive and finally downright annoyed at the non-appearance of the fireworks.

It was then that the Museum's directors realized they had made an unfortunate mistake. Although, as an abashed official announced, the Victorians never had fireworks, twentieth-century celebrators (especially when they had paid good money to attend) would not be satisfied by anything less. It seemed they were in for a rocket!

A quick-thinking custodian saved the day by slipping out and returning with his own private store of Catherine Wheels and Roman Candles. So finally honour, if not historical accuracy, was satisfied.

Ill Wind

Setting up a show is a notoriously dodgy business. Lesson number one in the Unofficial Organizers' Handbook reads: always *secure* your exhibits.

Those in charge of an exhibition at a North Wales Country Park failed to observe this elementary point and regretted the oversight when gale force winds, sweeping down off the surrounding hills, knocked over an old tram which stood in pride of place in the grounds.

Lesson two in the Handbook reads: always site your exhibits with due regard to possible mishaps. The Welsh team failed on that one too: the falling tram, transformed into a colossal nine-ton metal projectile, demolished the new Interpretative Centre which stood nearby.

Bad show, boyos!

Banking For Beginners

The imaginative head English teacher of a South of England comprehensive school reckoned without the zealous probity of his charges' parents when he introduced a distinctly unusual essay competition.

Pupils were invited to use plenty of imagination and write describing the perfect way to rob a bank. They were also given maps and plans (of an imaginary town) to assist in achieving the requisite sense of realism.

The headmaster was astonished, some days later, to receive a 'phone call from the local Chief Constable, who had been advised by an anonymous parent of a possible juvenile crime wave about to break in the area.

When the mistake was explained, the Chief Constable was understandably a little put out. He was mollified, however, when he received an invitation – to judge the bank-robbing essay competition.

Foulke Hero

Everyone has a breaking point. This lesson was learnt – eventually – by one of football's greatest eccentrics, 6ft 3 ins 22 stone goal-keeper, Willie Foulke. When he arrived at Chelsea Football Club in 1907, he soon established a reputation for his antics on and off the field.

On one occasion this jolly giant stopped a game by snapping the crossbar in half. On another, he grasped a member of the opposing team in his hamlike fist and stood him on his head.

These minor breaches of sporting etiquette the lenient club manager decided he could countenance. But when fun-loving Willie felt like a little pre-match snack, entered the dining room early and ate the entire team's dinners before they arrived, he really overstepped the mark.

A football team, like an army, marches on its stomach. Willie paid for his error of judgement – and his gargantuan greed – by finding himself on the transfer list.

He moved to Bradford Football Club, taking with him an additional 4 stones in weight accumulated during his sojourn in London.

410

. . . . .The Ayatollah's military leaders ordered aircrews to bomb American satellites when they appeared over Iran. . . . .

★   ★   ★   ★

Rouge-Faced With Embarrassment

The London firm responsible for labelling a consignment of French plonk called Vin Rude for sale to the United States were guilty of a gross marketing blunder.

The labels concerned showed naked couples enjoying a rather explicitly sportive romp – presumably inspired and invigorated by the brew contained within. The red bore the admonition: SERVE STARK NAKED; the white adjured: SERVE WITH A THRILL.

Having failed to obtain a single order from the upright (and sober?) wine-drinkers of the United States, a director of the firm finally concluded 'the whole thing was just too rude for the Americans'.

That sensible nation prefers its vin ordinaire!

Dyeing Swans

The scene: London's elegant Savoy Hotel. The occasion: the birthday party of an American millionaire in 1905.

To give the celebration a unique flavour, the hotel arranged for its courtyard to be flooded and a silk-lined gondola for the thirty guests to float on the water. A hundred white doves were set loose and flew over the Venetian replica, swans swam decorously alongside and a baby elephant deposited the five-foot-high birthday cake on the steps above the improvised lake.

The success of this artistic occasion was somewhat marred, however, when the swans began to keel over with wild and blood-curdling screams, dying in obvious agony.

It seems that a chemical that had been used to colour the water a delicate azure hue had been poisonous and had turned the poor creatures a whiter shade of pale.

411

Old King Cole

It is often a mistake to take unlikely-sounding statements at face value – especially if there is money involved and the speaker happens to be noted for his rather off-beat sense of humour...

At midday one bright spring day in 1910, a lorry broke down in the middle of the bustling Place de l'Opéra in Paris. Traffic ground to a halt, horns began to screech and Gallic tempers rose. The driver, however, quietly got out of his cab, lay down on his back and slithered under the vehicle to make the necessary repairs. 30 minutes – and a colossal traffic jam – later, he emerged, apologized calmly to the crowd of exasperated *gendarmes* who had rushed to the scene to cope with irate motorists, and drove away.

The man was, in fact, an Englishman, Horace De Vere Cole – the most notorious practical joker of the Edwardian era – who that night gleefully collected thousands of pounds from friends who had foolishly bet him that he could not lie flat on his back for half an hour at the busiest time in the busiest traffic centre in Paris.

No doubt the redoubtable Horace laughed all the way to the bank.

Ye Olde American Import

Immigration officials at Ellis Island, USA, decided in 1921 to greet the steady influx of people arriving to build a new home in the Land of the Free by serving them with a 'truly American dish'. A nice idea. Unfortunately, they chose ice cream, which originated in France in 1670 and did not reach the shores of America until well over a century later.

Moonshine

According to a survey conducted in 1969, over a fifth of the population of Morocco were unaware that man had set foot on the surface of the moon.

Over 50% of these angrily accused their questioners of trying to hoax them.

Scent To Pot

Florida students were delighted one year during their Rag Week festivities to welcome the offer of a local police officer to show off his tracker dog's remarkable sleuthing ability.

However, somebody blundered in selecting the venue for the event, for when, having concealed ten packets of cannabis about the room, the officer let his sniffing side-kick off the leash, the indefatigable bloodhound came back with 11!

Tripped Up

Holidays and holiday brochures are one area often responsible for anguish and dispute as the returning tripper complains that the sky was not so blue, nor the sand so golden as the brochure suggested.

Such complaints are usually dealt with in soothing tones, but the organizer of an Essex travel club is a definite exception to this rule. He received a letter of complaint from a bank manager who made the mistake of pointing out some shortcomings in his holiday to Portugal. The club organizer wrote back:

> As well as trying to improve our holidays, we are also trying to raise the standard of our clients. I'm afraid you do not come up to the mark and I should be obliged if you would make your arrangements elsewhere in future.

The astonished client commented: 'I was surprised at the tone of the letter. I've travelled with this firm many times in the past and have even written to them before, telling them how much I enjoyed my holidays. This time I complained about departure delays and the hotel food and I got this very rude letter.'

But the club man was unrepentant and adamant that his complainant could go and get sun-drenched with someone else.

'This man is a pompous ass,' he insisted.

413

Boozed Off

The history of live theatre is littered with classic clangers and first-night fiascos. None more dramatic, however, than that which took place at the opening performance, in London in 1875, of a French comedy of manners entitled *Écarté*.

The first Act opened with a drinking scene and the misguided producer decided to inject a little extra sparkle into the performance by filling the glasses with real champagne rather than the usual cold tea or coloured water. Not surprisingly, the cast took full advantage of this unaccustomed generosity and many of them fell before the first act curtain did! The entire play was cancelled before the beginning of Act Two and all the box office takings were returned to the disgruntled audience. The show never reopened.

The *débâcle* might perhaps have been foreseen by a producer more familiar with the French language. Roughly translated, the world *écarté*, appropriately enough, means discarded.

Killer Maiden

James Douglas, Earl of Morton, was proud of the recognition he received when he introduced a guillotine-like device called the 'maiden' into his native Scotland. He regretted it some time later, however, for he was himself beheaded by the cruel mechanism in 1581, after being convicted of complicity in the murder of Lord Darnley, first husband of Mary Queen of Scots, in 1567.

As It Is Written...

A certain young Frenchman thought that he had pulled off the perfect crime in Boulogne in 1942. But he was – quite unforeseeably – wrong...

The young man concerned was the nephew of a rich landowner. Having received many affectionate letters from his benevolent uncle, the youth harboured great expectations of a substantial legacy. Being unscrupulous and impatient, however, he decided to hasten the processes of Nature and poisoned the old man. Leaving nothing to chance, the nephew then forged a will naming himself as sole beneficiary, using his own letters as a handwriting guide. He then sat back to gloat over his newly-acquired fortune.

Justice intervened, however, in the shape of the old man's housekeeper. She went to the authorities and accused the young nephew of forgery. She should know – for apparently her employer had, in fact, been unable either to read or write and, for nearly 50 years, the faithful servant had preserved his secret by 'ghosting' all his correspondence and business papers. Including, of course, the very letters on which the murderous youth's original hopes had been founded.

Poetic Justice

In 1944 in Sydney, Australia, two young poets decided to engineer a hoax which they hoped would not only send up a pretentious *avant garde* literary journal called – believe it or not – *Angry Penguins*, but also ridicule the petty censorship that beset Australia at that time.

Stringing together words and phrases at random, they sent the resulting gibberish to the journal's proprietors under the guise of 'the complete poetic works of Ern Malley, who recently died in obscurity at the tragically early age of 25'. Deeply impressed, the editor published the 'poems' in a special edition of *Angry Penguins*.

As the hoaxers gleefully prepared to reveal the journal's blunder, things took a turn for the better, from their point of view at least, as puritanical police in South Australia confiscated the poems and arrested the *Angry Penguins* editor for publishing indecent material.

In the ensuing court case, the prosecuting detective directed the judge's attention to a reference in one of the poems to a man going about at night carrying a torch. 'There is a suggestion of indecency here,' he told the court. 'I have found that persons who go around parks at night do so for immoral purposes.' The great detective then turned to another of the gibberish verses. 'The word incestuous is used,' he declared. 'I don't know what it means, but I regard it as being indecent.'

The judge agreed, the editor of the journal was duly convicted, and only then did the two hoaxers (from a discreet and anonymous distance) reveal the true nature of this glorious series of errors and idiocies. Those concerned have been trying ever since to live it down-under!

Another Flynn Mess

Cornelius and Evelyn Flynn are movie fans of many years' standing – or rather sitting. Nothing, therefore, seemed more logical when Evelyn presented Cornelius with a son in 1968 than that the lad be named Errol, in honour of their favourite swashbuckler of the past.

However, Errol now laments his parents' decision. 'It can be very difficult,' he says. 'Once a referee in a football match booked me. He didn't believe me when I told him my name and just thought I was being cheeky. And new teachers are always suspicious of me, while the other kids just giggle. I'm fed up with it.'

Whoa, Tally-Ho!

Public Relations people at the Co-op probably thought they were on to a popularity-boosting winner when they loudly proclaimed their decision to ban fox-hunting over their many acres of farmland. However, they might have been wiser first to have checked up on the consistency of their public stand.

As hunt devotees were quick to point out, a hunting scene is depicted in glorious technicolour full cry on every plastic bag containing the Co-op's Cumbrian Loaf.

Clangers And Mash

With uncharacteristic ineptitude, advertisers of a private health insurance scheme much vaunted during the 1982 National Health Service dispute chose the signature tune of the television series *M.A.S.H.* as background music for their 2-minute slot on commercial radio.

As many TV viewers will know, M.A.S.H. is set in an army hospital during the Korean War where patients are treated in extraordinarily ill-equipped and slaphappy circumstances.

Although popular on the screen, such treatment might appear less so if one were actually to be on the receiving end!

★　★　★　★

. . . . A female crossword fanatic seriously overestimated the extent of her husband's patience when she continually woke him up as she struggled with the final poser through the night. On the fourth such occasion, the overwrought husband strangled her to death. A court acquitted him on the grounds of temporary insanity. . . . .

Hair-Brained Fashion

In Spain in the mid-fourteenth century a new fashion suddenly sprang up among the aristocracy. Soon everyone was doing it – old or young, politician or fop, every man sported an identical long black false beard.

The originator of this curious vogue can scarcely have guessed what a terrible and disastrous blunder it was to prove. Soon nobody knew who was who. Debtors escaped recognition by their creditors and villains hid behind cascades of hair while the innocent were led helplessly away to prison. Wives failed to recognize their husbands – until it was too late, and the market price of hair rose to astronomical heights.

Finally, King Peter of Aragon himself stepped in and called a halt to this hirsute chaos. A law was passed with all due solemnity, expressly forbidding the wearing of false beards in Spain.

Long Awaited News

National Westminster Bank Access cardholders were recently invited by an enterprising new wine company to enter a lucky draw competition. A note at the bottom of the announcement stated: 'The winner will be notified by telegram.'

He/she may be a long time waiting, since, as we all know (except, that is, for a certain wine merchant who shall remain nameless), the Post Office abolished the inland telegram in 1982.

Record Blunder

Thomas Edison (1848–1931) is best-known for his successful invention of the phonograph, forerunner of today's gramophone. Less fortunate, however, was a venture launched by him in 1888 – the talking doll. Fitted with a tiny phonograph in its body, the doll could recite a dozen favourite nursery rhymes. Yes, it *should* have been a sure-fire winner.

But – after making several hundred of the dolls – Edison discovered he had goofed. His firm had apparently sold the rights to make phonograph toys to another company some years earlier. Edison was compelled to halt production and have the dolls destroyed. The few that were saved have since become collectors items and only two are believed to be still in existence.

The Age-Old Problem

The United States is renowned for its prowess in sell-anything-to-anyone marketing techniques. One enterprising mail order firm company thought it had spotted a promising new target for its health and 'reinvigoration' products – the elderly. As an inducement they made an opening offer of a free book encouragingly entitled *Sex After Seventy*. After many complaints, they had to admit their error. They relaunched the campaign – still offering the same book. This time, however, it was printed in large type. Now, it was hoped, the old folk who had written in would be able to read the book with no difficulty.

Monkey Puzzle

During the war which raged between France and England in 1705 the people of England were constantly warned of the imminent threat of invasion from across the Channel. When a small ship was wrecked during a storm off the North West coast of England, therefore, the locals were suspicious to say the least.

The sole survivor of the wreck was the crew's pet monkey, which was rescued by local fishermen as it clung desperately to some floating timbers.

When the creature arrived in the coastal fishing village, the citizens, who were simple souls unfamiliar with such hairy primates, did not know what to make of it. But as soon as the monkey began to gibber weirdly and wave its long arms about wildly they recalled the descriptions of French agents that had been circulated by the government. Of course, they concluded, this must be part of a dastardly French invasion plot. The poor ape was then summarily tried and executed as a French spy.

Family Favourites

Fathers! Be warned: It may be a big mistake to allow a television set into your home.

According to a recent study at Michigan State University, given the choice of getting rid of the TV or their fathers, an astonishing 35% of four-and-five-year-olds opted to give dear old daddy the big elbow.

420

Don't Keep It Under Your Hat

It seems increasingly that there are no lengths to which shoplifters will not go in order to get away with their pilfered goods.

From the lady who secreted a 4lb joint of meat and a tin of tuna in her bra to the man who attempted to stuff a chainsaw down the front of his trousers, the tales of felonious derring-do seem endless.

But one woman went too far recently at a huge American-style hypermarket. Seeking to smuggle a large frozen turkey through the checkout without paying, she made the mistake of concealing the bird on her head – under a large and much-adorned hat.

She collapsed before she had the chance to leave the store and was later admitted to the intensive care unit of a local hospital.

It seems she had suffered a stroke brought on by the sudden exposure of her brain to below-freezing temperatures!

Gold Drain

Much was made of the impregnability of the new gold vault when the Bank of England moved into new premises in 1800. So that when a workman claimed that he could easily enter the stronghold undetected, the Governor of the Bank was so confident that he agreed to a wager of £2,000 that it could not be done.

Sure enough, however, when bank officials arrived the following morning they found a trap door open in the centre of the vault and the workman sitting patiently awaiting them. He explained to the horrified staff that one day, while undertaking some sewer repairs, he had come upon a ladder. On climbing it and pushing up the door to which it led he had found himself, to his complete amazement, gazing upon the massed hordes of England's gold reserves.

It was, indeed, fortunate for the Bank that the man was an honest fellow. The Governor, red-faced at this gross blunder, found his £2,000 wager a very small price to pay for such a narrow escape.

Bra Bar

In these days of women's liberation and equal opportunity, the life of the male employer is fraught with pitfalls and traps. Take the boss of an accounting firm in Nancy in Northern France for example.

Productivity in his erstwhile profitable accounting business began seriously to fall off when his 'token' female member of staff began to appear at the office quite obviously not wearing a bra. It seemed that this particular round figure 'disturbed' the day-to-day figurework of the male staff.

When the worried men tentatively suggested to the liberated demoiselle a change in her lingerie habits, she flatly (if that word does not sound too inappropriate) refused. Driven beyond endurance, the boss fired her.

That proved a very costly mistake. For, even in that deeply paternalistic society, such blatant *cochonnerie* is frowned upon, and the woman successfully sued and presented her account for substantial damages!

Braking Point

One of the most remarkable cases of 'mistaken identity' occurred of recent years in Pery, Ohio.

The chief of police was suffering from a severe shortage of manpower.

He did not have enough money in the budget to increase the force in the ordinary way, so he did the next best thing. He recruited a life-size tailor's dummy!

Every morning the dummy, which was dressed in full police uniform, was placed behind the wheel of a spare patrol car and left by the roadside. The citizens of Ohio were completely taken in.

Speeding motorists mistook the dummy for the real thing and, in the words of the delighted police chief, 'as soon as they see the car with the cop in it, they slam on the brakes and slow right down.'

He went on to reveal that 'this dummy is so convincing motorists have even been seen going over to it to ask for directions.'

★   ★   ★   ★

.............A nineteenth-century French construction company must win the all-time prize for perseverance – and incompetence. In their abortive attempts to build a canal across the isthmus of Panama between 1881 and 1889, they lost over £150 million and 20,000 men were drowned......

423

One More River To Cross

During the American Civil War battle of Antietam in 1862, Major General Ambrose Everett Burnside was in command of a crack force of Union troops.

During a forced march, the Unionists came to a broad river. Burnside scratched his hoary old head and hit upon the brilliant wheeze of sending his men single file across the only narrow footbridge.

Unfortunately, this exposed them to artillery fire from the Confederates posted on the opposite bank. They couldn't believe their luck – it was better than a rifle shoot at the local fair, picking off the poor boys in blue one by one. It was only when he had watched the greater part of his force destroyed in this way that Burnside decided to examine the mighty flooding river at closer quarters.

It turned out to be less than 3 feet deep. The men could have forded it with ease, lived to fight another day *and* kept their powder dry!

Texas Manger Rangers

When a Norfolk playgroup presented their 1982 Nativity Pageant, their audience was somewhat surprised to see the baby Jesus being visited in the stable by gun-toting cowboys!

It seems this novel interpretation of 'peace on earth and good will to men' was decided upon when the children declared they did not fancy dressing up as shepherds.

Naughty Auntie

The august British Broadcasting Corporation is usually the very essence of propriety in its dealings.

It was, therefore, greatly embarrassed when the news got out that it had paid white extras five times as much as their black counterparts during the African location shooting of an important documentary series.

The programme concerned was *The Fight Against Slavery*.

A Merry Dance

The RSPCA was hot on the trail of a hotel proprietor who had innocently been sending out a very jolly brochure advertising the Christmas holiday attractions his establishment had to offer.

The programme promised:

A mediaeval banquet, complete with wandering minstrel and dancing bear

Oh no you don't, said the local RSPCA and promptly sent around a gentleman in uniform to see about arrangements for the bear. The proprietor could hardly answer the officer's indignant questions without laughing.

He said later: 'We can only surmise that the apprentice chef, aided by a Brighton costumier, put on a better show last year than we thought at the time.'

Big Trouble For Ben

Schoolboy Ben enjoyed trying to cut a bit of a dash. And why not? If you aren't in the mood to stamp your individuality on this dreary old world at the age of 16, then you never will be.

Sadly for Ben, the officers of the law at Redland, Bristol, did not share his enthusiasm. They simply could not see that any young gentleman would swagger about with a silver-topped stick just for the sartorial fun of it. They therefore ran him in for carrying an offensive weapon! It took two hours to convince them that Beau Brummell lives.

Ben was justifiably furious about the whole thing. So was his father, who commented somewhat sharply: 'They'll be arresting people for carrying tennis rackets next!'

Solid Defences

Malcolm Finlayson is now a rich and successful businessman. But life was not always quite so easy.

On November 13, 1948, Finlayson was playing in goal for Third Division Millwall at an away match against Walsall. With his side 1 - 0 up, Finlayson was kicked in the face and had to be taken to a nearby hospital for stitches. Thus repaired and almost as good as new, the goalie returned to the ground.

By this time Millwall were losing 3 - 1 and the gates were firmly shut. Thumping on them did no good at all. He was well and truly locked out.

The unfortunate Finlayson, dazed, in pain, and feeling far from well, was obliged to climb over the fence to get back in, and when he did actually walk on to the field, he was so groggy that he set off for the wrong end.

He did wind up with some satisfaction, however, for his side eventually won 6 – 5.

Dog Day Afternoon

Stephen Winkworth, compiler of a popular book entitled *Famous Sporting Fiascos*, decided to call on the Voice of Cricket, John Arlott, to glean material for his volume. Mr Arlott, who has sadly now declared his innings closed and retreated to a fastness on the isle of Alderney, was, at the time of Mr Winkworth's visit, engaged upon the obituary of a very dear friend, and did not wish to be interrupted.

Pressing on regardless, the seeker after calamity ventured: 'Like if a dog ran on to the pitch and bit the wicket-keeper. That sort of thing, sort of…'

Arlott glowered at his unwanted visitor from beneath his Healey-style eyebrows and enquired dauntingly, 'Is that funny?'

Soon afterwards, and none the wiser for his trouble, Mr Winkworth went on his way.

The hand of Nemesis, however, never far from the heels of such dogged researchers, then revealed itself in the thoroughly unpleasant guise of a filthy mongrel cur, which scuttled across the road, as the unfortunate Winkworth was leaving the house, and bit him on the lower leg.

More Than They Could Chiew

When £2,000 worth of limp and soggy noodles were returned by angry customers to the Tai Cheong noodle factory in Lancashire, the bosses looked round furiously for the culprit. They found him in the shape of chief noodle-mixer Van Chiew Tu, who had mistakenly thought that nipping away from his duties for the odd quick smoke or drink would not affect the delicate balance of the recipe handed down from Tai to Tai over generations.

He blundered again when he decided to take his employers to court claiming unfair dismissal. The case was dismissed, leaving him to pay the costs of the proceedings.

Which all just goes to show the truth of the old Chinese saying (all old Chinese say it): Noodle mixer who get it wrong, get chopstick chop and wind up doing pancake roll into street chop chop.

Insoluble Tablet

A mysterious stone tablet was discovered among a load of prehistoric relics in 1838 by archeologists digging in the Grave Creek Mound in West Virginia.

For nearly a century over 60 linguists puzzled over the hieroglyphic characters engraved on the tablet. Controversy raged. Could it be Runic or Etruscan? Or was it, perhaps, a hitherto unknown ancient language?

There were red faces indeed in these academic circles when, in 1930, a young man endeavouring to get an unusually angled photograph of the now-famous 'mystery relic' discovered their mistake.

Quite decipherable from this perspective, the inscription, which was in English, read:

BILL STUMP'S STONE
October 14, 1838

A Dream Of Freedom

In 1880 Alessandro Saraceni was accused of killing a man whose body was found on the Naples road shortly after Saraceni had passed by on his mule. Saraceni hotly protested his innocence, but to no avail. The jury found him guilty and recommended that, in his case, life imprisonment should mean just that and nothing mamby-pamby like twenty years' hard labour.

So the unfortunate Alessandro languished in prison for thirty-two years. Then, one night, his warders were disturbed to hear the old man screaming in his sleep.

He told his captors he had seen King Victor of Italy on the brink of assassination. The warders informed the prison governor who thought, not unreasonably, that the whole thing was a joke, which he shared with the head of the state police. The police chief was a little more superstitious and was struck by the similarities in the dream to a ride through Rome that King Victor and Queen Elena were to take the following day.

Strange to relate, the next day, as the Royal couple drove through the eternal city, an anarchist named D'Alba fired three shots at the King. But the assassination attempt was foiled because the police were on their guard thanks to poor old Alessandro, still rotting in his cell.

Kings are very busy people and Saraceni spent another fourteen years in prison before Victor heard of the dream that had helped to save his life. The least he could do was to order that the case be reheard, so, in 1926, the old man was finally set free. He had been cleared at last, and in his place the mule was found guilty. Not that it bothered the homicidal animal. It had been dead for years.

★　　★　　★　　★

............There is absolutely nothing like a parade to get the average citizen of the United States lit up with excitement. Not, however, on the day in Ventura, California, when a drum major hurled his baton high into the air – where it hit a power cable, melted, blacked out ten blocks, put a radio station off the air and started a grass fire..

Seating Plan

Emperor Menelik II of Abyssinia was much impressed with a report of the first electric chair being used for executions in New York in 1890. Thinking this was just the thing to bring his nation sizzling into the modern era, he ordered three of the fearful machines.

When they arrived he was most disappointed, because he simply could not get them to work. The silly man had overlooked the fact that his country had no electricity supply.

However, he was a practical man and converted one of the chairs to become the Imperial Throne.

Tour De Force

Police at the charming Gloucestershire town of Cheltenham were called in to track down a missing tourist. Stanley Elsis from California had booked into a guest house and then vanished, leaving his two suitcases full of clothes.

The riddle was not answered for two weeks, when Mr Elsis turned up again. Red-faced, he explained that he had got lost journeying round the historic town. He could not remember where he was staying and so decided to carry on with his tour of Britain. His travels took him to visit friends in Wales and Scotland, before he wound up back in Cheltenham.

Jailbirds

Police near Sheffield learnt the hard way that abiding by the letter of the law can be a mistake. Answering a complaint, they took into custody eight ducks that had been found wandering nearby.

The feathered felons soon began disturbing the peace of the local nick, driving the boys in blue quietly quackers with their constant clamouring for food.

Regretting their initial zeal, the policemen had soon placed at the top of their Most Wanted list the owner of the noisy runaways.

Bureaucrackers

.................Errors concerning officialese
and gobbledygook ....

Look And Learn Dept

The Defence Ministry sometimes seems disturbingly simple. They once sent an order to Ladybird Books, the children's favourites, for a complete set of books explaining how computers work.

Messrs Ladybird, puzzled, responded by thanking the MoD for their offered custom, but begged to point out, most respectfully, that the target audience for the publication in question was the miniature boffin of around nine years of age.

The MoD wrote back right away, thanking Ladybird for this clarification, and confirming the order.

Gaucho Marks

You certainly can't trust the Argentinians, and we can all sleep more safely in our beds thanks to the beady-eyed vigilance of the Foreign Office, with a little help from the US State Department. The FO boys had words with those responsible for the heading over an item in the agenda for the United Nations General Assembly deliberations.

It was down as 'The Question of the Malvinas Islands'. Fearing a dastardly plot by the frightful Johnny Gaucho, our side bade the UN go away and retitle the item a little less controversially.

The final result, pleasing to all sides, was a masterpiece of diplomatic art. The English version referred to the Falkland Islands (Malvinas), while the Spanish-speaking contingent had it as Islas Malvinas (Falklands).

Rest Assured

The 1959 National Insurance Bill assured those of retiring age: 'For the purpose of this part of the schedule a person over pensionable age, not being an insured person, shall be treated as an employed person if he would be an insured person were he under pensionable age and would be an employed person were he an insured person.'

So *that* was all right.

............In 1954 the mayor of the
Châteauneuf-du-Pape community in France passed a by-law
banning all flying saucers from landing in the area........

★ ★ ★ ★

Baby Talk

Those attending a state-run training course on Civil Defence and Welfare wondered what they were there for when they read in a Section Bulletin on emergency midwifery the following encouraging injunction:

'It should be remembered that childbirth is a normal function and Nature should be allowed to take its course.'

Such advice, it might be thought, rendered redundant the very training scheme it illustrated.

A Vacancy Has Arisen...

The GCHQ at Cheltenham, the Government's top secret and highly leak-prone intelligence centre, advertised in November 1982 for a Russian linguist.

The ad appeared in *The Guardian* the day after superspy Geoffrey Prime, who used his post as a linguist to further his treacherous aims, was jailed for 35 years.

The centre would neither confirm nor deny that the timing of the ad was coincidental.

Watership Down And Out

It was more than enough to make Hazel's ears go on the droop when, to celebrate 1982 National Tree Week, Hampshire County Council decided to build wire fences around 1,000 young beech trees on the famous leporine beauty spot of Watership Down.

The object: to keep out rabbits.

As Easy As ABC

A Ministry of Defence publication informed an avidly waiting world:

'In reference A, the cover letter at Reference B is an error. The additions at Annex B to Reference B are already incorporated in Annex A to Reference B, and are those additional items per pack that will be required if the complete schedule at Annex A to Reference B are approved.'

Let us all hope with every fibre of our being that they never are.

Eightpenny Dreadful

After fourteen years working in a laundry and a further fourteen as a café waitress, Mrs Rosa Curran joined her husband in running a Whitbread pub in South London.

At the age of sixty-five, Mrs Curran decided it was time to call it a day, and was looking forward to a comfortable and problem-free retirement.

She was understandably concerned, and later furious, when the Department of Health and Social Security informed her that, after fifty years of paying stamps, she was entitled to a pension of – 8p a week!

A DHSS spokesman said: 'The 8p is based on contributions Mrs Curran paid to the graduated pension scheme between 1961 and 1975!'

The Currans must now live on a brewery – rather than a Beveridge – pension.

Don't Leave The Lab Without It

The credit card organization that is so anxious to ensure that you do not leave home without its passport to plastic happiness safely in your pocket issued a 'personal invitation' to Mr C. Cell, Mutation Unit, University of Sussex.

And it certainly did nicely as a source of hilarity for the team comprising the *MRC Cell Unit* at the university!

War And (At Last) Peace 1

The Pyrenean mini-state of Andorra is perhaps best known as an excellent spot for tourists to stop off for a carload of duty free goods on the way home from sunny Spain. However, it also has a war record second to none.

Because of an oversight, the Versailles Peace Treaty which ended the Great War of 1914-18 failed to include Andorra. So, in 1939, with the Second World War well under way, the tiny principality discovered to its horror that officially it was still fighting the first.

A quick and private treaty with Germany concluded hostilities.

Cross Bar

Councillors of the City of Oxford had hardly had time to pat themselves on the back for their conservationist and environmentally-conscious introduction of five miles of cycle-ways when they were brought up short by an accusation from furious feminists. It seems that the road signs showed only a man's bike with a crossbar – grossly sexist in anyone's highway code!

The prospect of Women's Rights demonstrations in the city of gleaming spires was too much for the councillors, who promised that in future all signs would show both a man's and a woman's bike.

Shell Shockers

Those wonderful eggheads at the Min. of Ag. Fish and Food Centre for Avian Epidemiology, (which those intelligent enough to be reading this book will not need to be told means the study of sick birds) down at Gloucester, got themselves into a rare old flap.

They were called out one day to a battery farm to crack the riddle of some erratic layers. The hens in the middle and upper tiers of the battery were not laying as many eggs as those on the ground floor.

What a puzzler! Could those on the two upper levels be coming down with some dreadful ague? The experts (I resist the temptation to call them eggsperts) at first suspected inadequate ventilation, and then vaccination problems, and still later infectious bronchitis. Heads were scratched late into the night.

The answer, when it came, was dazzlingly simple. A former employee of the battery had been stealing the eggs, and had left the bottom tier alone because he had a bad back.

★   ★   ★   ★

. . . .*United States President McKinley was assured by the Director of the US Patent Office in 1899 that 'everything that can be invented has been invented'* . . . .

★   ★   ★   ★

Weather, Or Not

A Governmental committee asked the Meteorological Office in Bracknell for a definitive ruling on when winter begins and ends. The Met waded in with an immediate answer: 'Winter begins when all the leaves have fallen off the trees,' they said, adding the further scientific ruling: 'And it ends when the bulbs start coming up again.'

No doubt the Governmental committee presented them with a very cold front and a severe touch of frost.

Turned Over By A New Leaf

Pensioners Sid and Sarah Coulson, and all their neighbours, were delighted when the thoughtful Sheffield City Council planted 11 lime trees along their road at Greenland Close, in Darnall.

But six years later they had changed their minds, for the trees had spread their roots, as trees are wont to do, and turned the Coulsons' home into a crumbling ruin. The council had to rehouse the couple while structural repairs were carried out.

They also gave the too vigorous trees the chop.

World Weary

The lugubrious-sounding and forward-looking End of the World Society decided to go down in style with a Doomsday Party at Bude in Cornwall. They called it all off, however, when local magistrates refused to grant a special late-night drinks licence.

Apparently the local beaks felt that the end of the world was not a special event.

★　　★　　★　　★

. . . . .Jean Cocteau's 1956 film The Seashell and the Clergyman *was banned by the vigilant British Board of Film Censors because 'the film is apparently meaningless, but if it has any meaning it is doubtless objectionable'. . . . . .*

437

There Were These Tree Fellers

Mr Hew Watt of the Nature Conservancy Council amazed, nay stunned, his audience at a seminar at University College, London, when he told them that he had grown weary of small boys with foul mouths intruding into his garden in order to steal conkers – so weary that he had chopped down his trio of venerable chestnut trees.

A Lot Of Awful Honesty In Brazil

Joao Damico, who proclaimed himself to be the most successful car thief in Brazil, was also destined to wind up as the most disgruntled. Interviewed after his ultimate arrest, he snarled: 'I do not understand the world any more. I have been a car thief for 25 years and this is the first time police officers have failed to accept a bribe. I am seriously disappointed by this unpatriotic behaviour.'

Senhor Damico went on to describe his local sheriff as 'a monster of honesty.'

438

Extended Credit

James Grant died on 29 June. His son Ronald was surprised, therefore, on opening his late father's credit card account some two and a half weeks later, to notice a debit of £7.56 paid to Travellers Fare Restaurant on 8 July. In a letter to the company concerned, Ronald enquired interestedly:

'I did not realize that such facilities were available, or indeed necessary, on the journey my father has just undertaken, nor indeed that the trip lasted so long. Do let me know for what period of time your credit facilities are extended in these circumstances.'

In their letter of apology, the company wisely declined to respond to the latter remarks.

★   ★   ★   ★

. . . . For those of you who have not heard, here is a news flash from the Compleat Works of the Department of Technical Co-operation Departmental Fire Precautions and Instructions: 'Most fires are caused by some igniting source coming into contact with combustible material'. . . . .

★   ★   ★   ★

Tube Boob

London Transport may pride themselves on the many and varied souvenirs and information leaflets they produce for tourists. Advertisements for T-shirts, country walk guides and the recently opened LT Museum emblazon every double-decker and tube escalator in the metropolis. However, a poster on display at London Bridge underground station cannot rank among the Information Office's most successful efforts. Advising travellers on how to get to any of the main line British Rail stations, the instructions for each possible route tell passengers to start off on the District or Piccadilly line. All well and good, you may think. But London Bridge is on the Northern line.

Safety Last

In furtherance of their campaign for safer toys, the United States Consumer Product Safety Commission had 80,000 fun badges made ready for distribution to the nation's kids.

Sadly, they had to junk the lot. The badges had sharp edges and pins that came undone with distressing and painful ease. And they were brightly coloured in lead paint.

No Mercy For The Angels

Student nurses at a West Country hospital received letters from their bosses offering them congratulations on passing their exams. The letters then went on to tell them that they were fired. Hospital administrators explained to the girls that they were being made redundant because there were no permanent jobs to offer them. However, if they had *failed* to pass their exams they could have stayed for another six months, while they studied for retakes.

The chief administrator said: 'We make it perfectly clear that we can't guarantee jobs.' But one of the student nurses was totally unimpressed by this argument. She said: 'I can't help feeling that we are being used as cheap labour.'

Danger! Woman Driver Behind

There are those who think that it is *always* a mistake to allow a woman behind the wheel of a car. In Memphis, Tennessee it *certainly* would be – you could get arrested for it. According to an old by-law, a female must not drive an automobile – unless she is preceded down the street by a man carrying a red flag!

★   ★   ★   ★

. . . .*Frenchman Paul Hubert was 21 years into a life sentence when, in 1884, his case was reopened because bungling bureaucrats realized that he had been convicted of murdering himself!* . . . .

They Must Be Inthane!

The Department of Education and Science was running a bizarre risk when it decided to close the Roman Catholic Newman College of Education. Not to put too fine a point upon it, the DES mandarins might have expected a rather nasty visitation from well beyond the grave.

The ghost involved would almost certainly have been none other than Wulfwine, an 11th century Saxon lord who owned the land on which the college stands. He decided that no one but the Catholic Church should use the land for all time on pain of a fearful curse. And Wulfwine seems to have been a dab, if bloody, hand at making sure the curse stuck.

When the Protestant Dudley family took over the land, they became spectacular victims. The hated Edmund Dudley was beheaded by Henry VIII, and his son, the Duke of Northumberland, went the same way attempting to put Lady Jane Grey on the throne.

Lady Jane and her husband, yet another Dudley, also lost their heads in the plot. Robert Dudley, Earl of Leicester, died of the fever while failing to lead an Elizabethan force to victory in the Netherlands.

Since these facts came to light, the Education Department, recognizing that discretion is the better part, has reversed its decision, the college land has been returned to Mother Church and peace reigns in Wulfwine's domain.

A Six Day Week Shalt Thou Labour

The canny framers of by-laws at Thurston County, Washington, certainly knew the time of day, if not the day of the week, when they were trying to avoid paying police and firemen overtime for Sunday working. The citizens of the County opened their local weekly newspaper one Sunday morning and couldn't believe their eyes. Although the date was correct enough, the paper proclaimed it to be *Monday*.

The explanation was simple enough: the powers-that-be had simply decided that Sunday was abolished.

Stone Blind

The City Corporation planning department really blew their cool when photographs of London's tallest tower block, the Nat West Building, landed on their busy desks. They never granted permission for those statues perched on the top storey, they expostulated. Then some sharper-eyed character pointed out that the figures in the snap weren't statues at all, but workmen!

...What The Left Hand Was Doing

During Prohibition (1920-33) in the United States the sale, manufacture and transportation of alcoholic beverages was rendered illegal by the 18th Amendment to the Constitution.

Somehow or other, however, nobody ever got round to informing the bureaucrats at the US Department of Agriculture of this. So, throughout the entire thirteen year 'dry' period, they continued to distribute leaflets detailing ways of extracting alcohol from apples, bananas, pumpkins, etc. It could only have happened in America – land of the Free and Speakeasy!

Video Fun And Games

When the Inland Revenue Staff Federation decided to produce a video cassette explaining to their members how the new technology might affect their future, the Inland Revenue Board (representing the employers' side) stepped in. They announced that the cassette could not be shown on government property (i.e. the 50 VHS video recorders specifically hired for the purpose) unless a video of Sir Lawrence Airey, the Board's chief, were played immediately after, putting an official reply.

The Staff Federation agreed readily enough, but when 50 video cassettes duly arrived from the Board, they were found to be totally unplayable.

Due to some 'unfortunate' bureaucratic blunder, Sir Lawrence's reply had been recorded on to Betamax cassettes, which cannot be used on the VHS machines. Talk about 'incompatibility'!

Trial By Duel

Sometimes, as we all know, the law is an ass. Such a case certainly occurred in 1817 when a certain Mr Ashford witnessed the murder of his sister by a man named Thornton.

The guilty man immediately challenged Ashford to decide the case by armed combat and appeared at the appointed time in full battle regalia, complete with a lance and a sword.

Not surprisingly, Ashford failed to turn up for the duel. He was busy with his lawyers preparing the case against Thornton. But

When he came before the court, however, the murderer claimed that he had already won the case by default.

The judge was forced to admit he was right. Parliament had foolishly neglected ever to abolish the medieval custom of trial by one-to-one combat.

Needless to say, the situation was at once rectified so that no such miscarriage of justice could occur again, but Thornton remained free.

Under English law, no man can be 'tried' for the same crime twice.

No Need To Worry

The spirit of the men who carry the mail seems to be unquenchable, and it spans the globe. At a recent House of Representatives hearing in Washington, Mr Ralph H. Jusell, the postal services civil defence co-ordinator, assured bemused Congressmen that a mere nuclear holocaust would not stop the mail getting through. He insisted: 'Those that are left will get their mail.'

Under the plan, drawn up in 1981, express, registered and other special delivery services might have to be suspended, for the time being at least. But first class letters would still get top priority.

Indeed, the optimistic Mr Jusell was able to go further, proving that those faceless legions who run public enterprise really do have an appreciation of the difficulties faced by the ordinary folk at times of inconvenience, such as during World War Three. The mail will still be delivered even if the survivors run out of stamps.

★　　★　　★　　★

. . . . *The census conducted in 1981 by the Australian Bureau of Statistics showed 3,287,035 men saying they were married. On the other hand, only 3,264,179 women declared themselves to be wed. Police are now looking for 22,856 missing wives!* . . . .

★　　★　　★　　★

Right On The Button

A new pressure group calling itself Lawyers v the Bomb has come up with the heartening news that, in the event of a nuclear holocaust, we may all have a very good case for legal action against those responsible. Their launch press release stated categorically that 'the use of nuclear weapons would be a clear breach of international law', while offering the opinion that 'the manufacture and deployment of these weapons may well also be a crime punishable in a court of international law.'

So now we all know what to do in that four minutes before the bomb drops – phone our lawyers!

Joint Board Bard

During 1982 a circular was issued by the Joint Matriculation Board Examinations Council. It declared that, because of a marked increase in 'the incidence of rubric infringements by Candidates', it had been decided to modify the format of the English Literature (Advanced) Paper I. In future, in order to avoid any possibility of confusion, section B will consist of essay questions on the plays of someone called Shakspaere.

No, this is not a recently discovered master writer of untold literary merit, but simply an 'infringement' of the accepted rules of spelling.

Defence Defect

When a British national newspaper published the tonnage of the Royal Navy's proposed new diesel-electric submarine, a flustered Ministry of Defence Press Attaché accused their Naval Correspondent of betraying an official secret.

Astonished, the journalist protested: 'There must be some mistake. It was you who gave me those figures.'

'Correction,' came the mind-boggling reply. 'We gave you the information calculated in metric tonnes – which is not secret.'

It would seem that the MoD fondly believes that the Russians do not possess such pillars of Western civilization as the conversion table or the pocket calculator – the necessary wherewithal for extracting the real tonnage from the elaborate coding of metric tonnes! It certainly makes you think...

Little Blacked Book

In 1930 a court in Boston, Massachusetts banned Theodore Dreiser's novel of murder and adultery among New York industrialists, *An American Tragedy* (1925), as 'an insult to a civilized society'.

Tough luck on students across the Charles River at Harvard University, where the book, regarded to this day both as a pillar of twentieth century American literature and an important sociological document, was required reading for some courses.

445

War And (At Last) Peace 2

1966 was a big year in the turbulent history of the charming border town of Berwick-on-Tweed, for it was only then that the town's 110 years of war with Russia came to an end.

Although the Crimean War was concluded in 1856, an oversight in the Paris Peace Treaty excluded Berwick (traditionally referred to separately in State documents) from this outbreak of non-aggression. Then, at last, in 1966 a Soviet Government envoy made a good will visit to the town and peace broke out under an official seal.

As the Mayor of Berwick put it: 'Now the Russians can sleep peacefully in their beds.'

Chequeing Out

Gerhard Koenig of Munich was not a frequent visitor to his bank. In fact, the officials of the branch with whom he had his account were a little puzzled that the only time their services were called into action was when his State pension cheques were paid in. It took the alert bank staff 7 whole years to realize that perhaps all was not as it should be.

Finally, they reported the inactivity to the authorities, who called at Herr Koenig's flat. They found nothing but a skeleton. The old gentleman had died – some seven years earlier.

Giro In A Spin

Definitely overworked and probably underpaid, the hard-pressed boys and girls at the social security office in Exeter, Devon, simply stopped answering the phones in the afternoons, because they were so far behind in their labours.

They knew that most of the calls were from people complaining that their Giro cheques were late, that lateness in turn being caused by the backlog.

A bewildered official said: 'If we answer the phone and then have to check out the queries, we'll just get even further behind.'

446

Board Stiff

July 29, 1966, was a red letter day for the Board of Trade Journal. True to its departmental terms of reference, it was splendidly international in correcting a previous entry:

In the list of films registered during the week ended 15 July, 1966, the title of the film *DeGaulle Stone Operation* should read *The Great DeGaulle Stone Operation* and the title of the film *The Great Napoleon Blownaparte* should read *Napoleon Blownaparte*.

Book now to avoid disappointment.

Yet More Hot News

The Civil Service is most concerned to protect its officers in the event of an igniting source getting anywhere near combustible material.

Hence this Minute (Civil Servicese for Memo) on the subject of fire precautions: 'Fire practice. This was discussed with the Fire Prevention Officer quite recently and the main objections were:

(1) that if the alarm bell rang, the occupants might think there was a fire and injuries could be caused among the old and infirm staff in trying to evacuate the building; and

(2) if regular fire practices were held, the staff would in time treat it as a joke and not in a serious manner.

There is more, but I feel the world is not yet ready to face it.

You Said It

.... *Errors concerning*
the spoken and written word ....

Snow Business Like Car Business

'I just pray to God that the UK Government spend their North Sea oil revenue intelligently, instead of continuing to pour money into subsidizing businesses that are losers from day one.'

The speaker, during a frank, free and fearless BBC Radio 4 interview on July 15, 1979, was John Z. De Lorean.

★　　★　　★　　★

. . . . .A woman walked into her local bookshop and asked the bewildered assistant: 'Have you got Thomas Hardy's Tess of the Dormobiles?'. . . . .

★　　★　　★　　★

. . . . .The Rules of Entry for the Miss Nude USA Competition included the stipulation that contestants must betray 'taste in clothing'. . . . .

★　　★　　★　　★

Deaf Ears

Lord Kelvin, President of the Royal Society, came to the following conclusion in 1894: 'Radio has no future.' At around the same time he also declared: 'Heavier-than-air flying machines are impossible.'

Time And Tim

1965 was not a particularly good year for Timothy Leary, the high priest of America's drug culture...but it was certainly a better one than 1980.

In 1965 he predicted the collapse of the United States within 15 years. When the deadline passed without too many signs of a wobble, much less a total collapse, he shrugged off queries by saying: 'What is time, my dears? You are talking to the man who brought you the 1960s.'

Request Bequest

The pressures of non-stop record-playing and compering can become too much for the average mortal. One disc-jockey certainly found it so as he announced on a request programme:

'This is for Mrs Brenda Jones who is one hundred years old today. But I'm told she's dead with-it.'

Shock Exclusive

In 1978 a British National newspaper stunned its readers with the headline:

...POPE DIES AGAIN...

★   ★   ★   ★

.............*Following the horrific financial disaster of his movie* Raise The Titanic, *Lord Grade was heard to remark of his mistaken venture: 'It would have been cheaper to lower the Atlantic'.*..

★   ★   ★   ★

A Tight Hand On The Reins

Advanced advertising material for a club's gala night contained the memorably phrased promise:

The evening will conclude with a toast to the incoming president in champagne kindly supplied by the outgoing president, drunk as usual at midnight.

No doubt there was soon an outgoing Press Secretary as well!

Doctor Death

A Paris newspaper once ran two unrelated paragraphs together to form the following howler:

'Dr F. has been appointed to the position of head physician to the Hôpital de la Charité. Orders have been issued to the authorities for the immediate extension of the cemetery at Montparnasse.'

Roads To Ruin

Several leading motor manufacturers have lost something (usually sales) in the translation of their car model names into foreign languages.

Ford have had considerable experience of this. They planned to introduce a glamorous new model in Mexico and eventually came up with the name Caliente. They were, however, obliged to have a rethink and call the car the S22 instead, for in Mexican-Spanish *caliente* is a slang word for street-walker. The company had yet another fearful disappointment when they discovered that Cortina in Japanese translates as the highly undesirable and unmarketable 'broken down old car'.

General Motors is another giant company which had its problems down Mexico way. They launched their Chevrolet Nova to a crescendo of hilarity: in Spanish, no-va means 'won't go'.

The Triumph Acclaim had to be renamed for the German market because the best translation available was the totally unacceptable 'Zieg Heil'.

However, first prize must go to the world's number one motor manufacturer, Rolls Royce, who did not realize that in Germany (East or West) Silver Mist meant nothing other than what one might tastefully describe as 'human waste'.

Bishop's Move

The Rt Rev. Timothy Dudley-Smith is Bishop of Thetford. He also became well known as the contributor of 46 of the new *Hymns For Today's Church*, which did not find universal approval among the faithful.

However, the Bishop caused even more scratching of heads when he announced: 'I'm tone deaf and cannot sing a note.'

★   ★   ★   ★

. . . . .A scathing three-word judgment was all that was vouchsafed to Hollywood heart-throb Clark Gable after his first screen test: 'Ears too big.' The author of the remark has wisely preserved his anonymity. . . . .

★   ★   ★   ★

Anything Could Happen

The effect was shattering for the big-selling vodka firm whose advertisement declared:

'I THOUGHT THE KARMA SUTRA WAS AN INDIAN RESTAURANT UNTIL I DISCOVERED SMIRNOFF.'

An executive, explaining why this particular ad was dropped from the campaign, said: 'We conducted a survey and discovered that 60 per cent of the people *did* think it was an Indian restaurant.'

★   ★   ★   ★

. . . . .In 1948 Warren Austin, the well-meaning but bungling United States Ambassador to the United Nations, implored the warring Arabs and Jews to behave 'like good Christians'. . . . .

Success On El Plato

Many Britons are, quite rightly, still dubious about foreign food, in spite of the proliferation of Indian, Chinese, Italian and other ethnic restaurants in this country. To many British eyes, not to mention stomachs, there is something especially ominous about what you get when you go abroad. (It is obviously all part of an extremely nasty plot to stop us taking over the Common Market.)

Conscious of the gastronomic culture gap, many helpful restaurateurs in the holiday hotspots now knock out a multi-lingual menu.

Unfortunately, the proprietor of one such eating house at Moraira, on Spain's sun-drenched (as they say) Costa Dorada, may have his heart in the right place, but his English phrasebook has clearly been left to languish in his other suit. Visitors to this palace of culinary delight will be presented with the following:

MENU

Aside Rice Ham Fish
Crumbled Eggs with Tomato

Goose Barnacles
Natural Fish Knife (piece)
Gordon Blu
Thigh Lambskin

Pineapple Wirsch
Special Ice from The House
Frost Pie

And to follow? Presumably, rampant indigestion!

454

Head's Roll

An advertisement for the headship of a junior school in London's East End appeared in the *Times Educational Supplement*. It revealed the following apparently contradictory information:

'The roll is largely Muslim. Strong Church of England links and a regular communicant preferred.'

★   ★   ★   ★

. . . . .In 1959 the head of the International Monetary Fund announced that world inflation was over. . . . .

★   ★   ★   ★

Dear Me

The *Chingford Classified*, surely one of the great news organs of our time, printed this sublime description of the Queen Elizabeth I Hunting Lodge in Epping Forest:

> It now stands mute, but if you stand still, eyes closed, willing the 20th century to roll back, can you hear the ghostly notes of an English hunting horn? Or the last swish of a Victorian petticoat? Can you catch an echo of its shrill, carousing, dog-baying heyday? When the open galleries on the top floors...echoed with the oaths...of noisy hunting fans. Where in later years, too worn to ride, the Queen and her favourites waited for dear after dear to come within bolt range of their crossbows.

The Word Of The Lord

A newly-revised edition of the Bible, which went on sale in 1982, almost appeared with a printing error which would have been a disastrous benediction for the idle among our number.

As I am sure you do not need reminding, Exodus 20, verse 9 should read: 'Six days you shall labour and do all your work.' However, in the new version it actually appeared as: 'Six days you should not work.'

Happily, this somewhat crucial error was picked up while the Bible was in proof form. A spokesman for publishers Samuel Bagster said: 'It would have been a disaster.'

Taxing Problems

John Maynard Keynes, the famous economist, took time off from diagnosing the problems of the modern world to offer the following philosophical observations:

'The avoidance of taxes is the only intellectual pursuit that still carries any reward.'

Alas Poor Schnozzle

John Barrymore, an occasional drinking companion of the great Jimmy 'Schnozzle' Durante, once told the melancholy man with the big nose: 'You should play Hamlet.'

Durante shook his head. 'To hell with them small towns,' he said. 'I'll stick to New York.'

★   ★   ★   ★

. . . . .During the hard-fought and exciting 1949 Oxford and Cambridge University Boat Race, BBC commentator John Snagge got so carried away by the excitement that he heard himself say: 'I don't know who's ahead. It's either Oxford or Cambridge'. . . . .

★   ★   ★   ★

456

Popsuey

Back in the halcyon days of the 1970s, when the spirit of good will was abroad in the air between the United States and the People's Republic of China, the new accord was celebrated with (what else?) supplies of Pepsi Cola to the yellow hordes.

The slogan 'Come alive with Pepsi' had been a great success in the West and seemed ideally full of Eastern promise too. So the company's ad men had it translated into Mandarin – or at least that was their intention.

Sadly, they were obliged to make a rapid return to the drawing board because the best translation that could be achieved was: 'Pepsi brings your ancestors back from the grave.'

Lipsmackinthirstquenchinggraverobbin...

Gun Law

A woman was committed under the Mental Health Act for shooting her husband with a .410 shotgun. After the judge had pronounced his decision, the prosecution – not unreasonably – asked that the gun be destroyed. The judge disagreed, declaring such an act both wasteful and unnecessary. He may have had a point, but his final suggestion must surely go down as a grossly insensitive blunder. Describing the weapon as 'a nice little folding .410', he went on: 'I think it should go to the son. It should give him a great deal of pleasure.' The mind boggles!

Fowl Play

Finger-lickin' good, but head-scratchin' puzzlin' was the sign which hung in pride of place in the window of a South of England Kentucky Fried Chicken dispensary.

It boasted:

OPEN SEVEN DAYS A WEEK, EXCLUDING SUNDAYS

What A Loo!

Those responsible for the placing of an official notice in the litter-strewn Ladies Room at London's National Film Theatre must surely have been mistaken – or *has* yet another of London's bridges found its way across the Atlantic? The notice read:

> *WE APOLOGIZE TO VISITORS FOR THE DETERIORATION IN THIS TOILET AREA. THIS WAS CAUSED BY MOVEMENT OF WATERLOO BRIDGE.*

Traffic Copped

The man from the Automobile Association who delights listeners to the London Broadcasting Company with descriptions of the misery they are going to face if they attempt to get to work in their cars, surpassed himself one merry morn.

He told the waiting millions: 'Traffic is very heavy at the moment, so if you are thinking of leaving now, you'd better set off a few minutes earlier.'

Do not adjust your trannies, there is a fault in the man from the AA.

Pieces Of Fate

.... **Errors concerning**
unavoidable misfortune *..*

Pastor Master

The Rev. James Boysell, hard-hitting pastor of a church in New Jersey, was a man who knew what to look for – and between which lines to read. When his car ran out of petrol in heavy traffic, he was suspicious. When the church chimes went out of order and the church central heating furnace exploded, he was suspicious and alarmed. When he entered the church one day and a board fell on his head, he was suspicious, alarmed and absolutely certain: it was the work of the Devil, Satan himself.

At the end of that demonic week in 1940 he startled parishioners with a pulpit denunciation of the Devil and all his sulphurous works. To assist the spirit of the meeting Rev. Boysell had engaged the services of a young man, who stood before him clad in Satanic costume. The pastor berated him with logic and ordered him to be gone. As a grand finale to the symbolic ceremony, the pastor then chased the 'Devil' down the aisle and out of the door.

Whereupon Rev. Boysell fell over and broke his arm.

Suspended Sentence

It is not customary to find much light-heartedness in the air on a hanging morn, but on February 23, 1885 at least one man managed to walk away from the execution shed with a decided spring in his step. The condemned man was 19-year-old John Lee who had been due to pay the supreme penalty at Exeter Prison. The thoughtful authorities had erected a brand new gallows for the occasion. Lee, hooded and manacled, stood on the trap awaiting the drop into eternity. And waited and waited, for the trap stubbornly refused to open.

The killer was taken back to his cell while engineers inspected the offending mechanism. The executioner had a test pull of the lever and the trap sprung open with awesome efficiency. Lee was brought back with due apologies for this unseemly hanging about. Again the trap refused to open. Again the wretched Lee was returned to his cell.

The process was repeated once more, with the same result, before the authorities decided to call the whole thing off and commute the sentence to life imprisonment.

Wrong Arm Of The Law

Police Constable Frank Melia called at an address in a run down area of Liverpool. The smell of the hovel was matched only by the scruffy appearance of the mother, father and five children who lived there. Melia, a fastidious man, politely and sensibly declined a cup of tea and perched uncomfortably on the edge of the greasy sofa. As he prepared to pursue his inquiries, he saw out of the corner of his eye a furry creature of verminous mien which was crawling up the arm of the sofa.

The constable knew a rat when he saw one and, with reactions as sharp as the creases in his trousers, whipped out his truncheon and walloped the tiny creature into eternity. The family gazed in silence for a moment before one of the urchins responded to Melia's triumphant glow with the words: 'Hey, Mister, why d'you kill my gerbil?'

★　　★　　★　　★

.............American golfer Elaine Johnson certainly started a bit of a storm in a B-cup when a shot hit a tree and landed in her bra. She told tournament officials: 'I don't mind taking a two-stroke penalty, but I'm damned if I'm going to play the ball where it lies.'......................

★　　★　　★　　★

Right Up And Away

Moira Haggerton wanted to keep her 9-year-old son amused while she was out shopping. What better than a video of one of the blockbuster *Superman* movies?

But when Moira returned to her house at Grindon, Sunderland, she could hardly believe her eyes. Her aim had been more than achieved, for there was the lad sitting still, enrapt, goggling at the TV screen. On which was showing an incredibly naughty porn movie.

The manager of the video hire shop admitted that his face was red over the blue movie. 'It was a slip-up,' he said. 'My assistant didn't check the tape before it went out.'

This Is A Stick-Down

A Scandinavian bank-robber who failed to check the efficiency of his shotgun paid the penalty for his carelessness when he tried to pull off a big haul in a city bank. On whipping the gun from under his raincoat with the familiar cry 'Don't move! This is a stick-up', he was appalled to see the barrel pointing innocuously at the floor. After several vain attempts to snap the barrel into its correct ready-for-action position, the robber threw the useless weapon to the floor with a disgusted 'Oh, forget it', and rushed out of the building!

Rail Fare À La Française

It is claimed that many a culinary creation has been born out of mishap and disaster. This is certainly true of the much-heralded French vegetable dish known as *pommes soufflées*.

A nineteenth century French chef was hired to prepare a celebratory banquet to mark the opening of a new railway line. As he was preparing the meal at one of the new stations, a message reached the *maître de cuisine* that the trainload of dignitaries would be delayed. Accordingly, he removed his half-cooked *pommes frites* from the oil and began philosophically to prepare a new batch.

Then he was told that there had been a mistake and that the train was even now pulling into the station, on time after all. In desperation, the chef plunged the half-cooked potatoes back into the oil and watched with amazement as they turned from soggy and unappetizing-looking lumps into puffy brown crisp ovals.

Later, on being congratulated on this culinary delight, the chef merely commented with typical Gallic *sang froid*; 'But, messieurs, they were only *pommes soufflées*.'

★　　★　　★　　★

. . . . .Robbers who held up a lorry at Lenham, in Kent, fled in empty-handed disgust when they discovered the cargo they were attempting to hijack was nothing more exciting than dog food and toilet rolls. . . . .

Prince Of Bails

Frederick Louis, Prince of Wales and eldest son of George II, was the first royal to take a big interest in cricket. In the end he was quite carried away by the game.

Having caught the cricket bug, an affliction impossible to cure, while watching Surrey playing their dreaded rivals from Middlesex in 1733, he went on to captain Surrey and London only four years later. When he died in 1751, his death was attributed to a painful blow in the side – from a cricket ball.

Home and dry

A thief who was surprised by the returning owner as he attempted to break into a house in Carlisle, hid his identity by swathing himself in the wet washing which hung on the line in the garden. He then coolly proceeded to a neighbouring house, broke in and stole a spin drier.
He got clean away.

Fishy Tale

Peter Fowler and his pal, Dennis Guest, became two anglers in a tangle when they were marooned on an island in the middle of a fast-flowing river. They used a ladder as a bridge in the River Trent at Torksey, but some other helpful anglers on the bank unwittingly took it with them when they knocked off after an enjoyable day's sport. Resourceful Dennis managed to climb up a rope to the top of a railway bridge, one of whose supports stood on the island. But Peter, who was a beefy 20 stones, was nothing like so lucky. The rope snapped as he tried to haul himself up. Dennis set off to find help, and four hours later the fire brigade turned up and managed to land their cold, wet and hungry catch.

LAUREL
AND
HARDY
RULE
O.K.

Not His Day

Joe Ramirez, aged 19, jumped into his car and drove to the New York courthouse where he was due to face a traffic charge. By the time his case was called, he realized that his parking meter was about to run out. However, the judge was a reasonable man and he allowed Joe to nip out to insert another coin or two.

At this point events began to take a surreal turn for the unfortunate Joe. As he tried to dash across the street, a policeman collared him and gave him a long lecture on the anti-social nature of jay-walking. He also gave him a ticket. When Joe finally got back to the car, he found that a highly-punctual traffic warden had already slapped on a parking ticket. The somewhat deflated young man went back to court, only to find that the judge had gone for lunch, leaving Joe to feed the meter until the court was ready to sit again.

When the case was heard, Joe was fined $5, but when he pulled out his wallet, he discovered that, what with jay-walking fines and feeding the meter, he had only $2 left. The court clerk agreed to accept the money on condition that the rest of the fine would be paid without delay. Joe went home and was only too pleased to be back behind his own front door, until he found a letter waiting on the mat. To complete a truly wonderful day, it told him: 'Please report for induction in the United States Army.'

★　★　★　★

. . . . .A course in public speaking at a Leeds adult education centre was given by . . .Mr A. Stammers . . . .

★　★　★　★

Canny Tale

Little-known Eastern proverb: it is a mistake to let your work take over your life – it can be dangerous.

Failing to heed this warning, a certain Mr Tin, aptly named Thai representative of the Pepsi Cola Company, paid the ultimate penalty when he was shot and killed during a business altercation by a Mr Thongyu Mauksuk of the rival Coca Cola firm. Well, they *said* things go better with Coke!

Sweet Smell Of Success On The Pavement

Monsieur Coty made millions as the founder of the famous perfume company, but he owed his great success to a lucky break on the pavements of Paris.

As a young man he was obliged to hawk his scents around the stores and one day he took a bottle of a new compound to the manager of a big *magasin*. The manager, smug and dismissive in black coat and striped trousers, rejected the young perfumier's sales pitch and personally showed him the front door.

As the dejected Coty left, he accidentally dropped the bottle and watch dismayed as the contents spread across the pavement. Another effort going down the drain. *Zut alors*! and all that sort of thing.

But then, as in all the best fairy tales, an extraordinary thing happened.

Several well-heeled and exquisitely-scented women customers gathered round and exclaimed: 'My, what a delicious scent,' and, 'Where can we get a bottle, or two?'

The manager did not bat an eyelid as he told the assembled Mesdames: 'Monsieur Coty has been showing me our new, exclusive mixture. We are expecting a large supply by the end of the week.'

Coty took the hint, and an order worth £3,000, and trotted off up the ladder to success.

Trunk Call

A visitor to Dudley Zoo in the West Midlands got an expensive surprise when she leaned over the barrier to give Flossie the elephant a pat on the head. The elephant was not in the least bit interested in gestures of friendship. A little snack was more in her mind.

Flossie reached out with her trunk, grabbed the woman's handbag, placed it decorously in her mouth, chomped it for the recommended dozen or so times and swallowed it – cash, chequebook, silver pendant and all. This impromptu nibble between meals cost the zoo £30 in compensation.

468

Crowning Glory

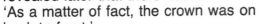

Edward VII waited a long time to be crowned King, and when he finally got as far as Westminster Abbey for his coronation in 1902, fiasco nearly ruined his big day.

The Archbishop of Canterbury was aged and infirm. He was handed the Imperial Crown by the Dean of Westminster, who was equally feeble. Onlookers feared that the Primate might drop the crown, for it shook in his hands as he held it over the King's head; but he got it on – somehow.

The Keeper of the Muniments and Sub-Librarian of the Abbey revealed later that there had in fact been a fairly glaring error: 'As a matter of fact, the crown was on back to front.'

In the overwhelming euphoria of relief that a total disaster had been averted, no-one appeared to notice the blunder.

'Everyone was so thankful that it was actually on.'

Cutting Up Rough

The *Gateshead Post*, famed for its fearless reporting of the truth, revealed that a local health centre had put toughened glass in its windows in an attempt to defeat the destructive pleasures of vandals.

Soon afterwards a mother complained to the amazed staff at the centre that her son's head had been cut when a brick he had hurled at the newly-strengthened windows bounced back and hit him.

How the Wrecktor Fell from Grace

Rector Max Williams turned into a wrecker when he took his car into a garage for a simple oil change.

The havoc got smartly under way when Rev. Williams trundled his Austin automatic into the garage at Newmarket, not far from the Suffolk village of Chevely, where he ministers to pastoral needs. Then his foot simply slipped from brake to accelerator, the car was transmogrified from harmless little runaround into snarling demon, as it fairly roared through the workshop.

Mechanics leaped for safety as the car hit a six-foot ramp, sending the car on top plunging to the ground, its horrified owner still sitting inside, no doubt giving up a quick prayer. Mighty Max then crashed into another car and hammered it into the wall. His own car finally slid gently to a halt, conveniently alongside a workbench.

The rector was unhurt in all but pride, but one mechanic and a customer needed the services of a doctor. The man in the stores was treated for shock.

The garage owner found it difficult to say anything that was not wholly blasphemous, while Mr Williams simply kept repeating to anyone who was capable of listening: 'My foot just slipped.'

IT CAN'T BE TRUE!

ILLUSTRATED BY BILL TIDY

CONTENTS

Legal Action

.... *Being matters of a legal or criminal nature*...

No Christmas

In 1649 when Britain was ruled by Oliver Cromwell and his Roundheads, a law was passed abolishing Christmas and declaring that it should be an ordinary working day, like any other. People, however, thought that the Puritans had gone too far and continued to celebrate as usual. Many congregations were arrested in their entirety for doing so, but the law was soon repealed and Christmas became Christmas once more.

Prison Pottery Classes

The governor of a Northamptonshire prison was very pleased with the success of the pottery classes that he inaugurated. He even went along occasionally to watch batches of pots going into the kiln. What he didn't know was that one of the prisoners had become so good at moulding and firing that he was able to pass his work off as that of a famous potter. So good were his forgeries that they even fooled the experts at famous London auction houses. So much for retraining!

Just A Reminder, Sir

At Saltcoats, in Scotland, a man has had thirty letters and several visits from Post Office staff, reminding him that he does not have a licence. As he says, 'Why should I have a television licence? I don't have a television.'

★   ★   ★   ★

. . . . *A Dallas under-cover policeman began to chat up an attractive but obviously provocative girl standing in a dimly-lit alley way. The girl suddenly slapped a pair of handcuffs on him. She was in the same job as he was. . . . . . .*

★   ★   ★   ★

A Well-Judged Remark

F. E. Smith, who later became Lord Birkenhead, was a barrister of international repute. During one trial he referred to one of the witnesses as 'being as drunk as a judge at the time of the offence,' implying that his evidence was therefore not to be taken seriously.

At this point the judge interrupted and told Mr Smith that he believed the expression was not 'as drunk as a judge', but 'as drunk as a lord'. On hearing this, Mr Smith bowed to the court and said, 'As your lordship pleases.'

I Was Trying To Get Back In

Authorities at a well-known London prison had to confess that a press report that stated that prisoners were taking it in turns to slip out of the gaol at night to have a drink in one of the local pubs, much patronized by the criminal underworld, was, indeed, true.

The matter came to light when police arrested one prisoner climbing up the wall trying to get back inside after a night's illegal revelries.

Nothing Smashed, Nothing To Grab

Brighton, the famous English seaside resort, is also the home of a bustling antique trade.

There are several streets filled with such shops, all boasting attractive window displays of valuable *objets d'art* and jewellery. Naturally there are many attempts, some successful, to break into the shops.

In 1981 one would-be raider attempted a smash and grab raid on one shop. It was a pity for him that the shop owner had had the foresight to have specially reinforced glass put in. The brick the robber threw bounced back off the glass and knocked him unconscious.

Stay Granted

An Arizona sheriff was convinced that a man awaiting execution was innocent of the crime with which he had been charged and found guilty. He wired the Governor requesting a stay of execution and was greatly relieved to receive the following wire:

STAY GRANTED STOP SIGNED H. SMATHERS, GOVERNOR.... BY E. RANDALL, TEMPORARY GOVERNOR.

It arrived a few hours before the execution was due to happen. The accused man was later proved to be innocent. What the sheriff did not know was that the telegraph operator who received the wire, appreciating the urgency of the situation, had taken the wire to the Governor's office in person, only to be told that he was terribly ill and could not see anyone. So the operator sent off the wire, having first signed it in his own name.

The Revenue's Revenge

In 1980, a woman wanted to register her 'practice' as a company.

The London-based Registrar of Companies was happy to accept her definition of the business as a provider of personal services. (The woman's services are those advertised as 'teachers' in the notice boards of seedy London newsagent shops.)

However, she desired to be more frank in the description of her business, and when the registrar refused, took him to court. The case was widely reported and the verdict went against the plaintiff.

Many people think that any publicity is good publicity, but one report of the proceedings caught the eye of the Inland Revenue who sent an inspector round to visit her premises. So, as well as having lost her case against the Registrar, the woman was faced with a tax bill of just under £11,000.

Any Excuse...

One dark December evening, London police arrested a lady of ill-repute and she was charged with soliciting. She asked to be released on the grounds that she was getting married the next day and had been out trying to earn some money to buy her husband-to-be a wedding present.

★　　★　　★　　★

. . . . .Duelling in Paraguay is quite legal, as long as both participants are registered blood donors. . . . .

BLAST...HIT HIS KIDNEY DONORS CARD!

An Escalating Battle

A Leeds postman was putting the finishing touches to smoothing some cement when a neighbour's dog walked across it. The annoyed postman set about re-smoothing the cement when the dog did it again. This time, the man threw his trowel at the dog and then kicked it. Unfortunately the kick landed on the wife of the dog's owner.

The incident was seen by another neighbour who decided to call the police. She ran across to the local telephone box and had just dialled 999 when the furious dog-owner's wife who had also decided to tell the police pulled her out of the 'phone box. A scuffle ensued and both ladies fell into the cement.

At this point, the postman's mother-in-law decided to intervene and although she was 86, she joined the scrap in the cement, pulling the poor postmaster in with her. Then the dog-owner himself came out of his house to see what all the commotion was about. He too was pulled into the cement.

They were all arrested for breach of the peace – all that is apart from the dog who had started it all.

★　　★　　★　　★

. . . . In New York City there is an old law that has never been repealed making it illegal for women to smoke in public. . . . .

★　　★　　★　　★

Happy Anniversary

The presiding officer in Leeds magistrates' court knew the defendant very well. It was the 500th time he had appeared in court on a charge of drunkenness. He had first appeared there in 1922. The magistrate decided to give the man an absolute discharge, and gave him another talking-to on the evils of drink. Two days later the same man appeared on the same charge. 'I was celebrating my 500th appearance in court,' he told the magistrate. This time he was fined 50p.

478

A Piece Of Positive Police Work

A climber in Glencoe found a camera wedged in an ice covered ridge. He had the film inside developed and handed the photographs and the camera to the police.

The police spotted a car registration plate in one of the snapshots and traced the owner of the car who lived in Cheltenham, Gloucestershire. He confirmed that it was his camera that he had lost eight months previously.

A similar story concerns a factory girl who lost a ring one day at work. She searched and searched for it but there was no sign of it.

She left the factory several months later. Eight months after that her ring was returned to her. It had slipped off her finger and gone into one of the pillows that she was stuffing.

The pillow was eventually sold.

The buyer, one night, felt something lumpy in the pillow and found the ring inside it.

Protest Against Pomposity

Most of the people in the courtroom in Rio de Janeiro thought it was a tremendous joke when the accused, Ricardo Forenza stood up in the dock to give evidence on his own behalf. He had been charged with malicious conduct, in that he had removed the soap from the men's washroom in the nearby local government building and substituted it with joke soap which made the washers' hands turn black.

He explained that he had been there to see the tax inspector about his tax return, and he had been so pompous that Forenza thought he had to do something to bring him down to earth.

The magistrate seemed to agree with Forenza and let him off with a warning about his future conduct. Minutes after leaving the courtroom, there was an awful smell of rotten eggs and the whole court had to be cleared.

Forenza was hauled back before the magistrate and confessed to dropping two stink bombs as he was leaving the dock.

His defence was that he found the court too pompous. This time he was fined £100.

No One Would Kill Him

During a case in Monaco in 1912 the judge
passed the death sentence on the accused who stood before
him. According to Monegasque custom an executioner was
brought in from France to do the job, but when he appeared he
asked for 10,000 francs in payment. The authorities said that this
was too much. The executioner refused to budge and went back
to France. No one in Monaco could be found to do the job, so
the execution was held up indefinitely.

Meanwhile, the condemned man had become quite
comfortable in jail. He was the only prisoner there and the cost of
guarding him night and day was beginning to mount up.

A delightful compromise was arrived at. The prisoner was told
that he could live in jail under minimum security if he promised
not to escape. In addition, he would be given a small allowance
to pay for his needs. The man agreed and lived in the prison,
being paid for the privilege, until he died thirty years later.

I Felt A Bit Peckish, Your Honour

A French robber broke into a house outside Paris in 1964. He went into the kitchen and opened the refrigerator where he found some of his favourite cheese. He then found some biscuits and three bottles of champagne. He was arrested the following morning, fast asleep in the spare bedroom.

Banned And Banned Again

An Essex man was disqualified from driving by magistrates at Southend Court.

A few minutes after he left court, he decided to risk driving illegally. Unfortunately, the magistrate who had banned him spotted him at the wheel.

The unfortunate driver had to reappear in court where he was fined £300.00 and banned for another year.

Look, No Hands

A Brentford man was fined £2.00 for careless bicycle riding. When he was arrested, he was riding without his hands on the handlebars reading a newspaper. 'It was,' he told the court, 'the only chance I ever get to read a newspaper.'

Stop Clipping

Frau Inge Bader's husband has an art studio in Vienna. He finds that the brushes on sale there are not fine enough for his style of painting, so he used to clip his wife's eyebrows to make fine brushes. She tried to stop him but he was insistent, so Frau Bader went to court and got an order restraining her husband's strange habit.

Let The Punishment Fit The Crime

In Monroe, California, two students were sentenced to walk for twelve miles. They had been found guilty of siphoning three gallons of petrol from a parked car, and the judge considered that four miles to the gallon was a suitable punishment.

Similarly, three football rowdies in the town of Burntisland in Fife were ordered by the magistrate to report to the local police five minutes before kick-off time and five minutes after the final whistle as punishment for a breach of the peace during a Dunfermline–Raith Rovers match.

The gleeful youths had been expecting a much worse punishment and calculated that they could report at five minutes to three, be at the game (provided it was being played at home) five minutes after kick-off, and rush back in time to report, as ordered, five minutes after the final whistle.

They realized that if it was a cup tie, and the game went into extra time they would have to leave before the final result was known. However, they took no account of the canny Scots police sergeant who was on duty throughout their sentence.

They reported, as arranged, five minutes before kick-off the following Saturday. The sergeant told them to sit down and wait for a couple of minutes as he was 'a wee bit busy, at the moment.'

A few minutes later, they again asked the sergeant to clock them in and got the same reply. This went on for more than an hour.

Eventually, at half-past-four, ten minutes before the final whistle was due to be blown, the sergeant found time to log the boys' arrival at the station. He took his time doing so and they did not leave until twenty to five. Just as they were leaving, he called to them not to forget to report back in five minutes.

This went on every Saturday throughout the football season.

★　　★　　★　　★

. . . . Several tourists in Majorca have literally had the coats taken from off their backs by wily Spanish thieves, who, having told their victims that pigeons have soiled their clothes, help them off – permanently – with their jackets. . . .

I Swear By Myself...

A Florida man claimed against his insurance company when he was injured by the collapse of a pavement. The company dismissed his claims on the grounds that it was an Act of God, so the injured party decided to sue God and issued a writ against Him, claiming $25,000. The defendant did not appear in court, although a local priest offered to give evidence on his behalf.

Dual Nationality

A criminal in Venezuela owns a house that straddles the border between that country and Colombia. If ever the police try to arrest him, he simply locks himself in his bedroom until they go away. His bedroom is in Colombian territory, and he has been clever enough to keep a clean record there.

Not For Sailor's Use

Captain Cook, the great English explorer, worried about the possibility of scurvy breaking out among his crew. He knew that German sailors never suffered from it, a fact they put down to eating sauerkraut. But he knew that his sailors would never be forced to eat the German food, so he had a large barrel of it placed on the deck of his ship and placed an impressive sign over it:

FOR USE OF THE
CAPTAIN AND OFFICERS
ONLY.

During the day none of the sailors went near the tub, but every night the level of sauerkraut went down slightly and not one of his men came down with the disease throughout the trip.

What? Fisticuffs

An argument broke out during a conference being held in Richmond, Virginia. Tempers flared and when it was all over, one man had been shot dead and three others had been seriously injured. They were all members of the security staff from the Fifth Federal Reserve Bank who had been discussing ways of making employees safe from armed attack.

It's Hard To Give Up The Habit

The accused woman gained the sympathy of Swedish magistrates when she appeared before them on a charge of shoplifting. She was given a suspended sentence, but blotted her copybook almost immediately when she left the court, taking with her one of the magistrates' fur coats that she had found in the cloakroom. Her case was not so sympathetically heard on that charge!

What A Way To Serve A Summons

Police in La Paz, Bolivia had to serve a summons on a stilt-walking circus performer. To meet the conditions of the law, the summons had to be handed personally to him. However the circus man refused to come off his stilts to receive the legal document. Undeterred, the police went off, found some pairs of stilts and came up to his level to deliver the summons into his hands.

Mia Culpa

Father Giuseppe was a model priest to his 300 parishioners who respected him as a devout Catholic and friend. Imagine their shock when the good father landed in court, sued by the local baker for £5,000. Father Giuseppe was addicted to playing poker and had lost the money IN ONE NIGHT. His only possessions were a kitchen table and his bed.

Looks Familiar

A Newcastle family were on holiday in Spain. The caravanette was broken into and the mother's handbag and all the money that had been lying around was missing. They found the police very unhelpful – the Guardia Civil could find no one to speak English and the family spoke no Spanish. The municipal police told them that they were far too busy to deal with the case, but eventually agreed to take down details. Five days later the family was told that the handbag had been found, minus the contents. The woman went to the police station to collect it and was asked to sign for it. She didn't have a pen with her so she asked if she could borrow the policeman's. As soon as she saw it she recognized it as her own.

Quite A Haul

Marseilles police were cock-a-hoop when they announced that they had found a quantity of heroin worth £200,000 and had arrested an Englishman for possession. They later had to release him and confess that what they had thought was heroin was, in fact, a chemical freely obtainable from many chemists. Its use? To be dusted over areas in order to discourage dogs from relieving themselves.

HE'S NEVER BEEN THE SAME SINCE SNIFFING OUT THAT STUFF!

All Because Of A Car

Jerome Findley of San Francisco, an automobile dealer, disapproved of his daughter's choice of husband.

Findley was a highly-decorated former naval officer who had built up a successful business. He was conservative, both politically and in his way of life, and was a staunch Episcopalian. His prospective son-in-law was anti-war and had been a leading member of a punk group and a Roman Catholic, to boot.

Barbara, Findley's daughter, was adamant and eventually won her father's approval. Findley even grudgingly gave the couple a wedding present – a brand new Chevrolet, from his showroom. He did however lay down two conditions: one, that he would never set foot in his son-in-law's house and, two, that the couple should have dinner with him and his wife every Sunday.

Things were all right for several months, but then, one Sunday, Barbara telephoned to say that dinner was off as she had a bad ear infection, and had been advised to stay indoors by her doctor. She telephoned again, the following Sunday, and told her parents that she had not recovered. Findley and his anxious wife decided to drive over to see their daughter. Standing in their driveway was, not the Chevrolet, but a brand new Japanese Toyota.

Jerome took an automatic pistol out of his glove compartment and began to fire at the car. First he knocked out the headlights, then the windscreen and all the other windows. He then reloaded his gun and began to pump bullets into the bodywork.

Barbara's husband, Vincent, ran from his house armed with a shotgun and began to blast away at his father-in-law's Chevrolet. Before the police were called, several thousands of dollars' worth of damage had been done to both cars.

The distraught Barbara told police that they had traded in their Chevrolet for the Toyota to save money on petrol and had not known how to break the news to her father. But why had Jerome reacted so violently?

'A few months after the wedding my Chevrolet dealership was forced into bankruptcy,' he explained to the police, 'by the competition of a nearby Toyota dealer. I never liked my son-in-law from the start and the sight of that damned Toyota in his driveway was the last straw.'

Prisoner X

Many people have read *The Man in the Iron Mask* by Alexandre Dumas, about a plot to replace the King of France with his identical twin.

The fictional story is actually based on fact. In 1669, a masked prisoner was turned over to the warden of a prison in France. The prisoner had been sentenced to life imprisonment and was wearing a black velvet mask. He was to be allowed many privileges not enjoyed by other prisoners, and was forbidden to remove the mask.

He died in the same jail 34 years later, never having removed the mask, and his identity never having been revealed – even to this day.

Anyone Interested In A Little House At The End Of The Mall?

In 1923, Scotsman Arthur Ferguson convinced gullible American tourists that Big Ben and Nelson's Column were to be demolished and that he was responsible for trying to sell them on behalf of the British Government. He got £1,000 for Big Ben and £6,000 for Nelson's Column. He was so smooth-talking that he managed to talk one couple into giving him a deposit of £2,000 – for Buckingham Palace.

Stop The Vandals

Councillors in Queensferry, a small village outside Edinburgh, were fed up with the regularity with which windows at the local primary school were smashed by vandals, so they decided to build a wall between the school and the community centre where the young vandals seemed to spend most of their time. Builders got to work and when they finished work on the first day the wall was two feet high. When they returned the next morning they had to start all over again, because the vandals had knocked the wall down. All that was left was a pile of bricks.

I COULD RING BUGSY MALONE ON THE MOON BUT HE'S NEVER IN...

Freephone

Convicts at top-security San Francisco County Jail broke a code that allowed them to use the long distance telephone system operated by a company called MCI. By the time the authorities realized what was happening, the convicts had clocked up bills of over $100,000. One man was regularly calling a friend in South America. A spokesman for MCI said after the crime had been discovered that they were really grateful that the men had broken the system because they had had no idea that it was powerful enough to reach as far as that.

He Tried To Blackmail The President

Gaston B. Means got away with murder as well as being a spy, and an extortionist. In 1916 when he was a seedy little private detective on the surface, he was in fact spying for the German Kaiser, reporting British ship movements from the United States.

When America entered the war, Means persuaded the

Bureau of Investigation to hire him as a special agent. When in Washington he ingratiated himself into the good graces of rich people, often little old rich ladies. One of them was Maude King. Means hired thugs to attack her, and while the assault was taking place, he rescued her from her assailants. She was so grateful that she made him her personal manager. In this position Means had the chance to swindle her out of many thousands of dollars and when she noticed that her account was going down, she demanded an independent audit. Means said that he could see no reason why not and suggested a pleasant trip to the country to talk things over. During the trip, Mrs King had an accident with Means' gun and was killed. At least that's what he claimed and the coroner went along with his story.

In 1921 he was taken back by the Bureau where he kept a little black book detailing the sins and indiscretions of his colleagues. He managed to steal a diary of an Ohio poetess with whom the President, Warren G. Harding had been having a torrid affair for some time. Means offered it to the President and his wife for $50,000. Harding seems to have wanted to pay, but his wife was made of sterner stuff. She had Means kicked out of the White House. After the President died Means took his revenge, by publishing a disgusting little book accusing Mrs Harding of murdering her husband to hush up the affair.

Although J. Edgar Hoover was determined to get Means put away, the con-man was too clever for him.... He always chose his victims with great care. The nice little old ladies who were too incompetent in business to realize that Means was taking them for a ride, or young and beautiful ones who were too vain to admit that they had been taken in by him.

However he chose badly when he selected Evelyn Maclean as a victim. At the time of the notorious Lindbergh kidnapping case, he told the lady that he could get the child back intact, if only he had $100,000 to bribe some friendly bootleggers, who knew where the child was being held. Kind-hearted Mrs Maclean gave him the money in cash as he had requested.

The next time she saw Means was in court. She went to the police when she realized that she had been conned and the evil man was given eighteen years in jail. He died there, in 1938, with FBI agents clustering around his bed, trying to make him tell them where the money was.

He died with his wicked secret intact – and the money has never turned up.

489

Not A Very Neighbourly Neighbour

A Maryland man did not get on very well with his neighbours, in his home town of Glen Burnie. He had a minor dispute with three of them and whenever they passed his house he jumped out of his front door and shouted dirty names at them. The three neighbours took him to court where he was ordered to pay them $70,000 (£45,000) each. At just over £135,000 in total it was a very expensive row for the argumentative man.

A Ghostly Solution To A Ghastly Crime

Inspector Bhadule was sitting dejectedly in his office puzzling over the senseless killing of a pretty, 25-year-old schoolteacher. Suddenly a farmer from the nearby village of Kuhi, in the Maharastra area of India, came in and told the inspector that he knew someone who could tell him how to solve the case.

When the inspector asked the farmer who it was, he replied 'A ghost who insists on talking to you.' The policeman was understandably sceptical and dismissed the man; but he returned the next day and the day after.

The inspector decided that he had nothing to lose so with two local doctors to act as witnesses he went back to the farmer's village with him. The farmer took the three to a deserted field where stood the ruins of a temple.

When they arrived there the old man recited some mumbo-jumbo, blew a conch shell and called for the spirit to appear. Much to the astonishment of the sceptical inspector he heard a voice inside his head tell him where he would find the weapon that killed the girl.

The next morning the inspector went to where he was directed and dug. To his amazement he found a blood-stained knife and lab tests showed that the blood matched that of the victim. When the owner of the yard where the knife had been found was faced with the weapon, he broke down and confessed to the crime.

If you don't believe this, contact Inspector B. M. Bhadule at the police station in Maharastra in India and he'll tell you it's true.

Police . . . The Store's Being Robbed

In Frankfurt in 1979 three people broke into a department store. There were two men and one of the men's girlfriend. As they passed through the bedding department, the two lovers' desires became so strong that they passionately embraced on one of the beds there. Their embrace led on to rather more intimate things and the other man asked if he might join in. When he was told no, in no uncertain terms, he left the department, found a telephone and called the police to report that the department store was being broken into. Police arrived shortly afterwards and found the man and woman, literally with their trousers down. The caller had, naturally, left the scene of the crime but the arrested pair felt no sense of disloyalty at giving his name and address to the police.

★ ★ ★ ★

. . . . The citizens of Kentucky, USA, are required by law to take a bath once a year. At least they would be cleaner than King Louis XIII of France who had a grand total of five baths in his whole lifetime. . . . .

★ ★ ★ ★

Who's Sleeping In My Bed?

Golden Beach is an exclusive area in South Florida. Many rich and famous people live there and they hire security guards to ensure that their privacy is not invaded and to protect their homes while they are out of town. All the strict security did not deter a 29-year-old Canadian beach boy who simply dodged the guards, went up to the windows of the house of a wealthy Lebanese businessman, bent back the bars on a bathroom window, climbed in and looked around. He must have liked what he saw, for he stayed there for three weeks despite the gardeners and caretakers who were working in the grounds every day. While he was there he drank £900 worth of liquor, ate everything in the larder, most of what was in the freezer and ran up a £250 air conditioning bill. When the owner returned he found his uninvited guest fast asleep in bed – just like Goldilocks.

491

Talk Less Loudly, That's The Thing To Do

A New York businessman had to make a call from Chicago airport and asked the operator to put him through on his telephone credit card number.

When his wife got their monthly telephone bill she was horrified to see that it totalled $20,000 and most of the calls were to girls.

The man was shocked when his wife presented him with it on his return home. The bill ran to 334 pages and looked like a telephone directory.

After an investigation by the phone company it turned out that when he had quoted his credit card number over the phone, two marines in the next booth had overheard him and taken down the number. They had passed the number on to their buddies in the corps.

The unfortunate man had been paying to support the collective love life of half of the US Marine Corps.

Fortunately, he will not have to pay for the calls.

The Wild East

Train robbing Indians may, you probably think, belong to twentieth-century Hollywood movies.

You're wrong.

In India's rugged northern frontiers, bandits are holding up trains at an alarming rate.

In 1981 370 trains were robbed, 160 passengers were injured and 36 were killed.

The most common method is for a partner-in-crime to board the train as a paying passenger and pull the communication cord at some pre-arranged spot to allow gun-toting cohorts to board the train when it grinds to a halt. In other cases, bandits blow up sections of tracks to derail the trains – board them, pillage and make off with their booty.

So next time you're waiting for the 8.30, look at your watch, see that the train is 20 minutes late and curse, just thank the gods that you're not in India.

At Least The Police Didn't Put The Punters Away

Ladies of the night, who also work during the day, in and around the notorious squares of London's King's Cross district considered that they were being harassed by local police. The police claimed that the girls were operating outside the law and they were doing their job. Some of the ladies took over a local church hall by way of protest and created some publicity. The local council decided to appoint a monitor to protect the girls' interests. For her work she is paid £160 per week. The girls are most unhappy. Their trade fell off when the scheme was announced. 'After all,' said one, 'if a man is discussing terms he doesn't want someone standing over his shoulder taking notes.'

HAVEN'T HAD A CLIENT ALL WEEK BECAUSE OF HER!

493

Not On The Table

A group of Edinburgh golfers sat despondently in a bar in the small town of Gullane, a few miles to the east of Edinburgh and home of some of the best and most challenging golf courses in Scotland.

They had been looking forward to their game but the rain was coming down in torrents. After a few hours drinking one of them was rather the worse for wear, but suddenly the clouds cleared and the rain stopped. The others decided to play a few holes, but their companion was in no fit state, so they walked him back to their car, laid him across the back seat and left him sleeping peacefully.

An hour later they came back and there was no sign of their friend. They waited and waited, thinking that perhaps he had gone for a walk to clear his head, but there was still no sign of him.

They were becoming quite worried when a policeman came up to them and asked if they knew the driver of the car. When they said yes, the policeman told them that he was in the local prison on a charge of breaking and entering and gross indecency!

It turned out that he had woken up feeling a bit cramped on the back seat so he had decided to go for a walk. During his walk he had felt the need to relieve himself and being unable to find a public convenience had decided to ask at a house if he could use the lavatory.

There was no answer to his knock so he tried the front door. Being a small, quiet village the residents never bothered to lock the door when they went out. The man entered the house and searched for the lavatory, which he found.

He was unfortunately overcome with tiredness on his way out. So he lay down to sleep for a few minutes. He doesn't quite know how it happened but when the poor woman who owned the house returned she screamed when she saw the young man, lying completely naked on top of her dining room table.

After she had gathered herself together she telephoned the police who arrived within seconds and promptly arrested the still-sleeping man. He was fined £100 a few days later. The sheriff told him that in fining him so lightly he had taken into account several things including his age and background, which was very Edinburgh middle class. He was warned that if ever he was in trouble again, he would be punished much more severely.

The young man took the sheriff's words to heart; the next time he was in trouble he did not wait around to answer the consequences. He absconded with £10,000 of his employer's money and went to South America, leaving behind many debts – including £10 to the compiler of this book.

The Nails Gave The Game Away

Shortly after the First World War, the Frick Collection in New York paid more than $100,000 for a fourteenth-century carved wooden madonna.

In 1927 the carving was X-rayed as part of a routine check and was found to be a twentieth-century imitation. Investigations proved it to be the work of a man called Dossena who one day had sold a marble madonna to a man called Fasoli.

Fasoli, knowing it to be brand new, but also being a man with a criminal turn of mind sold it for a substantial profit. He contacted Dossena and bought more of his work and, unknown to him, sold it for more, passing it off as of antique value. Over the years Fasoli sold Dossena's work for more than £50,000 and paid Dossena next to nothing for it. One work which sold for $60,000 saw Fasoli pay the unwitting sculptor $600.00.

When all this came to light many museums had to admit that they had been fooled, but there was a vogue for Dossena's work and at an auction in New York in 1933 each buyer received a certificate from the Italian government that the purchase was an authentic Dossena forgery.

.... *When thieves broke into a church kitchen and stole two dollars, and cooked and ate five dollars' worth of hamburgers and two dollars' worth of ice cream, the local priest was a little upset at the theft but was pleased that the thieves had had the courtesy to wash up everything behind them.* ....

★ ★ ★ ★

The Price Of Sin

Police in Tennessee, Illinois, were called to rescue a man who was trapped waist deep in the cess-pit outside a toilet by a local roadhouse. When they arrived he was almost dead. His body temperature had fallen to 91°F and he was unconscious. He claimed that he had been beaten and mugged by unknown attackers and thrown into the pit. At first the police believed him but became suspicious when they found his wallet, cheque book and credit cards lying in a neat pile in the men's room.

When asked about this the man confessed that he had been standing on top of the ladies lavatory roof watching through a 'glory hole' and had slipped and fallen into the pit. He had taken his personal possessions out of his pocket when he had gone to the men's room to wash, because, he told police, he liked to be clean when he went a-peeping and did not want to have anything on him to identify him in case he was caught.

Impractical Joke

Cincinnati citizen John Simon got rather too drunk one day and thought it would be fun to play a practical joke on a ten-year-old boy who was a common sight in the town, wandering around scraping a living by begging and selling pieces of crochet.

The boy was selling some crochet in the bar where Simon was drinking and the man told him that he wanted to buy one. He said that he was out of money and scribbled a note which he told the boy to take to the bank across the road.

The innocent boy did as he was asked and gave the note to one of the tellers. It was in fact a hold-up note and the teller pushed the alarm. The police arrived a few seconds later and promptly arrested the boy. He protested his innocence and took the police across the road to the bar where Simon was still sitting drinking. Simon found himself in court later in the week charged with malicious behaviour.

The judge, taking pity on the boy ordered Simon to buy him some warm clothes for the winter. Simon agreed to do so, but did not carry out the order. The judge had him thrown in jail and Simon very quickly found the money to buy the boy a splendid new winter wardrobe.

Allow Us, Sir

The Waldorf Astoria is among the grandest hotels in New York and is staffed with security men and detectives, among other, more usual hotel staff, whose job is to protect the wealthy residents who stay there. One night the hotel detective saw a man stumble as he came down the staircase into the lobby. In falling he dropped his suitcase which burst open and spilled out precious jewels all over the hallway. He summoned a porter and the two hotel men helped the grateful guest put everything back into the case, held the door open for him and hailed a cab... Only after the guest was safely away was the theft of more than half a million dollars' worth of gems reported to the desk clerk.

French Promises

At a dance in Foix, Aix-en-Provence, in France the band leader offered a prize of a television set to any woman who would remove her clothing. At first there were no takers, so he increased the offer to a television set and a tape recorder. This tempted one woman who stripped off in front of the assembled dancers. Police were not amused by the display and the woman found herself in court being fined 2,000 francs for immoral behaviour.

Unfortunately, the band leader was not forthcoming with the prizes and the poor stripper found herself with nothing at all for her labours.

AIX GENDARMERIE ANNUAL DINNER DANCE

LAST TIME I COME TO A DANCE WITH YOU!

The Religious Thief

A twenty-five-year-old burglar in Madras confessed to a string of robberies when he was arrested by police. He said that half of his loot could be found in the vaults of the temple of the Goddess Amman at Mangadu, near Madras. The police checked his story and found it to be true. When asked why he had donated half of his loot to the goddess, Venka replied, 'I have to steal to live. But I was brought up to believe in donating half my income to the temple. And I am still a very religious man.'

No Escape For Manson

Charles Manson, the madman who masterminded the Hollywood murders, is, thankfully, in jail in California. When he was assigned to clean the prison chapel, his guards became suspicious when they spotted the chapel door ajar but could not open it because it was being held by an electric cord. Manson came out when the guards ordered him to do so, but there were some odd things lying on the chapel floor.

A search of Manson's cell astonished the prison authorities, for they found that Manson was half-way through building a hot air balloon which he intended to use to escape from prison. He had simply written to a do-it-yourself balloon manufacturer and bought a kit by mail order. No one in the prison had bothered to check the package when it was delivered.

Only An Irishman (Sorry)

An Irishman toured dole offices all over Wales and southern England and claimed Social Security payments, using 24 names. The swindle netted him more than £500. He was eventually arrested and pleaded guilty of obtaining in one case £97 and in another £74 by fraudulent claims. He asked for eleven other offences to be taken into account. An inquiry revealed that if he had used his own name and made legal claims over the same period of time, he would have been legally entitled to £800, over £250 more than he had obtained fraudulently.

498

Arrested For Sweeping Up

A little old lady who lives in a small town in New York State liked the stretch of pavement in front of her house to be clean and tidy, and although the streets were cleaned by town authorities their work was not to her satisfaction. So, first thing every morning for ten years she got out her broom and set to work. The sidewalk was always scrupulously tidy. Until one day a new policeman was patrolling her area and saw her standing in the road sweeping rubbish into the gutter. He promptly gave her a ticket for jay-walking (a finable offence in the United States) and the eighty-two year old woman found herself in court. Fortunately the judge let her off – but only after making her promise to sweep the pavement without standing in the road. He didn't, he said to her, want to see such a public-spirited old lady as herself get knocked down and injured.

Black Market Money

Kevin Butler was an ordinary London mini-cab driver, whose radio-linked cab drove around North London picking up fares. One day he took a Nigerian businessman, Kizoto Idehem to a bank and waited for him while he withdrew cash from his bank. The money was in a black bag which Mr Idehem laid on the back seat. He asked Butler to stop outside a shop and went in to buy something. He never saw Butler again. As soon as his back was turned, Butler drove off – with £241,000 belonging to the Nigerian. To date, he is still free.

★　　★　　★　　★

. . . . The man in the dock in a Scottish court looked shamefaced as his girlfriend claimed that he had hit her on the head with an axe, twice, while she had been lying in bed. Not satisfied with that, he then assaulted her with a can of soup. Having done so, the can was then opened and the couple warmed it and had it for supper. . . . .

★　　★　　★　　★

Mere Technicalities

.... *Being matters of a mathematical, statistical or technical nature.................*

Movable Months

In the Western world the month of December always falls in winter, but, because they use a different calendar, a Moslem month that occurs in winter one year will fall in summer thirty years later. Interestingly enough, it would be possible for a Moslem who converted to Judaism to celebrate his first birthday 4,340 years later. This is because of differences in the systems the two faiths use to calculate the year. Moslems calculate the year from the date of Mohammed's flight to Mecca in 622 (in the Christian calendar). Jews calculate the year from the time when they believe the world was created – 3761 years BC. Therefore 1982 is 1403 to Moslems (if you decide to work that out, you must remember that the Moslem year contains only 354 days!) and 5743 to the Jews. Complicated, isn't it?

I'm Millions Of Thingies Tall

The smallest unit of measurement is called the attometre. It is only used in the microest of micro calculations and is so small that you could never see anything one attometre long. The average human thumb is 7,000,000,000,000,000,000 attometres long – and that's an awful lot of attometres.

★　　★　　★　　★

. . . . *$11,111,111^2$ equals 123456787654321* . . . .

★　　★　　★　　★

News Travels Fast

If a rumour was started at midnight and repeated within two seconds by everyone who knew about it to two people and those two people told two people and those two people told another two people ... everyone on earth would know about it by 6.30 in the morning.

Underground Wonder

In 1900 a Sicilian immigrant entered the United States, penniless, although he came from a wealthy family. He had been disinherited after a family quarrel. He worked hard as a farm labourer and eventually saved enough money to buy a piece of land on which he intended to build a house for himself and the girl he intended to marry.

The land, however, turned out to be a barren piece of rock with a small wooden shack on it. The man decided that it was too hot to live in the shack, so he built an underground cellar where he could go to cool off. The cellar was so successful that he built another room adjoining it. Then he added a kitchen, hallway, bedrooms and a library.

The rooms were lit by natural light let in by fanlights sunk in from above and there was even an air conditioning system based on a ventilation duct that brought cool air up from below. There was also a garden, again lit by a skylight, which is still, today, filled with exotic plants and shrubs.

However, he took so long about building it – 39 years to be exact – that his fiancée got fed up and ran off with another man. The heart-broken man died alone in his underground palace in 1946.

A Shortage Of Hotel Space

The Japanese, pioneers of miniature radios and electronic gadgets are also the pioneers of miniature hotel rooms.

Building space in Asaka is at such a premium that a new hotel has been built which contains 411 sleeping capsules, each equipped with a reading light, a television set, radio and transistor radio and digital alarm clock.

The 'rooms' are three feet high, thirty inches wide and six feet deep.

Every capsule has been filled every night since the hotel was opened in 1979, mainly by businessmen who have been out drinking and have missed their last train home.

Square Earth

Apart from a few people who still believe that the Earth is flat, everybody believed that the Earth was round – until photographs taken from American space shots proved that actually it is pear-shaped. Recent research has, however, shown that the Earth in fact has four CORNERS, one in Ireland, and three in the oceans near Peru, South Africa and New Guinea. It really is a square world after all.

★ ★ ★ ★

..............*If the 4½-billion-year history of the Earth were to be measured in proportion to one year, man did not appear until 8.30 pm on December 31.....................*

504

Enter A Different World

Harrods, one of the smartest shops in London, has always prided itself on caring well for its customers – pandering to their every need. In 1898 Harrods installed the very first escalator in Britain in their Knightsbridge store.

But in case any of their wealthy customers found the moving staircase too much for their nerves, liveried attendants were positioned at the top to offer smelling salts or brandy to anyone who wished it.

We do not know how many customers went straight back down and up again ... and again ... and again ...

Hoot Mohammed

Bagpipes, which are associated with Scotland more than any other nation did not originate in that country. They were first played in Persia hundreds of years before the Scots first played them, and spread from there to many parts of Europe. Many people probably wish they had stayed in Persia.

The Drachma In The Slot Machine

Machines operated by coins, such as cigarette machines or chocolate dispensers are, you may think, a twentieth-century invention. Well, you would be completely wrong. Nineteenth century? No. Eighteenth? No.

Slot machines were actually invented by a Greek scientist called Hero, in the first century AD.

Holy water was sold in temples. The water was contained in urns with a short pipe leading out from the base. The top end of the pipe, inside the urn, was closed by a plug which was fixed to one end of a horizontal bar.

The other end was directly underneath an opening where coins could be inserted. When the coin dropped in, it hit the end of the bar and caused it to move down. This caused the plug to open and the holy water to trickle out.

A Good Banking Service

The Bank of England, in London, has a special department that deals with claims for reimbursement of ruined banknotes. One of the most common causes of damage is – washing machines! Long-forgotten notes still line the pockets of many a dirty pair of trousers, and emerge from their ordeal clean but unusable. Other culprits are dogs, and lawnmowers, but there have been a few really weird claims.

One Church of England vicar tore up a fiver during a sermon to demonstrate the worthlessness of money, and then filled in a form claiming the money back from the Bank. A magician borrowed a pound note from a member of his audience and put it into a shredding machine, assuring the lender that it would be all right. The trick failed and the conjurer sent the shredded money to the Bank and was reimbursed.

One family whose house was broken into found that their safe had stood up well to the heat of the robbers' acetylene torch. But the heat had been so intense that the cash inside had burned. The charred remains were sent to the Bank and the family got their money back.

In 1981 the Bank paid out £607,890 in this way.

★   ★   ★   ★

. . . . *Mount Everest, at 29,000 feet, is one foot higher than it was one hundred years ago. The earth's forces that created it are still working.* . . . .

★   ★   ★   ★

A Shaving Success Story

In 1895 King C. Gillette had a wonderful idea. He was fed up with having to use a cutthroat razor every morning so he set about designing a wafer thin, incredibly sharp blade that could be held together by a safety clamp. It took him eight years to perfect the design and when it went on sale in 1903, he thought he had been wasting his time for in that year only 51 razors and 168 blades were sold. The following year, however, he knew it had been worthwhile. 90,000 razors were sold and *12,400,000 blades*.

France To England – By Horse And Coach

Several French and British governments have studied the feasibility of linking the two countries by means of an underwater tunnel. The last one, which was abandoned in 1974, would have cost £846 million. But work was actually started on the digging on an earlier project in 1881. The tunnel is still there. The workers dug a tunnel, seven feet high and 879 yards long, from Kent out under the Channel. The idea was to link Dover with Calais and to transport people between the two in horse-drawn carriages along the candle-lit passageway. Work was abandoned shortly after it had begun.

★　　★　　★　　★

. . . . The average human being produces two to three pints of saliva every day. That is almost 8,000 gallons during the course of an average life. . . . .

★　　★　　★　　★

Spring Will Be A Little Early

The Russians have a novel way of making snow melt earlier than it would normally. When the first weak spring sunshine appears, they spray the solid snow fields with coal dust. The black dust absorbs more heat than would otherwise get to the snow, so it melts quickly.

Dry Lakes

Oklahoma legislators decided to build several new reservoirs and ordered the state cartographer to redraw tourist maps with large blue splodges where the lakes were planned to be. Unfortunately funds ran out before the first lake was completed so motorists who drive out to the country expecting to be able to picnic beside an attractive lake are met with barren, bone-dry basins.

507

Better Late Than Never

The Camden librarian opened the letter on his desk and read:

I suggest that all those disgusting books by Mr Havelock Ellis and other similar dirty-minded men posing as psychiatrists be removed from your shelves. Nay sir, I do more than suggest it – I demand it! You are contributing to the undermining of the fibre of the English people – and if war comes, we shall be in no fit state to wage it.

Mr Cole, the librarian, received the letter in 1977. It had been posted in 1938, one year before World War II broke out.

A Crowning Achievement

An American scientist asked several people to identify the subject of a photograph he had taken in 1937. Most of them said that it was an elaborate hat or a crown. In fact it was a drop of milk splashing into a bowl, which he had photographed at a flash exposure of 1/10,000th of a second.

★   ★   ★   ★

. . . . .If all the telephone lines under New York City were straightened out, they would reach from here to the planet Venus. . . . .

★   ★   ★   ★

Small Is Beautiful

Most people have heard that the Lord's Prayer can be, and often has been, written on the back of a postage stamp, but how many know that microfilm technologists in Dayton, Ohio, have put every book in the Bible on to cards 1 inch square? Each book can be read quite clearly under a microscope.

Perhaps even more miraculous is a new Japanese camera that is 1.14 inches long and 0.65 inches thick.

508

Amazing What A Body Can Make

The human body contains enough iron to make a nail, enough carbon to make the lead of 9,000 pencils, enough phosphorus for the heads of 2,000 matches, fat for seven bars of soap, as well as three pounds of calcium and one ounce of salt.

Blue Moon

In 1883 after the volcanic eruption at Krakatoa, near Java, so much dust was thrown up into the atmosphere that the moon appeared to be blue in the night sky. The dust scattered the light which became richer in short wavelengths, thereby intensifying the blue light.

Just To Make Sure

William Dewer's mother-in-law was not at all impressed when he showed her his new invention – the vacuum flask. It would, he assured her, keep things at a constant temperature for hours. Not only did she disbelieve him, but to make sure that the one he gave her worked effectively, she knitted a woollen cosy to fit over it and retain heat.

Power By Rubbish

Nashville, Tennessee City Council collect lorry loads of rubbish from the city tip every day and feed it into an incinerator boiler where it is burned and converts water into high-pressure steam. The steam is used to spin the rotors of a turbine which generates enough electricity to provide heat and air conditioning for 38 office blocks.

The plant cost £6.8 million to build in 1974, and paid for itself within a year.

★　　★　　★　　★

. . . . .Office space in central London is now so expensive that it costs £50 a year to rent the space taken up by an average wastepaper basket. . . . .

★　　★　　★　　★

A Sweet Victory

Scientists who developed the limpet bomb during World War II came up against a serious problem that threatened to jeopardise its success.

No matter what chemical they tried they could not find one that dissolved at a constant rate in both salt and fresh water, which was essential to activate the trigger mechanism.

Then one of the scientists had a brainwave. He tried it out and it worked. The magical chemical – ordinary aniseed, exactly the same as is used to make aniseed balls.

It's Worth About Ten Pounds!

In 1886 a South African gold prospector sold his claim in the Transvaal for the equivalent of ten pounds.

Ever since then, the mines that have been sunk there have realized seventy per cent of the Western world's total gold supply.

Talk about being short changed.

Stretching A Point

If all the tiny tubes in the human kidney were stretched out and laid end to end, they would run for forty miles. (In similar vein, Dorothy Parker once said that if all the debutantes in Yale were laid end to end she would not be at all surprised.)

A Few Surprising Facts In The Day In The Life Of The World

Every day your heart pumps enough blood to fill the fuel tanks of about 400 cars. The population of the world increases by about 200,000. Nine million cigarettes are smoked. 740,000 people fly off to foreign countries. International trade brings in $1.5 billion. Enough water evaporates from the oceans to fill five million average sized swimming pools. In America 10,000 serious crimes are committed and in Japan twenty million commuters cram into trains. In Russia 1.3 million telegrams are sent. 20,000 aircraft take off carrying almost one and a half million passengers and fly a total of 13 million miles. 200,000 tons of fish are caught and 7,000 tons of wool are sheared off sheep. Enough tobacco is produced to give everyone in the world two cigarettes and the equivalent of 23 million tons of coal is burned to produce energy.

Read It Quick

By the time you have read this paragraph (assuming that it will take you about half a minute) 50 people will have died and 120 will have been born. The human population increases at a rate of 140 per minute.

★   ★   ★   ★

. . . . .Eskimos use refrigerators. Not to keep food fresh as we do but to prevent it from freezing solid, as it would if left outside in the ice and snow of the Arctic. . . . . . .

★   ★   ★   ★

A Dream Come True

A Colombian priest dreamed that his little flock of men and
women would one day have their own cathedral to worship in.
The town was poor and most of the people in the parish were
employed at the local salt mine, the largest salt producer in the
world. Eventually his dream came true. It took six years to build
the Cathedral of Our Lady of the Rosary. It can seat 5,000
worshippers. Its nave is 400 feet long and 73 feet high. It is
supported by columns 33 feet square. Outside there is parking
space for 200 cars. The cathedral is built entirely of salt and is
800 feet down the mine beneath the summit of the salt mountain.
It is reached by a deep tunnel more than one mile long.

A Fishy Story

If a man or woman wants to gain one pound of weight by eating
fish, more than one thousand pounds of other living things must
die first. The person would have to eat ten pounds of fish, which
in turn would have to consume one hundred pounds of small fish
creatures, which would in turn have eaten more than one
thousand pounds of plankton.

Hot Stuff

There are several authenticated stories of unfortunate people
spontaneously combusting. One gruesome photograph shows all
that remains of one poor man who burned to death in his
bathroom – his calliper. Experts are puzzled by the phenomenon.

They reckon that the heat necessary to destroy the human body so completely is 3,000°C and the heat is always localized in the part of the room in which the combustion takes place. The fire never spreads.

Pity therefore the poor young man who was dancing with his fiancée at a disco in Chelmsford. Suddenly, in front of the horrified assembly, she burst into flames in her fiancée's arms.

Travelling Theatre

The Royal Exchange Theatre in Manchester is one of the most famous companies in Britain. The stage there, in the 700 seat theatre, is such that the plays are always performed in the round. This makes it difficult for them to take their productions on tour, but the demand for them to do so has been so great that they have designed a portable aluminium structure which, when erected, can take a stage the same size as the original, seat 400 people, and use the complete lighting and sound systems as used in the original productions. When it is dismantled, the theatre can be packed into TWO lorries.

I Don't Want To Know

Shoppers in Stop and Shop, a grocery chain in Massachusetts gave the thumbs down to new cash registers which, when the total button was pressed, announced how much was due. The reason, according to a survey, was that shoppers did not want to *hear* how much they had spent, it was bad enough having to pay anyway.

Sheer Croppers

.... *Being matters of an accidental or calamitous nature*...

Stuck – By The Lips

A Lancaster driver returned to his car one day and found that the lock had frozen. Being a non-smoker he had neither matches nor lighter to defrost it, so he went down on his knees and breathed on it hoping that his warm breath would do the trick. It didn't. Instead he became stuck to the lock for twenty minutes!

A Fishy Tale

A 51-year-old company director was relaxing at home one evening while his wife was in the kitchen preparing their supper – a fine six-pound pike that her husband had caught six hours earlier on a fishing trip. Suddenly, he heard his wife scream. He ran into the kitchen and found her crying and trying to staunch a wound on her arm. The pike had bitten her as she lifted it up to clean it.

Such A Sad Waste

German stevedore Wilhelm Schmidt of Hamburg had never suffered or caused any accident during the 43 years he worked at the docks. On the day he retired, his workmates presented him with a case of whisky. Unfortunately it proved too heavy for him and he dropped it on his foot, breaking three toes.

One In The Eye For Justice

A customer of a certain fish and chip shop found himself in court charged with assaulting the owner. It seems that as he was queuing for his supper, he sneezed and his glass eye shot from its socket into the hot fat-filled deep frier. The owner was forced to drain the tank and clean it. He picked out the eye with a pair of tongs and threw it on the floor. This was too much for its unfortunate owner who promptly leaned across the counter and slapped the owner's face.

Smoking's A Headache

An American soldier was accidentally shot through the head while serving in the army. Surgeons removed the bullet but could not sew up the hole in his brow. The unfortunate man lived for many years with this hole, through which he could blow out cigarette smoke.

Suicidal

A New York painter decided to end it all by throwing himself off the Empire State Building. He took the lift up to the 86th floor, found a convenient window and jumped. A gust of wind caught him as he fell and blew him into the studios of NBC Television on the 83rd floor. There was a live show going out, so the interviewer decided to ask the would-be suicide a few questions. He admitted that he'd changed his mind as soon as he'd jumped.

★　　★　　★　　★

.... *'Of course the water's safe to drink,' said English novelist Arnold Bennett in Paris one day in 1931. He promptly drained a glass of unboiled water, caught typhoid and died.* . . . .

★　　★　　★　　★

A Hot Christening

Guests at a christening party in Peterhead near Aberdeen gasped in astonishment when the godfather of the child being baptized performed a spectacular rugby tackle on the priest in charge of the ceremony, brought him to the ground and pulled his vestments off him. What they had not seen, that only the godfather had noticed, was that the cleric's robes had brushed against a candelabra and flames were licking up his back. Everyone else had been doting on the baby and had not seen the fire start. The baby slept throughout the service, not waking up once.

Not Again, Pierre

Pierre Joilot backed his fork lift truck over the wharf edge at Toulouse Docks where he worked. His employers were understanding and took no disciplinary action against him. Not even the second time he did it, nor the third, fourth or fifth. However, after the sixth truck in two years went into the water, the unfortunate M. Joilot was dismissed.

A Cold But Fortunate Escape

Two fishermen were out one night in their 40-foot boat, when it was hit by a sudden storm and wrecked. They were found two days later, well fed and not too badly hurt. Their craft did not have a lifeboat, so when it went down they threw the refrigerator overboard and clung on to it as it floated along. When they were hungry, they simply opened it up and had a snack.

Please Don't Do It Yourself, Darling

Tony Thompson is an avid do-it-yourself fan. One day, after watching plumbers install a new bathroom in his house, Tony decided to fit a shower curtain. Unfortunately, his electric drill slipped out of his hands and cracked the new porcelain sink. As he reached out to stop it falling he fell off the ladder. His hammer left a huge hole in the new bath and the ladder fell on top of the water closet, cracking the tank and several of Tony's ribs.

When he came out of hospital and was feeling ready for action again, he decided to remove an old fireplace. This went slightly better. Tony survived unharmed, but a sharp piece of flying concrete shattered the television set in the corner.

He then decided to paint his carport, so he tied his ladder securely to a window frame and set to work. Unfortunately, he slipped off and fell through a fanlight, covering himself and his car with a gallon of paint. As he fell he grabbed on to the window frame and pulled it right off the wall.

Undeterred, Tony decided to tile his hallway and bought some expensive Italian tiles for the job. He stored them at the foot of the stairs ready for work the next morning. But he slipped on his way down and smashed every one.

You'd think he'd give up, but no. Shortly afterwards he was drilling a hole under his kitchen sink. It's a pity that he forgot to empty it first. When the drill went through the sink Tony was covered in a torrent of dirty dishwater, and the drill blew up, almost electrocuting him in the process.

Fortunately, his wife understands his obsession and refuses to leave the house when he gets to work – she always hovers close by with the first-aid box in her hand – just in case.

Fore

The pilot of a plane taxiing along a runway in California suddenly collapsed over the controls and the co-pilot had to land the plane. The pilot's collapse was the result of a freak accident – he had been hit on the head by a golf ball struck on the adjoining golf course by someone who, I suspect, lost the hole.

Asleep On The Job

A Heathrow Airport baggage handler was in the hold of a Tri-star waiting for the last bag to be loaded. He lay down for a few seconds' rest and unfortunately fell asleep. When he woke up the plane had taken off. He cried for help and was freed by the flight crew, using a trap door that led from the baggage hold into the lavatory inside the plane. They led him to a seat and gave him a hot meal.

When the plane landed in Bermuda, the accidental passenger was put on the first return flight by immigration officials. He returned to London not just to face the ribbing of his workmates but also a bill for £298 from British Airways for the cost of the flight.

Killed – By A Fish

In the 1930s a Canadian angler fishing in one of the many Canadian lakes was delighted when he landed an extraordinarily large pike. He duly despatched it with a heavy stick and laid it down on the bank beside his shotgun. Unfortunately, the fish was not properly dead. It began to thrash about and its tail caught on the trigger. The gun went off – sending the angler to the happy hunting ground in the sky.

An Expensive Accident

Near the city of Bikaner, in Rajasthan, India there is a temple dedicated to the goddess of poets. The poets who are called Charans have a strange belief. The temple courtyard is a swarming mass of rats, around 100,000 of them.

The Charans think that when they die, they become one of the temple rats, and that when a temple rat dies, it returns to earth as a Charan poet. If one of the poets accidentally steps on a rat and kills it he is fined for his accident – an amount of silver equal to the weight of the poet to whom he has gone to pay his respects.

A Slight Headache

In 1955, *The Times* reported that a South African had been shot in the head. The bullet had entered the back of his head, passed through the lobes of his brain and come out above his eyes. The man walked to hospital and, apart from the flesh wounds, was found to be perfectly all right. He did have a headache.

★　　★　　★　　★

. . . .*The registrar at Toulouse General Hospital in France told the man standing in front of him that the hospital would be pleased to accept his body after death for medical research, whereupon the elderly gentleman shot himself.* . . . .

An Odd Accident

A Somerset man parked his car on a hill and went to a nearby telephone box to make a 'phone call. As he was in the box, another car swerved into his and released the handbrake. The man watched in horror as he saw his car come closer and closer and closer until finally it crashed into the telephone box and, with him still inside, knocked it over.

Trapped In The Loo

A sixty-year-old Liverpool woman decided that her bathroom needed cleaning. She set to work but had some difficulty in reaching the wall above the lavatory cistern.

She decided to stand on the rim of the lavatory bowl, so she put her bucket down, clambered and stretched her arm up. Suddenly, she slipped on the wet porcelain. Her right foot went into the bucket of water and her left plunged straight down the toilet. She fell backwards and her foot became trapped in the S-bend.

Try as she might, she couldn't pull it free and no one answered her cries for help. She eventually managed to remove her right foot from the bucket but could do nothing about her left one. Finally, one almighty yank did the trick and she hobbled round to her doctor who treated her for a badly bruised toe.

A Volcanic Romance

The Island of Reunion is the ideal place for a honeymoon. Tropical climate, balmy nights, romantic beaches – they can all be found there.

A young Frenchman certainly thought so when he took his bride there in 1977. They hired a honeymoon cottage and at first everything was quite perfect. One evening, however, the newly-married man decided to vault over the fence around the cottage and surprise his wife of three days. Unfortunately he had lost his way in the tropical darkness, plunged headlong into a crater of the Ganga Volcano and died.

An Expensive Loss

Prince Urussoff was an extremely rich Russian nobleman who was extremely superstitious as well.

While honeymooning with his bride on the Black Sea, her wedding ring slipped off her finger and disappeared beneath the waves.

The Prince believed, according to an old family superstition, that the loss of a wedding ring would bring about the death of the bride, so he bought both shores of the Black Sea, believing that if he owned the sea, he still owned the ring lying on the sea bed. He spent $40 million buying the shores.

But when he died, his family did not want the ring, so they decided to re-sell the Prince's property – and they got $80 million for it.

In Sickness And In Health

The guests at a wedding in Rochester, New York were sorry for the obviously still-recovering bridegroom when he was led to the front of the church to await his bride. They knew that he had been in an accident and was slightly concussed. They nodded sympathetically when the bride hobbled up the aisle, her foot in a splint because of a broken toe as a result of the same accident. The head bridesmaid, also in the accident, was sporting a black eye and limping slightly because of a sprained ankle. The other two bridemaids each had an arm in a sling – one because of a fractured humerus and the other due to a dislocated shoulder: victims, not of the same accident, but of separate skating disasters.

★　　★　　★　　★

. . . . .In 1666 much of London was destroyed by a fire which started in a baker's shop in Pudding Lane and spread quickly, devastating building after building. Amazingly only six people died in the conflagration. . . . .

★　　★　　★　　★

Exploding Soup

An Aberdeen woman decided that the broth she was preparing needed some hot water added to it. She lifted her electric kettle, tilted it forward and – WHAM. She had forgotten to disconnect the plug from the kettle and as she tilted it, the live plug became free and landed in the soup. The soup went everywhere – even covering the ceiling. Somehow, she hasn't really wanted to make soup since.

Oh, What A Picture

A woman who lived in San Diego in California and some friends were having a fun day on a picnic. The girls were preparing the food and their boyfriends went off to do some target practice with their hand pistols. When they came back someone suggested taking a photograph and everyone lined up in front of the camera.

One of the men thought it would be a fun idea if he dropped his pants in the photograph. Unfortunately, as the pants hit the ground, the pistol in his pocket went off and struck the girl and his wife. The wife was furious with her husband, not only at the time of the accident, but a few months later when a judge awarded the girl $260,000 damages.

A King's Road Caper

A well-known newspaper editor was dining with some friends in a fashionable King's Road restaurant. The restaurant employed a violinist to move between the tables serenading the customers. One of the party saw that this was causing some embarrassment to a lady in the group, so he decided to tip the fiddler with a ten pound note, hoping that he would move on. He leaned back and without looking at what he was doing, tried to push the note into the violinist's pocket.

The guests watched with a mixture of hilarity and astonishment as he pushed and pushed, apparently having difficulty in getting the money into the pocket. Hardly surprising, he was trying to push it into the violinist's trouser fly!

Sorry, Wrong Number

A New York housewife in the 1960s had the same digits in her 'phone number as that of the White House in Washington. To make matters worse, the area code for New York is 202 and that of Washington is 212. The woman therefore often got calls that were meant for the then president, Lyndon B. Johnson.

She received a letter from the President saying that he could not be more grateful for the diplomatic way she handled the White House calls. In receiving the calls, Mrs Brown of Glendale, Queens, had always been polite to the sometimes distinguished callers.

Mr President promised that he would try to be just as polite in his reception of calls that were meant for Mrs Brown and her family.

A Nice Long Bath

A young Edinburgh housewife was on holiday for a week and one morning after her husband had gone to work, she decided to take a nice long bath. She put some of her favourite magazines and books on a chair alongside, turned the tap on and poured in some of her favourite bath salts. She went into her bedroom and undressed and walked naked to the bathroom, forgetting to take a towel from the airing cupboard in the hall.

She was just about to step into the bath when the telephone rang so she went to answer it. She grabbed the door handle, and to her horror the doorknob came off in her hand. Worse, the bar that worked the latch on the other side slipped out and fell on the hall floor. There she was, marooned in the bathroom with no clothes, not even a towel to wrap around herself. All she could do was jump into the bathtub; and whenever the water became too cold, she topped it up with hot water.

Her nice long bath lasted eight and half hours until her husband came home from work.

★　　★　　★　　★

. . . . *As the industrial lift in which he was working crashed sixty feet towards the ground, a Liverpool glazier waited until the very last second before he jumped out, escaping with a slightly twisted ankle. The other four men in the lift were all seriously injured.* . . . .

★　　★　　★　　★

A Matchless Achievement

A German man's hobby was making models out of matchsticks. He entered a competition held each year in Cologne, but his efforts were never deemed worthy of a prize, so for two years he burned the midnight oil and produced a stunning matchstick model of Cologne Cathedral – perfect in every detail.

The night before the contest he decided to stay up all night and guard his model in case anyone tried to steal it. He made himself comfortable, lit his pipe – and unfortunately fell asleep. His pipe fell into the model and set fire to it, destroying it completely, as well as half of his house. He has now given up smoking – and model making.

Where's He Gone?

The dramatic critic of a well-known London newspaper was walking along a small street in Torremolinos with a friend. Neither had been there before and as they walked they pointed things out to each other and chattered happily, neither paying much attention to what the other said.

At one stage the friend turned round to say something to the critic and was astonished to find that he had vanished.

Assuming that his companion had turned into a side street to explore something of interest, the friend returned to their hotel, expecting the critic to turn up in time for dinner.

Four hours later, long after the meal had been consumed and when the friend was beginning to think about contacting the police, the critic turned up at the hotel, his head swathed in bandages.

It turned out that he had been so busy looking at the sights, he had not noticed that a manhole cover had been removed from the pavement and had simply fallen down it while his friend carried on talking, completely unaware of what had happened.

A Very Narrow Escape

In March, 1958, a B-47 plane took off from Hunter Air Base in Savannah, Georgia, on a routine flight to North Africa. At 14,000 feet the plane was over the small town of Florence, South Carolina travelling at 450 knots.

Suddenly a bright red light on the console told the pilot that the cargo that was being carried in an undercarriage, was rocking rather violently. A few seconds later the electric locks failed and the shackle opened allowing the cargo to fall out and smash down to the ground below. It struck the earth a few yards away from the home of one of the residents of Florence. He was awarded $50,000 compensation after a long court battle.

What was the cargo? A live atomic bomb. When it crashed to the ground, the triggering mechanism went off with a force of several hundred pounds of TNT. The blast tore up trees, wrecked Mr Gregg's house and damaged a church half a mile away. Fortunately the nuclear warhead didn't go off, but there was a crater 35 feet deep and 75 feet wide in the garden.

Wholly Matrimony

.................Being matters of a marital nature.........

It's A Man's Life

George I of Great Britain never brought his wife from Germany when he inherited the throne. Because of her adultery, he had her imprisoned for 32 years at Ahlden Castle in his native Hanover. He, however, arrived to take up his throne accompanied by his two mistresses.

Peter the Great of Russia was equally unforgiving of his wife's unfaithfulness. When he discovered her guilty secret, he had her lover executed and decapitated. The head was then preserved in an alcohol-filled jar and placed in the unfortunate queen's bedroom as a lesson to her.

Nisi, Nisi

On 17 July, 1975, a London High Court judge granted a decree nisi against a Muslim security officer who worked in Walworth. Fifteen minutes later he granted a decree nisi against the same man. Under Muslim law, a man is entitled to have four wives.

The Meat Was Undercooked, M'lud

A 54-year-old Frenchman, believed that cooking was the most important duty for any housewife. In 1956 his first wife served him an undercooked roast. A row followed that went on until the couple went to bed. He continued the argument and eventually became so angry that he threw her out of bed so violently that she broke her neck and died. He was jailed for seven years after which time he was released for good conduct.

Ten years later he was in court again. He had remarried on coming out of prison. One night a row broke out over a religious television programme. The Frenchman was so incensed by the programme that he fell into a foul mood. Later on in the evening, his wife presented him with an overcooked roast for supper. He was so angry that he struck her. She fell and broke her neck and died. He was sentenced to eight years' imprisonment.

I Do. But Why? Because I Love Him

The row that Eleanore Giacolone had with her boyfriend Johnny Campagna would have finished most romances. In a fit of rage one night he bashed her with a pole, then assaulted her with an ice-scraper and then stabbed her with a pitchfork. She was rushed to hospital and treated for broken ribs and a damaged spleen. She was lucky to be alive at all, the medics in the hospital thought when she left hospital a few weeks later. Two weeks after that she smiled serenely as she repeated her wedding vows in front of the minister who married her to Johnny.

'Why did I marry him?' she said afterwards. 'I love him. He's very like me in a lot of ways and I'm crazy about him.'

★　★　★　★

. . . . .The women of Ancient Greece used to count their ages from the day they were married rather than the day they were born. It was considered that life only began for women after they were married. . . . .

★　★　★　★

Don't Be Late, Wife

Mr Parkinson of Los Angeles owned a news stand quite close to his house. From there he could see his wife leave to do the shopping and come back in with her groceries. He allowed her exactly one hour a day to do this. If she was as much as five minutes late he would beat her black and blue. He was so obsessed with the idea that some other man would try to steal his wife that, apart from her one hour's shopping, he refused to let her go out, unless he accompanied her.

On one occasion he saw a delivery man leave the house and, so convinced was he that he'd been up to no good with his wife, he asked a passer-by to watch the stand for a few minutes, ran back to the house and ripped up every flower in the garden and chopped down a tree that his wife had grown from a sapling. This was the last straw for Mrs Parkinson. She packed her bags and left him. How long had her husband been behaving like this? THIRTY YEARS.

Speech bubble: SHE'S YOURS BUT I'M HAVING CUSTODY OF THE CEMENT MIXER!

It Always Ends In Tears

The scene: a unisex hairdressing salon in San Francisco. The characters: James and Dorothy, two customers, and Archibald, Dorothy's husband.

James was very attracted to Dorothy and when he struck up a conversation with her, she responded happily. She was, Dorothy told James, a model in Hollywood and her husband was an executive in a large public relations company, also in Hollywood. James told Dorothy, in a smooth upper class accent that he was divorced and owned a prosperous manufacturing company. Both believed each other implicitly.

In fact James came from a humble family and worked as a bicycle salesman; true, he was divorced. He had once had dreams of becoming a Hollywood movie star, and the more Dorothy talked about her connections there, the more his old dreams came back to him. Here was his passport to fame and riches, provided he could charm her enough. He did not have to try very hard, for Dorothy had never modelled in her life and her husband was the owner and operator of a concrete mixer. As she listened to James's smooth line of talk she found herself thinking that here was her chance to move into a better class of society. Here was a man who could satisfy her craving for fashionable clothes and expensive jewels.

The two, I suppose inevitably, became lovers but before they found out the truth about each other, Dorothy's husband became suspicious of Dorothy continually coming home late every night, and one day followed her to James's one-storey house on the outskirts of San Francisco. His suspicions confirmed, he decided to take his revenge, and when James came home two nights later he found his bedroom window open. What he discovered inside filled him with horror, for Archibald had backed his cement mixer up to James's window, forced it open and emptied two tons of concrete into the room, leaving a solidly set floor, four feet thick from wall to wall.

Archibald was given a six-month suspended sentence, ordered to pay $15,000 in costs and damages and is suing Dorothy for divorce. James and Dorothy don't see each other any more, not even at the hairdresser's.

★　　★　　★　　★

. . . .*An English High Court judge ruled that a woman found guilty of unlawfully killing her husband with a kitchen knife was not eligible for a widow's pension because she had, he said, brought her widowhood on herself.* . . . .

★　　★　　★　　★

Here's My Address, What's Yours?

A New York girl decided to go down to Miami for a holiday. While she was there she met and fell in love with a handsome man, also on holiday. As the vacation progressed, so too did the romance and near the end, the man asked the girl to marry him. The delighted girl said 'Yes', amazed that a simple holiday should turn out to be a whirlwind romance. The two exchanged addresses and found out that they both lived in the same apartment building in Brooklyn, New York.

A Strange Beginning To A Courtship

Bill Fralick was grateful to find a job as maintenance man at a hotel in Laconia, New Hampshire. After a few days he was called to check out a problem in the ladies room. He thought it was a blocked sink, but when he investigated, all the sinks were in perfect working order.

Then he heard a woman's voice shout, 'I can't get out, I'm stuck.'

Bill got to work with his screwdriver, slipped the lock mechanism and turned it from the outside. On the other side of the door, looking very embarrassed, was the Head Housekeeper. Without exchanging a word, the two left the ladies room.

A couple of days later they passed each other in the corridor and smiled at each other – still very embarrassed by what had happened.

However, seven months later they thought they had got over their embarrassment and they were married. But the first thing they did when they moved into their house was take the lock off the bathroom door.

I Do Because I Suppose I Have To

A Birmingham salesman was invited to a wedding at Avon. The invitation said that his best friend was being married. He duly turned up in church and was met by his girlfriend who smilingly handed him a wedding ring.

'You'll be needing this,' she said sweetly and before he had time to argue, the 'wedding guest' found himself exchanging vows and being married to Rosemary.

He said later that his new wife and he had been living together for more than two years and he had often asked her to marry him, but she had always refused.

The proud bride said, 'I thought it would be jolly good sport to surprise him.'

Age Is No Barrier

Curtis Petty Jr grew up two houses away from Mary Hillman in Flat Rock, Michigan. He often did chores for her – he mowed her lawn and ran errands for her. Eventually the couple decided to get married, much to the fury of Mary's children – and her grandchildren! In fact Curtis was younger than Mary's grandchildren. He was 24 when they got married – his bride was 83.

★　　★　　★　　★

. . . . A High Court judge granted a divorce on the grounds that the plaintiff's wife had acted unreasonably in insisting that, when he came home, he kiss first her, then her sister – and then the cat. . . . .

★　　★　　★　　★

Will You Marry Me – Ouch

The thirteenth-century Tartar princess, Aiyavuk, used to challenge all men who wanted to marry her to wrestle with her. She would agree only to marry the man who could beat her. If the man lost, he had to forfeit 100 horses to the princess. By the time she was eventually beaten, she had acquired 10,000 horses.

Don't Throw Rice At This Wedding

Every day for twenty-two years a Turkish wife served her husband rice twice a day for lunch and supper. She died and the not-too-upset widower met and fell in love with another woman. They have since got married, but before they did he made it a condition that not so much as a grain of rice should ever come into his house again.

I Don't Like My Son-In-Law

A certain English woman did not approve of her son-in-law. He was constantly hard up and her daughter was forced to scrimp and save in order to run the house. The woman offered her daughter £25 if she would leave her husband, and the girl took it, packed her bags and went home to Mummy. At least that's what the heartbroken husband is claiming in court where he is suing the woman for breaking up his marriage.

A Record Divorce

A 32-year-old German woman obtained a divorce from her husband in a Munster court on the grounds that her husband cared more about his collection of records than he did about her. On the day he came home with his 6,000th disc, she decided that that was enough and packed her bags.

She told the judge that the money she gave him to buy clothes for their daughter, Kerstin, was spent on records and he played Rolling Stones records at most inappropriate moments in their married life.

The judge ordered the man to pay £96 a month maintenance to his wife and daughter.

Hearing this, the man muttered 'I could have bought 20 new albums for that.'

His ex-wife has now married another man who doesn't own a record player.

A Kitchen Sink Drama

A Jugoslavian plumber was called out one morning to attend to a blocked sink in the house of a newly married couple. The wife was out when he arrived at the house and when she returned she saw a pair of legs sticking out from under the sink. She thought that they belonged to her husband and being very newly wed did something rather intimate.

The astonished plumber jumped up and banged his head on the sink, knocking himself out. The panic-stricken girl called an ambulance and by the time it came the plumber had recovered consciousness. He was placed on a stretcher and while he was being carried down the stairs one of the stretcher-bearers asked what had happened.

He thought it was so funny that he dropped the stretcher and the unfortunate plumber tumbled down the stairs and broke a leg. The woman's husband was also slightly disturbed – his wife was so upset by what had happened that she withdrew from the marital bed for quite some time, saying that the incident had completely put her off sex.

Limelight Cordial

***.................Being matters of a kind
concerning famous people.....................***

An Ill-Fitted Match

Before she met and married Prince Rainier of Monaco, the late Princess Grace was the well-known film star, Grace Kelly. Throughout the 1950s she was one of the most popular of all Hollywood actresses. Her name was linked romantically with Clark Gable, perhaps the most famous of all post-war Hollywood heartthrobs. It is said that they were on the point of marriage (before Ms Kelly had met her prince) but there was one thing about Mr Gable that she found immensely irritating. He wore a very ill-fitting set of dentures which clicked together whenever he talked.

Lucas — Aid

George Lucas was a young Hollywood film director who had a great idea for a movie. He budgeted it and decided that it could be filmed and edited for around $700,000. He found a backer in United Artists, but they withdrew at the last minute. Eventually, after a great deal of dithering, Universal Pictures backed the movie which went on to be one of their most successful films of the 1970s – *American Graffiti*.

Having finished the movie, Mr Lucas then came up with another idea which he thought was a winner. But even Universal, who had made a lot of money out of *American Graffiti*, turned it down. Eventually Twentieth Century Fox gave him some backing. The men at Universal must still be kicking themselves, for the film eventually grossed more than $300 million even without television and video rights. The film? STAR WARS.

A Painful Experience

John Dillinger, the notorious prohibition gangster, decided to change his fingerprints as a way of evading prosecution. He dipped his fingers into a bowl of acid and went through weeks of agony while his burnt fingers healed. He was more than slightly distressed to find that his 'new' fingerprints were exactly the same as the original ones.

Fair Exchange?

It is the custom when the British Royal Family make State visits overseas or receive foreign Heads of State in Great Britain, that gifts are exchanged. When the Queen and the Duke of Edinburgh visited the Middle East in 1980 they received some beautiful jewellery.

But perhaps the oddest exchange occurred when the British Royal Family gave President Geisel of Brazil and his wife a set of Charles Bentley sketches, a 1648 edition of the *Natural History of Brazil*, a gold and enamel brooch and a carriage clock. In exchange they were presented with six toucans, two giant ant-eaters, a sloth, an armadillo and two black-necked swans.

Sit Up Straight — Forever

Poet Ben Jonson was honoured with a place in Poet's Corner in Westminster Abbey when he died in 1637. Unfortunately the space allocated to him was too small to allow him to be buried in the traditional way – so he was buried in a sitting position.

No Smoking

Annie Oakley, of *Annie Get Your Gun* fame, was one of the most famous marksmen – sorry markswomen – of her day. The crown prince of Germany, Prince William, once allowed her to shoot the ash from a cigarette that he was holding between his lips – from one hundred feet away.

★   ★   ★   ★

. . . .*His Grace, the Archbishop of Canterbury, when he was Bishop of St Albans, used to dread wearing his purple robes in the street in case, if he was knocked down, he should be taken for a transvestite.* . . . .

★   ★   ★   ★

Curtains For The Lady Of Lyons

Lord Lytton, an eminent Victorian literary figure, was very proud of a play he had written called *The Lady of Lyons*. He was convinced that it would run for a respectable length of time. The first night audience was full of literary and society people. After waiting for one hour they all left the theatre as no one could raise the safety curtain. The play never opened.

..AND I'VE SEEN BETTER SAFETY CURTAINS!

But Was It Worth The Money?

James VI of Scotland became King of England on the death of his mother's cousin, Queen Elizabeth. Like many kings, he had his favourites and took them with him when he went to London. Many of his subjects were furious at the privileges that he granted them; feeling was especially strong against the Earl of Stirling who was granted the lands of CANADA for an annual rent of ONE PENNY PER ANNUM.

542

The First US President Served In The British Army

George Washington served for nearly six years in the British Army and rose to the rank of colonel. It was during these years that he became a skilled leader of men, a talent he used to full effect when he led the American Army against the British during the War of Independence.

Rain Stops Play (Almost)

At the Royal Opera House, Covent Garden one night in October 1982 during a performance of Mussorgsky's opera *Khovanshchina*, raindrops were seen falling on the chorus on stage. It seems that the roof, which had recently been repaired, was leaking. The chorus bravely carried on singing.

Coincidentally, thousands of miles away at about the same time, the Queen was visiting the island of Kiribita in the South Seas. For days before her visit the rain had poured down in torrents. In order to ensure that it cleared up for Her Majesty's arrival, the authorities called for a local magician, Iosiabate, to stop the rain. In great secrecy the magician worked his spells and then, by custom, disappeared to make them work. Ten minutes before the Queen stepped ashore, the rain stopped.

Third Time Unlucky

Oliver Cromwell won two of his greatest victories on the third of September, one at Dunbar and one at Worcester. If he began to think of it as his lucky day he was wrong. For he died on the third of September in 1658.

★　★　★　★

. . . . *Lord Nelson chose to be buried in St Paul's Church in London rather than in Westminster Abbey because he believed that Westminster was sinking into the nearby River Thames.* . . . .

At The Count Of Five

Former Prime Minister James Callaghan was usually very kind to press photographers who wanted to snap him. He did not mind stopping for a few extra moments to make sure that the paparazzi had good shots of him.

During a visit to the new Anglo-Australian premises in London in 1978 he was asked to unveil a wooden plaque to commemorate the event. He told the press that he would count to five and then pull the ribbon.

The cameras focused on him and the Prime Minister duly counted one ... two ... three ... four ... five.

When he said 'five' all the flashlights went off and the cameras got a perfect picture of Mr Callaghan pulling the plaque right off the wall.

Shoo, Your Majesty

During a visit to Toronto, the Queen was invited to a horse-shoeing competition. The competitors were instructed that under no circumstances were the horses' rears to be allowed to face Her Majesty, 'for reasons of protocol'. The Queen took great interest in one of the competitors, but her interest was disastrous for the 'smith. As Her Majesty walked around the horse the 'smith was forced to hop around away from her in order to keep to his instructions.

A Deadly Obsession

Sarah Bernhardt, the famous French actress was obsessed with death.

When she was a teenager in Paris one of her favourite occupations was to visit the city morgue and look at the unclaimed corpses of derelicts who had been dragged from the River Seine.

Before she was twenty, she persuaded her mother to buy her a rosewood coffin lined with white satin. She often slept in it and was buried in it when she died aged seventy-nine.

Sorry, Ma'am

Lady Diana Cooper was, and still is, one of the greatest society beauties of the twentieth century. Unfortunately, her sight has failed slightly with the advancing years, and without her glasses she is very short-sighted.

At a concert to celebrate the hundredth birthday of Sir Robert Mayer, Lady Diana found herself talking to a chatty little woman who came up to her and seemed to know her quite well. It was only after a few minutes that Lady Diana realized to whom she was chatting.

'I am sorry, ma'am,' she blurted out, 'I didn't recognize you without your crown,' and desperately tried to bob a curtsy to Her Majesty the Queen.

A Common Investiture

In 1843 William Wordsworth was appointed Poet Laureate. For the ceremony at Buckingham Palace he had to borrow a suit from fellow poet Samuel Rogers. Seven years later, his successor Alfred, Lord Tennyson went to the Palace to be formally appointed to the same honour. He borrowed the same suit from the same poet. Poor Mr Rogers' suit seems to have lasted longer than his poetry.

The Spirit Of The Lord

At the end of the Battle of Culloden in 1746, the devoutly Roman Catholic Lord Strathallan lay mortally wounded on the battlefield. There was no bread or water available for the priest who was attending to administer the Holy Eucharist – so oatcakes were used in place of bread – washed down with malt whisky.

★　　★　　★　　★

. . . . Gustav III of Sweden was so convinced that coffee was poisonous that he ordered a convicted murderer to be executed by drinking cup after cup of it. He didn't die. .

A Floating Experience

Dame Janet Baker is still one of the greatest female singers of today. Although she has retired from the opera stage, she performs frequently at concerts.

Shortly after her retirement from opera, she was singing in Berlioz's *Damnation of Faust* at the Festival Hall in London. The previous evening there had been a Hallowe'en concert during which members of the audience had floated helium-filled balloons around the hall.

Unfortunately, during Dame Janet's performance some of the balloons which had not been removed floated against the lights and exploded with loud bangs. The laughing audience then watched as two of the balloons floated harmlessly down to the auditorium - one fell among the audience and the other into the orchestra. Dame Janet, being a true professional, carried on singing as though nothing had happened.

It Wasn't Cheating – Exactly

Mary Pickford was only five feet high and became the most famous star of her day. Many of the roles that she played were children and the sets of her films were specially built to make her look smaller than she really was. All the furniture and props were made one-third larger than usual, windows and doors were bigger than normal, and doorknobs were placed slightly higher to make it look as if she had to stretch to get up to them.

Reheaded

The Duke of Monmouth was executed in 1685 for his part in the unsuccessful plot to overthrow his uncle, King James II.

It was only after he had been beheaded that it was decided to paint an official portrait of him. His head was skilfully (if ghoulishly) stitched back on to his body. The corpse was then dressed in his own original suit of clothes and posed carefully for the artist.

WE APOLOGISE FOR THE LATE ARRIVAL OF THE 11.35 UNIFORM ON PLATFORM 3...

And The Band Played

The royal train carrying King Edward VII of Great Britain, drew into the station at Rathenau in Germany on February 9, 1909, during the King's state visit. The welcoming military band struck up God Save the King and the reception committee shuffled nervously, expecting the King to step down from the train before the National Anthem was finished. The band played it once through, but there was no sign of the King ... so they played it again, but still the King did not appear. The conductor raised his baton and the Anthem was played for a third time ... and a fourth ... and a fifth ...

Sixteen play-throughs later, the King eventually appeared at the door of the carriage, resplendent in the uniform of Field Marshal of the Imperial German Army. The reason for the delay was that the uniform was so tight the portly King had been struggling to get into it all the time the band had been playing on the platform.

★   ★   ★   ★

. . . . Albert Einstein, one of the most formidably clever men of this century, failed the entrance exam for Zurich Polytechnic when he was sixteen. . . . .

Professional Jealousy?

Ernest Hemingway was a keen amateur boxer and when in Paris often worked out with a fellow American called Morley Callaghan.

One day when the two were getting ready to box at the American Club, fellow writer Scott Fitzgerald stopped by and Hemingway asked him to keep time.

The first round began and Hemingway and Callaghan were evenly matched. After three minutes, Fitzgerald called time and allowed the usual minute's rest before beginning the second

round. The fight began to go in Callaghan's favour, and he drew some blood from the American writer. This infuriated Hemingway who began desperately to counter-attack, but Callaghan was more than a match for him.

Fitzgerald was so spellbound by the fight that he forgot all about the stop-watch in his hand, until after about four minutes Hemingway was knocked to the ground. He yelled out that he had let the round go on far too long and Hemingway, picking himself up, shouted, 'All right, Scott. If you want to see me get the hell knocked out of me just say so. Only don't say that you made a mistake.'

Prince Uncharming

The young man walking along one of Monte Carlo's exclusive beaches recognized the beautiful television and film star relaxing on her own in the Mediterranean sun. He had read that her romance with one of Hollywood's most famous Romeos was in shreds and thought that he might be able to ingratiate himself into her company.

He sat down and had a waiter page him – Prince Urbano Barberini. The actress was impressed when she saw the handsome prince answer the paging call and the two struck up an instant friendship.

She was bowled over by his charming manners and the friends whose names he dropped into the conversation – including the daughters of the local royal family. For three days the two were inseparable, lunching and dining together.

They even flew to Paris, the actress picking up the bills all the way. It was only there that she discovered that her prince was, in fact, a nineteen-year-old ne'er-do-well with not an ounce of royal blood in his veins. She prefers not to talk about the incident today.

★　　★　　★　　★

. . . . *In 1857 the French poet Baudelaire was fined for publishing six obscene poems in* **Les Fleurs du Mal.** *He was later pardoned – in 1949, 82 years after his death.* . . . .

★　　★　　★　　★

Not Again, Crew

The crewmen of the *Bounty* were not the only ones who mutinied against the infamous Captain Bligh. When he later became Governor of Australia, he did his best to eliminate rum smuggling. A rebellion resulted from his high-handed attitude and the officers of the New South Wales Corps arrested Bligh and held him prisoner until a replacement governor arrived in Australia the following year.

A Sentimental Phonebox

A very famous Welsh pop-singer who now lives and works mainly in the United States grew up in comparative poverty in a small Welsh town where very few people had the telephone installed in their houses. When he wanted to call his girlfriend, now his wife, he had to use a callbox on the corner, and very often the couple used the box to carry on their romance if there was nowhere else to go.

When he bought a huge mansion in Bel-Air, California he contacted the council of his home town, bought the telephone box from them and had it flown over to America and installed in his $4,000,000 residence.

A Really Quick Worker

Enid Blyton was one of the most popular children's authors of her generation. Her books still sell in vast quantities, more than fifteen years after her death. She wrote more than 600 books in her lifetime and was an amazingly quick worker.

But her agent did not realize just how quick until one Friday afternoon when he telephoned her and asked if he could come down and see her that evening to discuss some business. She said that it would not be convenient as she was planning to start one of her well-known Famous Five books that day and she planned her whole weekend around her work schedule; why didn't he, she said, come down the following Thursday for lunch? He agreed to do so and turned up on the appointed day.

'I'm so glad you came today,' she said when he arrived. 'We can kill two birds with one stone.'

At which she gave him her new manuscript, which she had not started until after she had talked to him the previous Friday. It was a 50,000 word manuscript which was duly submitted to her publisher who produced it without changing so much as one comma.

★   ★   ★   ★

. . . .*Henry VIII loved gambling but was often short of money to pay his gambling debts. He once lost the bells of Saint Paul's Church.* . . . .

Odd Bods

*.................Being matters of a medical
or physical nature..*

Nor Yet A Drop To Drink

A 35-year-old Somerset man has, as part of a strange diet, to eat lots and lots of juice-bearing fruits and vegetables, such as apples, oranges and tomatoes. Nothing odd about that you may say; after all, many diets specify large intakes of fruit.

But the reason for this one is that the unfortunate man is allergic to all liquids – including water. He last drank a glass in 1980 and it made him terribly ill.

Some friends gave him a bottle of special mineral water. He took a sip which immediately gave him a dreadful headache and affected his legs so badly that he could not walk for the rest of the day.

So he's sticking to his odd diet until doctors work out a cure for him.

It's A Boy . . .

Little Gregory was a healthy baby boy. EVERYTHING about him was perfectly normal. When he was thirteen months old, he had to be taken into hospital for a hernia operation. Doctors discovered that a vital piece of the little boy's identity was in fact an enlarged piece of a little girl's identity and Gregory was actually a girl. He ... sorry she, is now called Marjorie.

All Join In The Last Verse

When a missionary called Herr Schwartz died in Delhi at the end of the nineteenth century, a large crowd turned up for his funeral, so highly regarded was he.

Herr Schwartz had specified in his will that his favourite hymn was to close the ceremony. His wishes were duly respected and the congregation, many of them openly moved, began to sing the hymn.

When they reached the last verse, they were thunderstruck to hear Herr Schwartz's voice coming from the coffin, joining in the singing. He had been incorrectly certified as dead, and came to just in time.

Something Nasty Under The Sink

Before moving to Atlanta, Georgia, a certain Mr Rodrique used to rent an apartment in Hamden, Connecticut. He occasionally took his work home as he found he did not have enough time where he worked to do everything that he wanted to. When he moved he unfortunately left some of the work behind and the new tenants were horrified when they looked under the sink and found a pair of nicely dissected human arms there. Mr Rodrique is an orthopaedic surgeon and had taken the arms home from Yale School of Medicine because he was not getting enough laboratory time for study. In the haste of packing up and moving he had simply forgotten that the arms were there.

★   ★   ★   ★

. . . . The funny bone is not a bone, but the ulnar nerve which runs in a shallow groove close to the skin on the inside of the elbow. . . . .

★   ★   ★   ★

Don't Be Shy

The nurse in the emergency ward in an Edinburgh hospital was quite used to men being shy when she had to ask them to remove their trousers, but the burly young man who had come in with a badly cut leg was extremely reluctant to do so.

'Come on,' she said, 'I'm a trained nurse and am quite used to this you know.'

'Very well,' said the man eventually, 'but please don't get the wrong impression.'

The nurse watched as the embarrassed man removed his pants to reveal that he was wearing a black suspender belt, holding up dark stockings. He had been dressing to go to a fancy dress party with his wife. He had intended to go as a nurse and had put on the unusual undergarments.

While putting on the dress he had tripped and fallen, cutting his leg very badly. He pulled on a pair of trousers and a sweater and his wife had driven him to hospital forgetting that he was wearing her underwear.

I THINK HE'S GONE OVER THE TOP WITH THAT EYEPATCH AND TELESCOPE!

A Leg Bye

At Greenwich Hospital, a home for retired sailors, two teams organized a cricket match. At the end of the day, the winners had won by 103 runs. Nothing unusual about that, you might say. Well, the losers had all lost an arm – and the winners were all one-legged.

Stand By Your Desks

Two of America's top business executives, the Chairman of Kelloggs and the President of IBM, as well as the Vice-Chairman of the Federal Reserve Board, all had something in common apart from being successful. They all suffered from bad backs, brought about, their osteopaths said, by spending too long each day sitting at their desks.

So, too, did the Chairman of Prudential Insurance Co. of America. He realized that although his dentist stood all day he never suffered from a bad back, so he had a special desk designed for himself that allowed him to work and stand at the same time. It worked so well that the other top executives mentioned did the same.

All now heartily recommend standing desks not just for those with bad backs, but for anyone who does not want to feel physically exhausted at the end of the day.

Thanks To The Cigarettes

The voice of the phenomenally successful *ET* (extra-terrestrial), Steven Spielberg's record-breaking money-spinning film, was something of a problem. Technicians could not come up with a voice to match the appearance of the model star of the film. By pure chance, Mr Spielberg happened to be in a store one day when he heard a lady ordering something. Her voice, he thought, was exactly what he wanted, and so unknown American housewife Pat Welsh's voice became part of the biggest money-making movie of all time. Mrs Welsh used to be a speech trainer – but excessive cigarette smoking caused her voice to crack up, leaving her croaky and gasping for breath – exactly what Mr Spielberg had in mind.

May I Borrow Your Breast, Madam?

A Zimbabwe businessman was attempting to remove a dangerous cobra which had slithered into the engine of his car, when the snake spat at him and with deadly accuracy landed her stinging venom right in his eye. This usually causes blindness.

Fortunately, a lorry driver who had parked nearby saw what had happened and pulled the agonized man into the cabin of his truck, where his wife was breast-feeding her baby. He pushed him over to the astonished woman and told her to squirt some milk into his eyes. This diluted the venom and the 'victim's' eyesight was saved.

Oh Brother

A Moscow woman has given birth to ... wait for it ... sixteen sets of twins. That makes 32 children. As well as seven sets of triplets (another 21) and four sets of quads (another 16). That makes 69 children altogether.

An Odd Mouthful

There are many instances of seeds becoming lodged between the teeth of people whose oral hygiene could be better, and which take root and sprout. But there is only one recorded instance of an unfortunate woman whose fillings are so arranged that when the atmospheric conditions are right, they pick up commercial radio signals, particularly long-wave ones.

A Near Miss

Peter Lenz, a twenty-year-old West German, received his call-up papers one day. He did not relish having to spend two years in the West German Army and he knew that he could only be excused on medical grounds. Fortunately, his girlfriend was diabetic so when he went to the Medical Officer to be examined, he took with him a specimen of her urine. When he was asked to supply a sample, he switched his girlfriend's urine for his own.

He went home confident that he would be told not to report back. He was astonished therefore a few days later to receive a letter telling him that he had been passed fit and to report to his unit.

When he did so, the recruiting officer told him, 'We would have believed that you were diabetic, but not that you're pregnant, too.'

★   ★   ★   ★

.............In 1941 Elaine Esposito of Florida, USA, unfortunately lapsed into a coma. She died without regaining consciousness – 37 years later in 1978.................

★   ★   ★   ★

No Conception

The natives of a part of northern India listened intently as a member of the World Health Organization talked to them about contraception. To demonstrate the use of a condom sheath, the doctor rolled one over a convenient piece of wood. The natives nodded in understanding and the doctor left, convinced that the birth rate in the area, which had been dangerously high, would begin to fall. A few years later he revisited the place and was surprised to see more children than ever before. 'But haven't you been using contraceptives?', he asked the people.

'Yes,' they replied. 'We did as you said but they don't work.'

He asked them to demonstrate how they were being used, and, sure enough, one of the men produced a sheath and ceremoniously rolled it over a convenient piece of wood.

I'll Get You In The End

John Hunter was an eighteenth century surgeon who was keen to dissect the body of a local giant, Charles Byrne, who because of a tumour in his pituitary gland had grown to a height of more than seven feet. Byrne did not like the idea of having his body cut up after death so he refused his permission. Undaunted, Hunter simply hired a private detective to follow Byrne everywhere.

He eventually died of tuberculosis in 1783 and the undertaker was bribed to take the body to Hunter's hospital.

For Love Of A Cuppa

The tea in the hospital where a woman lay waiting for an operation was not to her liking. So, before she was due to be operated on, she got out of bed, went home, made herself a decent cuppa and returned to hospital – all in her dressing gown.

★   ★   ★   ★

.............The normal human body temperature is 98.4°F. The highest temperature where the patient survived is 112°F...

A Varied Diet (Or An Iron Tonic)

In 1960, the Journal of the American Medical Association reported that a patient checked into a hospital to have treatment for a swollen ankle. X-rays revealed that he had swallowed 26 keys, 39 nail files, 88 coins – as well as a three-pound piece of metal.

That's Her Foot

An old lady died after a long illness that necessitated having her foot amputated, in a hospital in Florida. Her body was put into the morgue locker with a plastic bag containing her personal belongings and another containing her foot. A funeral undertaker collected the body and the two bags, not realizing that one of them contained the foot. He took the parcels round to Ada's relatives where her son-in-law reached into the unmarked parcel and withdrew the amputated foot, to his own horror and the screams of his wife and sister-in-law. Embarrassed hospital officials have agreed in an out-of-court settlement to pay more than $10,000 compensation.

Eye, Eye

The eyes are the most sensitive of all the body's organs. It has been estimated that they are capable of differentiating 10 million different shades. The average eye can see an object 4/1000th of an inch long from ten inches away, and some people with extraordinarily good vision can see light shining through a hole 1/6000th of an inch across. People with such excellent sight can recognize human faces from one mile away. Wonderful if you want to avoid someone coming towards you.

★　　★　　★　　★

. . . . When Berkshire mothers-to-be received forms asking if they wanted polio injections, they were amused to see that as well as their age, name and address, they were asked to fill in a box indicating their sex. . . . .

. . . . .An American strong man, has such powerful stomach muscles that when he once had a 104 pound cannon ball fired at him from close range on stage, it did him no harm whatsoever. . . . .

The Ear Fairy

A Northamptonshire woman, who lived in Higham Ferrers, was quite hard of hearing, so in 1979 she went to her doctor and asked to have her ears syringed. The obliging doctor was astonished when he pulled out a baby tooth. It had been there for thirty years. When Janet was five she had lost the tooth and, following the time honoured custom, had put it under her pillow hoping that the tooth fairy would leave the usual sixpence (2.5np). After she fell asleep, the tooth had lodged in her ear, and stayed there for the next thirty years causing her no pain whatsoever.

561

Animal Crackers

.... *Being matters of a kind concerning animals...*

The Call Of The Wild

Noel Macabe of Derbyshire was relaxing one day in his home, listening to a record called *Cry of the Wild Geese*. There was a sudden breaking of glass as a Canadian Goose, eager to find its hidden noisy brothers, crashed through his window. Another two were apparently so overcome that they fell into the garden.

Only The Queen

The queen termite which is about 100 times larger than the other termites and which can lay about 1,000 eggs daily, secretes an acid that makes the other females sterile. If the queen becomes sterile, she is deprived of food and dies. Another female, deprived of the fluid, can then reproduce and become queen.

An Unwanted Passenger

A Midlands businessman was on a trip to Malaysia. He decided to take a few days off and see something of the country so he hired a small pick-up truck to drive from Singapore to Kota Bharu, a trip of around 350 miles.

At first everything went perfectly, but suddenly the weather changed and he found himself in the middle of a tropical storm. Driving became impossible so he pulled into the side of the road and waited until the rain had stopped before driving off again.

A few miles further on, changing gear he felt something warm and smooth move across his wrist. He looked down and saw a large python slithering through a gap in the floorboards. He slammed on the brakes, wanting to get out as fast as possible, but the snake was too quick for him and within seconds had wound itself round his body, squeezing the breath out of him.

The terrified businessman managed to grab the snake's head and tried to smash it against the car window. But the snake was too strong and the man thought he was going to die.

Suddenly he heard a screech of tyres and saw a lorry draw up alongside. The Malaysian driver jumped out and shouted at him to let it go.

The man did so and threw the snake's head away from him. Instantly the lorry driver cut its head off with his sharp knife. He then explained that the snake must have wound itself round the axle when the car had been parked and then got in through the floorboards. Apparently it happens quite often.

The lorry driver then asked if he could take the dead snake with him.

'Whatever for?' asked the businessman.

'Supper,' replied the lorry driver.

* * * *

.............It has been estimated that, between them, all the chickens in the world lay an awful lot of eggs every year – 400,000,000,000 to be precise. ....

565

Dinner Is Served — Woof Woof

The eighth Earl of Bridgewater used to give lavish dinner parties for his best friends. They were all dogs, and were dressed up in silk coats, satin breeches and leather shoes — the same clothes worn by aristocratic Englishmen of the day.

Hopped Off With My Wallet

An Australian farmer found a kangaroo caught in the wire fence around his property. The poor beast was shivering with fear as the kind-hearted farmer took off his waistcoat and slipped it onto the animal — impulsively fitting its paws through the armholes.

He set to work freeing the 'roo, which took about three hours. As soon as it was free, the animal hopped away, still wearing the farmer's waistcoat. He wasn't too upset as it was an old working 'coat anyway. But three hours later, while searching for his wallet, he remembered that it had been in the waistcoat pocket.

So, if you're ever in Australia and see a kangaroo hopping around wearing a waistcoat, try and catch it — it could be well worth your while.

Skunkorella, Or Is It Skunkorissima?

It is well known that the skunk emits a disgusting smell if it is frightened or in danger. At first it will growl and stamp the ground to warn its enemies. But if this is unheeded, the skunk turns its back, lifts its tail and squirts the secretion at its foe. The odour can be smelt half a mile away. The same secretion, with the foul odour removed, is used as a base for making expensive perfumes.

★　　★　　★　　★

. . . .*The rarest dog in the world is the Tahl-Tan bear dog. In 1982 there were only three of them living.* . . . . . .

566

Trapped

The sixteenth century Dean of Hereford, a Dr Price, considered that he was socially superior to the other clergy and so decided that during a regular religious procession he would not walk with the others, but instead would ride on the back of a mare and read his prayer book as he went. Unfortunately a stallion broke loose and mounted the mare, leaving the embarrassed Dean completely trapped by 'horseplay'.

Not Biting Today, Boys

The anglers of the National Ambulance Service Championships held at Kidderminster in 1972 took up their places eager for a good day's fishing. There were two hundred of them altogether. Five hours later, when not one fish had been landed by any of the fishermen, they were told by a local passerby that they were wasting their time – all the fish had been moved to other waters three weeks earlier.

★　　★　　★　　★

.............*In Buenos Aires, a cat called Mincha ran up a tree and stayed there for six years. Whilst up there, she gave birth to three lots of kittens.*.....................

★　　★　　★　　★

Dead Heat

Punters at a New South Wales racecourse cheered wildly as the three leading horses galloped towards the finishing line. None of the horses managed to put in that extra something necessary to win the race and the judges declared a triple dead heat. The race was re-run with only the three joint winners – High Flyer, Loch Lochie and Bardini – running. The expectant racegoers watched astonished as the three horses tied for first place again.

Better Than Paying Taxes

A tribe of Idaho Indians were given complete tax exemption when their lands were confiscated by the American government in the nineteenth century.

All they had to do was present the Governor of the state, once a year, with 20 beaver pelts in lieu of taxes. When beavers became more difficult to trap, this was amended to one deer and a turkey, which are still handed over to this day ...

I wonder if the Chancellor of the Exchequer would be interested in a frozen chicken or something similar.

I Don't Want To Know That

The South-east Asian cave swiftlet makes its nest from its saliva which hardens on the cave walls where the bird lives. It is these nests that are used to make bird's nest soup which is a great delicacy in some parts of the world.

FIRST TIME ANYBODY SENT THE BIRDS NEST SOUP BACK!

Come Home ... By Post

Pigeon racing is a popular sport all over the world. Owners take their birds to pre-arranged places, release them and the pigeons with unerring ability find their way home. In 1953, a keen pigeon fancier released his bird in Pembrokeshire expecting him to be home that evening. Eleven years later the bird turned up dead, in a box bearing a Brazilian postmark.

Snails Save Lives

To determine blood groups, there is a method of extracting a chemical from human blood which, when mixed with a sample of the blood in question will react in a particular way according to the blood group. However, to get enough of the solution a great deal of human blood is required. But fortunately, snails' eggs, which are the size of a pinhead, contain the same chemical – in fact, the blood of five donors would be required to supply the same amount of the chemical as is found in one of the snail's eggs.

He Dyed Hunting

An American millionaire on a deerstalking trip in Scotland decided that his white horse could be seen too easily by the deer. He bought two black dyes from a local hairdresser and set about changing the horse's colour with the aid of two brushes. The operation was successful. The black dye changed the horse's appearance completely. Unfortunately, the dye had such a powerful smell that the deer could smell it miles away, and the luckless millionaire returned empty-handed to America.

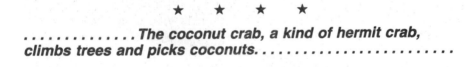

★ ★ ★ ★

............*The coconut crab, a kind of hermit crab, climbs trees and picks coconuts.* ....

★ ★ ★ ★

An Inside Job

The hagfish has a unique way of killing its prey. This eel-like creature ties itself in a loop and attaches itself to a fish's gills by biting it with its sharp teeth. Twisting its knotted body around and around, the hagfish buries itself deeper and deeper into its victim until it is completely inside. Then it begins to eat its prey from the inside until only the skeleton and skin are left.

★   ★   ★   ★

. . . . .The natives of Hawaii call one of the largest of their local fish by the simple name 'O'. By contrast, they call one of the smallest 'homomomonukunukuaguk'. . . . .

★   ★   ★   ★

Roommates Unwanted

Even the cleanest home contains approximately 452 species of assorted insects and vermin. But don't worry. A survey of a house in Kent carried out in 1860 revealed that there were 3,287 assorted 'animals' living there, including pinhole borers, cockroaches, booklice, bookworms, Pharaoh's ants, wasps, houseflies, bluebottles, greenfly, ladybirds, carpet beetles, moths, wood beetles, pipistrelles, bats, mice, rats, dormice, toads, millipedes, cellar beetles, mosquitoes, black beetles, black ants, flourworms, leather beetles, silverfish, steam flies, grain weevils, cheese mites, mealworms, earwigs, woodlice, slugs, earthworms, snails, spiders, firebrats, sparrows, house martins, centipedes . . . and the human owners.

A Balanced Diet

When one of the ostriches in London Zoo died unexpectedly, the keepers decided to hold an autopsy. In its insides were found two handkerchiefs, three gloves, a film spool, part of a plastic comb, the winding key of an alarm clock, part of a rolled gold necklace, two collar studs and a Belgian franc piece.

Hard To Swallow

Vets have often been called out by distressed pet owners when the unfortunate animals have got something stuck in their throat. But Dr Deke Beusse was surprised when he was asked to remove a fish that got caught in the throat of a Tiger Shark.

High Freeze

One morning in 1974, an American housewife was astonished to see frozen ducks fall out of the sky in Arkansas. It turned out that a flock of ducks had flown so high that they had frozen to death in the air.

A B. . . . . . Painful Death

A recent Hollywood disaster movie about a killer swarm of bees is based on fact. A beekeeper in Sao Paolo, Brazil decided to cross gentle European bees with larger, more aggressive ones. His idea was to improve productivity, but unfortunately the vicious tendencies of the African bees were stronger than the European ones. Twenty-six swarms escaped and, led by their African Queens, began to attack animals and occasionally human beings, with fatal consequences.

Here, Boyo

£65 seemed reasonable for the trained sheepdog being advertised in a farming magazine. At least the Surrey farmer who stumped up thought so. Unfortunately for him the dog had been trained in Wales and could only respond to commands (other than whistles) in the Welsh language.

★ ★ ★ ★

. . . . When cats hear a dog barking, the soles of their paws very often perspire. . . . .

Breed Like Rabbits

Rabbits are the biggest animal pests in Australia. There are literally millions upon millions of them. They are all descended from six rabbits, three males and three females, who were let loose in the 1850s.

ER...I THINK I'LL ATTACK RUSSIA INSTEAD...

Not Tobite, Josephine

After the wedding celebrations were over and Napoleon had withdrawn to the bridal chamber with his bride, Josephine Beauharnais, her pet dog, mistaking the Little Corporal's amorous advances on his mistress as an assault, jumped on to the bed and bit him.

★   ★   ★   ★

. . . . *Sea hedgehogs, usually about a foot long, can kill sharks more than twenty feet long.* . . . .

Compassionate Leave Granted

Billy Smart, the late circus owner, had a grandson who became very fond of a whale that was part of the Smart menagerie. The young man was eventually called up to do his National Service. Unfortunately, the whale began to pine for him. Mr Smart contacted the authorities and requested that his grandson be given compassionate leave. The request was granted and the youth and the whale were happily reunited.

That's A Nice Insect You're Wearing

Women of Cuba have a most unusual way of making themselves attractive. They hang fireflies on their dresses and around their necks as decoration. Actually, the firefly is not a fly, it's a beetle. Inside its stomach there are five chemicals. When oxygen enters the firefly's body, it stimulates a nerve reaction which causes the chemicals to combine. This makes the firefly glow. A few seconds later another chemical combines with the other five and switches the fly off. Men travelling in tropical forests sometimes collect fireflies in jars and use them as emergency torches.

Roses For The Lady

Like most other ladies, a resident of Canterbury called Killa, enjoys being presented with a lovely bunch of roses now and again. But unlike most women, Killa eats them. She also has a taste for expensive chocolates and is always happy with a bunch of celery. Killa is a 60 pound female gorilla. One of her male companions in the zoo where she lives enjoys the odd gallon of beer.

★　　★　　★　　★

. . . .*In Kuala Lumpur an elephant once beat a team of 100 farmers at a tug o'war contest.* . . . .

573

Hundreds Of Thousands Of Ducks

Le Tour D'Argent is one of the smartest restaurants in Paris. Since it first opened in 1582 the rich and famous have flocked to it to sample the renowned cooking and superb wines. In 1890 Frederic Delair became Master Chef and began a tradition which is still in existence today. The speciality of the house is duck, and he decided that every duck that is served should be served with a card giving the bird's number.

In October 1982, the restaurant's 400th anniversary, the 600,000th duck was served.

★　　★　　★　　★

. . . . *During the All-Ireland Frog Swallowing Championships, John Macnamara of County Clare was declared the winner after swallowing five live frogs in 65 seconds.* . . . .

★　　★　　★　　★

He Had No Right To Be There

In 1872 the viceroy of India was on a hunting trip and one night when he went to bed he woke up when he felt something heavy on his body. He opened his eyes and saw a huge cobra coiled up on his chest.

He knew that if he moved the cobra would strike and kill him, so he lay dead still for almost an hour, when suddenly someone came into his tent. The man saw the snake and left the tent. A few minutes later he returned carrying a jugful of steaming hot milk. He put it down as close as he could to the cobra's head and within a few minutes the snake, sensing the warmth coming from the pot, uncoiled itself from the viceroy's chest and slithered into the jug. The man rammed the lid on and trapped the cobra.

The viceroy was astonished when his saviour asked him to say nothing about the escapade. It turned out that he was a wandering thief who had been looking for rich pickings from the viceroy's camp.

574

Two Whites Don't Make A Black

It is not possible for two pure white dogs to produce a litter of black pups, according to a judge in a recent litigation suit.

A wealthy 74-year-old woman owned a beautiful white poodle called Caro. She paid £100 to a breeder in Wales to have Caro mated with his pedigree white poodle. She drove Caro up to his stud in Wales and the dogs were 'introduced'; but there was no interest on the part of either party.

After the first meeting, the woman told the court that she had been asked to wait outside the kennel and the breeder took the two dogs into a clipping room.

He came out of the clipping room 30 minutes later and said that the mating had occurred. Nine weeks after the breeding session Caro gave birth to six jet black puppies.

The owner of the stud, after testifying that the two white poodles had mated, suggested to the court that Caro had been unfaithful to her pedigree.

The judge said that this was unlikely as the dog was kept, alone, behind two six-foot fences. He awarded the woman more than £1,000 damages as black poodles have less than half the market value of white ones.

★　★　★　★

. . . . There's a South American earthworm that's over six feet long. . . . .

★　★　★　★

Here Pet

Gator Bait of Houma, Los Angeles, California was slightly worried when her grandmother refused to listen to her worries that her baby daughter, who was at the crawling stage, might be injured by gran's pet. Grandma has had her pet for two years and it has complete freedom of the garden. She feeds him every day, plays with him affectionately and says that he would not hurt a fly. Gator is not convinced. You see Cajun, the pet, is a five foot long, sharp toothed ALLIGATOR.

Killed By A Bite

A fourteen-year-old cattleboy called Edward, who worked in Richmond, South Africa, was walking through the plantation one day when he tripped over what he thought was a rope. Seconds later he was horrified to see a huge python begin to coil itself around his legs.

The boy could do nothing as the snake coiled itself right up his legs and round his chest, crushing every ounce of air out of his lungs as it did so. As the horrendous coils circled towards his throat the boy realized that there was only one thing to do.

He managed to snap at the snake with his teeth. The first time the snake slipped out of the boy's mouth, but at the second attempt he got a good bite and managed to hold on.

The harder he bit, the less the snake squeezed. It stopped shaking its head and the boy chewed on. Eventually the snake stopped squeezing completely and slid to the ground. Dead.

Police were astonished a few minutes later when the boy calmly walked into the police station and told them what he had done. They refused to believe him until he took them outside and showed them the body of the snake with its head almost chewed off.

A Shaggy Dog Story

Neighbours of Ginete Franke in Cleveland, Ohio were distressed by the smell that often came from her house. 'It's only the dogs,' she would say reassuringly. 'I'll see to it.' But the stench got no better so residents called in the police. When police knocked on her door the smell was so overpowering that several policemen were sick. But Mrs Franke had been telling the truth – it was the dogs causing the smell – all 127 of them.

A Lot Of Litter

In 1944, an American foxhound called Lena began to give birth to a litter of pups. Her anxious owners watched with delight as the first pup emerged, then another, then another, then another, then another ... there were 23 altogether.

★ ★ ★ ★

. . . . .The eagle can see straight ahead, although its eyes are on the side of its head. . . . .

★ ★ ★ ★

A Secured Loan

The manager of a Detroit Bank was quite willing to lend the pretty woman sitting across the desk from him the $1,000 she requested, but had to ask for some security. 'No problem,' the prospective borrower replied. 'I'll be back in a moment.' A few minutes later she returned with the collateral – a 25-pound tiger cub called Tinker Bell. The woman was an animal trainer. The tiger cub was insured at Lloyds in London and she told the bank manager that the loan would be repaid from payments she received from people who rented the tiger cub. She got her loan.

Worm Eats Dog (Biscuits)

Researchers at Dublin University wanted to do some work that needed woodworms – plump ones. The only ones that were available were too thin so Dr Sean Thompson, leader of the team, fed them on dog biscuits. Within one month they had grown to twenty times the size of an average woodworm.

WOOF WOOF!

You've Heard Of Raining Cats And Dogs...But

In 1973 the villagers of Brignoles in France were astonished when there was a freak storm and thousands of toads fell out of the sky. They had been whisked up into the sky by a whirlwind which blew across their nearby breeding ground, and, having blown itself out, left the toads to fall to the ground over Brignoles.

The Word Of The Lord Spreads

A shark caught in Antigual waters was found to have some odd items in its stomach when local natives cut it open. There was a human skull, a pair of suede shoes, and a copy of the Gospel According to St John printed on polythene.

Birds VC

In the grounds of All-Hallows-by-the-Tower, in London, there is a strange memorial. It was dedicated in 1946 by the then vicar the Rev. P. B. Clayton, and was organized by a Miss Nancy Price.

The memorial takes the form of a small rowan tree trunk with forked branches set in a rough stone base which forms two pools for water. Between the branches at different heights are wooden troughs for crumbs to feed the birds. On its branches are carved wooden pigeons, canaries and sparrows.

The memorial is dedicated to the memory of the pigeons that died on active service during the Second World War. Apparently, in one operation 27,000 pigeons were used, and it was a pigeon that brought the first news of the fall of Tunis to the British Army Headquarters in North Africa.

★　★　★　★

.............The dragonfly flies with its legs together forming a basket in which to capture insects that it eats while in the air.....................................

578

Strange Tastes

Some dogs are said to take exception to postmen and other
people who invade their territory. Others seem to develop
fixations for motor car wheels and if off the leash, tend to chase
them. But Otto, a bulldog in Virginia Beach, Vermont has
something against skateboards. Woe betide any unaware boy or
girl 'boarding through Otto's territory. His score so far: an
uncountable number of boards – two broken arms, one fractured
leg and a smashed kneecap – as well as quite a few bloody
noses.

A Lion's Tale

Judson Brown, a zookeeper at Prospect Park in Brooklyn was
attacked by a lion that had somehow managed to escape from
its cage. The animal was mauling Mr Brown on the arm and
hand and would undoubtedly have killed him were it not for
quick-thinking Dennis McCarthy who happened to be passing
the bloody scene. He simply whipped off his belt and beat the
lion once across its back. The lion was so astonished that it
stopped its attack and the lucky zookeeper was pulled free.

★　　★　　★　　★

.............*An American airliner flying at 20,000 feet
over South America was hit by a condor.*................

★　　★　　★　　★

Cat And Mouse

The family cat of M. and Mme Blond of Nevers in France was a
happy, peace-loving animal who would never do any harm. Until
one night when the family were seated around the television
watching a Tom and Jerry cartoon. All of a sudden, during a
sequence when Tom was chasing Jerry, the cat went berserk
and attacked the family. When police were called, the cat was a
spitting ball of fury being kept at bay by M. Blond with the aid of
a chair. The unfortunate animal refused to calm down and had to
be destroyed.

In A Word

.................Being matters of a verbal, linguistic
or etymological nature........,..........................

Well Named

A Montreal bank-clerk, appropriately named Gerry Cash, fell in love with one of his attractive colleagues and was delighted when she accepted his proposal of marriage. So Mr and Mrs Cash now work side by side in the bank. She was actually quite relieved. Her married name, Cash, is much more acceptable than her maiden name – Crook.

Tea-Clipping Whisky

One of the most famous export brands of Scotch whisky is named Cutty Sark – all because the patron of a lunch club in London won a bet.

Over three hundred years ago the firm of Berry Brothers and Rudd opened a coffee mill at St James's Street in London. (It is still there.) They also served fine Scotch whisky to such famous people as Lord Byron and Beau Brummel – the whisky was simply called Berry Bros Scotch Whisky.

One day in the 1870s when members were having a luncheon party it was suggested that a more suitable name could be found for the popular drink. One of the guests had just won heavily on a race between some tea clippers coming back from India to England with their cargoes – the winner was called Cutty Sark.

The other guests gave this suggestion their unanimous approval, and an artist who was present immediately tore a sheet of yellow paper from his pocket and sketched the beautiful ship and her name. Both the name and the drawing are still used today.

Abuse Of Language

A New York surgeon was interviewed outside Belle Vue Hospital after an old lady of eighty-two had been knocked down while waiting for a bus, and had tragically lost her leg. The interviewer asked the surgeon if there was any likelihood of the limb being sewn back on to her body. 'No,' the surgeon replied. 'We have examined the lady and the leg and they are not candidates for reattachment.'

I Command It

People who bought an edition of the Bible printed in 1631 by Barker and Lucas were surprised (some may have been pleasantly so) when they came to the following verse in the Book of Exodus:

20:14 *Thou shalt commit adultery.*

The printers had inadvertently left out the word 'not'. The English monarch, Charles I, was horrified, recalled all 1,000 copies and fined the printers £3,000.

Revenge From Beyond The Grave

The sixteenth-century Countess of Seafield was not amused when a local clairvoyant known as the Brahan Seer, told her that her husband had a mistress in Perth. She was so angry that she ordered that the unfortunate man be boiled in tar. As he was about to be cast into the bubbling liquid, he prophesied that the line of Seafields would die out with a deaf and dumb girl, and that the estate would be inherited by a 'white-clothed lassie who would kill her sister.'

Two centuries later Francis Mackenzie, who was last in the line, was struck deaf and dumb. His eldest daughter, recently widowed, inherited the estate and arrived to claim her inheritance wearing white from head to toe. Later while she was out driving, the horses reared up and her sister was thrown from the carriage and died instantly.

★　　★　　★　　★

. . . .*Salt was so valuable in Roman times that Julius Caesar paid his soldiers in salt rather than money. The Latin word for salt is 'sal', thus giving us the word 'salary'.* . . . .

★　　★　　★　　★

Sent To The Louis

Many people think that the traditional French method of
executing criminals was named after Joseph Guillotin, who
invented it. Wrong. It *was* named after him, but not because he
invented it but because he was the man who recommended that
a device for executing people swiftly and as painlessly as
possible be developed. It was actually invented by Dr Antoine
Louis and was originally called the *Louisette*. But somehow being
sentenced to death by *Louisette* does not have the same sinister
ring to it.

★　　★　　★　　★

. . . . *The Indian name for Lake Webster in Massachusetts is Chargogatmanchaugagochaubunagungamaug,
which, when translated, means 'You fish on your side, we
fish on our side, nobody fishes in the middle.'* . . . .

★　　★　　★　　★

There Are No Such Things As Sardines

When you buy a can of sardines you are not getting any particular kind of fish. Sardine is the name given to several different species of herring which are caught when young, and packed in flat tins for sale in shops and supermarkets around the world. In California the sardine is usually a young pilchard. In England it is usually the young of the Cornish pilchard and in Norway, sardines are normally sprats or brisling.

Sounds Painful

The Japanese words for 'four' and 'death' sound almost identical. So, too, do their words for 'nine' and 'suffering'. Because of any unfortunate confusions resulting from this, many hospitals in Japan do not have any wards numbered 4 or 9.

A Gobbledygook Explanation

The editor of the National Taxpayer's Union, an American organization that takes a keen interest in how the taxpayer's money is spent, is up in arms at a grant of $45,000 to the National Science Foundation. The latter august body want to study how the Caribbean lizard competes with birds and other lizards for food. They freely admit that the lizard has already been extensively studied but justify the grant as follows:

> *The Research is pertinent to applied ecology because the government of the Lesser Antilles is attempting to inventory its biotic wealth preparatory to the establishment of a cohesive national party policy.*

Mr Eric Meltzer, the editor, said in reply, 'Instead of funding such a programme we should do basic research on what motivates bureaucrats to fund such unnecessary projects.'

The Most Famous Cook In America Doesn't Exist And Never Did!

The manufacturers of Gold Medal flour decided to publicize their product by publishing a picture puzzle in several national magazines. When it was solved, the puzzle showed a scene depicting customers carrying sacks of Gold Medal flour to their lorries.

More than 30,000 people sent in the completed puzzle and, along with the answer, many of them sent in questions about baking with the flour. Each letter received a personal reply but the question of who was to sign it soon arose. A well-loved secretary-director of the company had recently retired, so it was decided to use her surname and a cosy-sounding first name was then added.

Since then the name has been seen on cookery books, household hint books, recipe cards, and there is a department of five specially-trained correspondents, 23 trained home economists using five special kitchens who constantly test products and create new recipes bearing it. They receive between four and five thousand letters every month as well as 1,200 guests from all over the world.

The name that was made up to answer all these questions so long ago is now one of the most famous in all America – Betty Crocker.

★　　★　　★　　★

. . . . *'I would rather,' declared a distinguished academic, when addressing a gathering in Kentucky in 1956, 'sit at the feet of the Lord than dwell in the house of the mighty.' Whereupon he promptly died.* . . . .

★　　★　　★　　★

. . . . *In 1945 the bursar of Magdalen College, Oxford was named Cook, the cook was named Butler and the butler was called Chamberlain.* . . . .

★　　★　　★　　★

Odd Censorship

The Turkish government was very sensitive about allowing reports of foreign events to appear uncensored in the newspapers. When the American President William MacKinley was assassinated in 1901, it was reported that he had died of anthrax, but this was nothing compared to the official version of the deaths of the King and Queen of Serbia who were assassinated in 1903. Turkish readers were very sorry to read that their Royal Highnesses had died of indigestion.

A Curate's Egg

Samuel Johnson, the English lexicographer, was once sent a manuscript from an unknown author and asked for his advice. The great man wrote back:

Your manuscript is both good and original. But the part that is good is not original, and the part that is original is not good.

A Dash Of Sandys, Sir?

Over one hundred years ago a British nobleman, Sir Duncan Sandys, returned from India where he had been Governor of Bengal. He brought back with him the recipe for a sauce made of several Indian spices.

When he returned home he sought out two chemists near where he lived, gave them the recipe and asked them to make some for his own use. As a lavish host, Sir Duncan entertained often and well and the sauce became much talked about.

Eventually the two chemists asked his permission to manufacture the sauce on a small scale for sale. Sir Duncan gave his permission and today the sauce is used throughout the world, still made to the treasured secret recipe. The two chemists decided to name the sauce after the county in which they lived. Worcestershire. And the chemists' names? Mr John W. Lee and his partner, William Perrins.

Thank Goodness She Wasn't Called Boneta

The word 'money' comes to us from the Latin. The ancient Romans used to store their gold and silver in the temple of the goddess Juno Moneta - hence 'money'. Just think; had she been called Juno Boneta, we would be walking around with bunnies in our pockets.

A Lot To Do In Such A Short Time

A North of England newspaper once advised its readers that if news of a nuclear attack being launched broke, they should paint their windows with a mixture of whitewash and curdled whey in order to deflect dangerous rays, and soak their furniture in a solution of borax and starch to prevent fire. What the readers were expected to do with the remainder of the four-minute-warning, the paper did not say. Try the crossword, perhaps?

You're Not Going To Believe This

Scott Raoul Sor-Lokken has a pretty daughter called Snow Owl. At least that's what she's called by her family and friends. But, her real name is something very different.

Scott was so upset by government bureaucracy when he filed his tax return the year that Snow Owl was conceived that he decided to throw a spanner into the works and cause some confusion when he registered her name.

At first the Washington State registry office refused to accept the name, but Scott insisted and said that that was the name he had chosen for his daughter and that was the name he wanted on her birth certificate.

He was so adamant that the department relented – very reluctantly.

Not surprising really when you read Snow Owl's official name – Snowowlwolfeschlegelsteinhausenbergerdorffvoralternwarenge wissenhaftschaferswessenschafewarenwohlgepflegeundsorfg-faltigkeitbeschutzenvonangreifendurchahrraubgierigfeiene-welchevoralternzwolftausendjahresvorandieerscheinenvanderer-steerdemenschderraumschiffgebrauchlichtalsseinursprung-vonkraftgestartseinlangefahrthinzwischensternartigraumaufder-suchenachdiesternwelchegenabtbewohnbarplanetenkreise-drehensichundwohinderneurassevonverstandigmenscklich-keitkinntefortplannenundsicherfreuenanlebenslanglichfreude-undrehemitnichteinfurchtvorangreifenvonandererintelligent-geschopfsvonhinzwischensternartigraum Ellen Georgianna Sor-Lokken.

A Bad Choice Of Words

In Hollywood, during the shooting of a film, it used to be customary for parties of sightseers to be allowed into the set when shooting was finished for the day. They could wander around and, if any of the actors were there, could feel free to approach them. One famous English actor was approached by such a party. His latest film, *Witness for the Prosecution*, had just been released. An effusive American lady walked up to him and gushingly said, 'Oh Mr ...... I just loved your performance in *Witness for the Prostitution*.'

Enigma Variations

..................Being matters of a supernatural, coincidental or mysterious nature..........................

The Curse Of Tutankhamun

Most people scoff at the idea of curses coming true, but the events that followed the opening of Tutankhamun's tomb by Howard Carter in 1922 may make them think twice before laughing.

The story of the curse began when the last man climbed out of the tomb. It is said that a sudden sandstorm blew up and that the men in the party saw a hawk, the ancient royal symbol of Egypt, fly overhead.

Local Egyptians took this to mean that the spirit of the dead king had left his tomb, cursing those who had opened it. Five months later, the man who had financed the expedition, Lord Carnarvon, was bitten on the cheek by a mosquito. Normally nothing too serious! But the bite became infected and Carnarvon caught pneumonia and died in an Egyptian hospital.

At the precise moment of his death all the lights in Cairo went out, and thousands of miles away at the Carnarvon mansion in Hampshire, his dog began to howl – and died that night. Doctors who examined the mummified body of Tutankhamun reported that he had a small depression on his cheek, just like a mosquito bite, in exactly the same spot where Carnarvon had been bitten.

Strange deaths also befell many people who visited the tomb. Lord Carnarvon's half brother died of a burst appendix. An Egyptian prince whose family claimed descent from the pharaohs was murdered in London and his brother committed suicide. An American railway tycoon caught a cold while at the tomb and died of pneumonia.

The man who helped Howard Carter to catalogue the items found in the tomb committed suicide, and a few months later his father jumped to his death from a balcony at his London flat. There was an alabaster vase from the tomb in the room that he jumped from.

In 1966 the government of Egypt agreed to lend the treasures to France for an important exhibition. The Director of Antiquities fought against the decision, for he had dreamed that he would die if he allowed the treasures to go out of Egypt. When he left the last meeting, still trying to make the authorities change their minds, he was knocked down by a car and died two days later.

And Howard Carter who was the first man into the tomb? He died – of natural causes – in 1939.

Not Another One

In 1982 Helen Patterson won the £983 jackpot in a Scottish bingo club. Her husband won £13.00 on a fruit machine on the same night. A few days later, Mrs Patterson had three small bingo wins and her husband took another £20.00 from the fruit machine. A few weeks later Helen had another win, taking their joint winnings up to £1,900.

A few days later Robert Patterson, no relation, won £70.00 and several days after that his wife hit the jackpot with a bingo win of £853. The next day, she had four more small wins.

Later in the same week, an elderly lady was being presented with a cheque for £500 which she had just won. The manager jokingly asked her if her name was Patterson. The lady looked completely taken aback. 'No', she said. 'But it used to be. It was my maiden name.'

★ ★ ★ ★

.............In Redruth, Cornwall in 1906, two cars crashed into each other. Nothing unusual in that you may say – but they were the only two cars in the town at the time...

★ ★ ★ ★

.............The author of several books promoting clean living, including one called Nutrition for Health, *died of malnutrition...*

★ ★ ★ ★

Where Exactly Are We?

Walpole in Somerset is a tiny hamlet whose residents are up in arms against the local council. The hamlet was not listed on the last official census and is not on any maps. The postal address is Dunball, a nearby village. Ecclesiastically it is in the parish of Pawlett. Telephone numbers for the hamlet are coded under Puriton and it has recently been earmarked as an official rubbish tip.

An Unfair Fare

An Athenian taxi driver was more than a little surprised when the man he had stopped to pick up gave him his own address as his destination. The taxi driver did not say anything, but drove the passenger as requested. He got out of the car and let himself into the driver's house with a key. A few minutes later, the driver crept into his house and found his passenger and his wife making love. Out of the thousands of taxis in Athens, he would have picked that one.

Home Sweet Home

A Margate couple were in Wales on holiday. They decided to take a day trip on a British Rail Mystery Tour. As the train travelled towards its secret destination, the countryside became more and more familiar and the couple realized that they were about to arrive at their own home town.

594

Too Close For Comfort

On April 14, 1912, the 'unsinkable' *Titanic* struck an iceberg on her maiden voyage. It was packed with rich passengers, many of whom lost their lives as there were too few lifeboats to accommodate them all.

In 1898 a novel was published, called *Futility*, by journalist Margan Robertson.

It was about an unsinkable liner sailing from Southampton on her maiden voyage. Full of rich passengers, it struck an iceberg and sank killing many of those on board. The name of the ship in Robertson's novel was *Titan*.

Six years before *Futility* was published W. T. Stead, a well-known reporter, wrote a short story which also amazingly foreshadowed the sinking of the *Titanic*. Stead was one of the 1,513 who died when the great ship sank.

Twenty-three years after the *Titanic* went down, a young seaman called William Reeves was standing watch on a steamer bound from Tyneside to Canada.

The water was calm and there was no sign of any icebergs, but Reeves couldn't help but worry about what had happened to the *Titanic*, which had gone down in similar circumstances, and he wanted to shout a warning. The only thing that prevented him from doing so was the ribbing that his shipmates would give him.

Suddenly he remembered the date, April 14. It was his birthday.

Not only that, but it was the date that the *Titanic* sank – the very day that Reeves had been born.

Unable to stop himself he shouted a warning and the ship came to a halt a few yards away from a huge iceberg that loomed high above the ship.

The ship's name? *The Titanian*.

A Strange Premonition

A Gottenburg seaman often dreamt that he would die on his fiftieth birthday. The day came and he was happy to survive it – so happy that he gave a delayed birthday party to celebrate the fact that his dream had not come true. Unfortunately he got exceedingly drunk, had a heart attack and died.

Family Purse-uit

Alexi Sogmorov was cleaning the roads in Moscow one day when he found a purse with some money in it.

Being honest, he decided to return it to the owner whose address, but no name, was in the purse.

He was more than a little surprised when the door was opened by his sister Svetlana whom he had not seen for fourteen years.

What Happened To Them?

In 1858 a group of 18 Englishmen landed in Roanoke Island near the coast of North Carolina. Encouraged by Sir Walter Raleigh's example of two centuries before, they built a fort and houses, and planted crops. But hostile Indians made life impossible for them and they were forced to return home. The following year, another group re-settled on the island. After a few weeks the leader of the group, John White, sailed back to England to get more provisions. When he returned, all he found was a mysterious word carved on a tree:

CROATOAN

There was absolutely no sign of any of the settlers.

Well Oil Be Blowed

A bomber crew who happened to be carrying a chaplain among its numbers ran out of fuel and was forced to land on a Japanese-held island in the Pacific ocean. The crew resigned themselves to the fact that they would be captured and imprisoned by their Japanese enemies. The chaplain, a firm believer in the power of prayer, knelt down and asked his God to help them.

The next morning one of the crew felt a strong compulsion that he should go and take a walk down the beach. When he did so he found a huge drum of aviation fuel bobbing in the waves of the incoming tide. He ran back to the rest of the men and got them to help him carry the oil back to the plane. A few minutes later the bomber took off and returned to base.

They took note of the name on the drum and when they were safe they made inquiries about it. It turned out that the fuel had been part of a cargo that had been thrown overboard from an American barge after a Japanese attack. All the other drums had been lost, but this one had floated for over 1,000 miles past more than twenty other islands and miraculously turned up where it was sorely needed.

★　★　★　★

. . . . Residents of Panther, West Virginia swear they know when a fire is about to break out because they see Big Red, the fire truck, racing down the street – which is strange, as Big Red went out of service several years ago and sits rusting and unable to move in the Volunteer Fire Department. . . . .

★　★　★　★

A Lot Of Coincidence

At an auction to raise funds for the Society for the Preservation of Rural Wales, a friend of Baroness White the organizer, decided to bid for five machine tapestries showing views of Venice and London.

He was surprised when he got the lot for £50.00. He had decided to spend more than that in aid of what he considered was a good cause, but everything else he bid for went for more than he was prepared to pay.

He was just about to leave when he saw two bottles of his favourite wine, a 1955 Gevrey Chambertin, were about to go under the hammer. His bid was accepted and he returned home quite happy with all he had bought.

The next morning he telephoned the Baroness to thank her for a pleasant evening and to tell her what he had bought.

'How very peculiar,' said Lady White. 'I was staying with friends last week and told them about the auction. They insisted on giving me something for it – five machine tapestries of Venice and London and two bottles of 1955 Gevrey Chambertin.'

Mr Otis Regrets...

One cold, blustery night towards the end of the last century, the British Ambassador to France, Lord Dufferin was visiting Ireland. One night he was unable to sleep. He left his bed and drew back the curtains from the window to see if the strong winds were doing any damage to the well-kept gardens. He was startled to see someone carrying a coffin across the lawn. He tapped loudly on the window and the man turned round. He had the most hideous face Lord Dufferin had ever seen – 'as if', he said to his wife, 'a long dead corpse had risen from the grave.'

A few years later Dufferin was back in Paris and had to go to a diplomatic reception in the Grand Hotel, which had recently installed one of the new-fangled lifts. He went to enter the lift and drew back in horrified amazement. The operator had the same face as the man he had seen running across the lawn some years before. The terrified lord drew back from the lift and decided to walk up the stairs.

A few seconds later there was a resounding crash as the cable snapped and the lift crashed to the basement. Everyone in it was killed – including the lift attendant.

Lightning Strikes

In Canada, during a fierce storm in 1934, the tombstone of an officer who had served in the First World War was shattered by a bolt of lightning. The unfortunate officer had been invalided out of the Canadian Army after being struck by lightning in 1918. Six years later he was struck by another flash while fishing, and his right side was paralysed. He recovered and two years later was taking a walk through a park when ... this time paralysing him for good. The gods must have had it in for him.

What A Coincidence

A Derbyshire lady and her husband were motoring south one day when they stopped at a motorway lay-by to rest. They got out of the car and fell into conversation with another couple. The second man happened to mention that a few months before he had lost his wallet containing credit cards, cash and other personal items. As he was talking he took the wallet out of his pocket and the astonished Derbyshire lady looked at it in amazement – it had been she who had found it and handed it in to the police, and the two couples lived more than 60 miles away from each other.

Dead Man's Tales

A Warwickshire builder was quite surprised to bump into a cousin he hadn't seen for some time in a pub. But not half as surprised as his cousin, who had been at the builder's funeral service in Dublin some time earlier. It turned out that former workmates had wrongly identified him as the victim of a car crash and had telephoned his family in Ireland. The family decided that rather than come over for the funeral, they would hold a mass for him there.

Hello, Father

Johann van Vliet, a Dutch tourist, was on holiday in Austria when his car broke down just outside Innsbruck. A local farmer's wife kindly stopped her car and offered him a lift to the nearest garage. It turned out that she was his daughter who had run away from home 23 years earlier.

A Ghostly Experience

Nell Wood of Redwood City, California, swears that the following story is true.

She woke up one morning with her stomach in knots. She was certain that something awful was going to happen and the feeling stayed with her all day.

When she went to bed that night she had a strange dream. In her dream her sister came to her and told her that there had been an accident. Two had been critically injured and one only slightly. Nell did not know what her sister meant by 'two' and 'one', but she sensed that her mother was involved. At that time her mother lived three thousand miles away.

The next day Nell's sister telephoned and told her that their mother had had a fall.

'She's broken her pelvic bone, her hip and the small bone in the leg. The small bone is not critical but the other two are.'

Nell's dream flooded back to her and she understood the meaning of the 'two' and the 'one'.

A few weeks later, Nell was lying in bed thinking about her mother's accident and how much she would like to visit her; she closed her eyes and dropped off to sleep.

She dreamed that she was in her mother's bedroom, standing at the bottom of the sleeping woman's bed. She did not want to waken her mother, but the old lady opened her eyes, smiled at Nell and went back to sleep.

The next morning her mother telephoned. She said she had dreamed in the night that Nell had been in her bedroom wearing a pale pink nightgown.

Nell was stunned, because she *had* been wearing a pale pink nightgown that night – a new one that her mother had never seen, and a colour she had never worn before.

600

A Good Gamble

Mr George Epp, a former policeman with Atlantic City Police Department quit the force because of his gambling debts. He felt it was giving the police a bad name, so he took a job as a taxi-driver to give himself time to get over his addiction. He worked hard to pay off the $25,000 he owed his creditors, but still found it hard to stop dicing with Lady Luck. Just as well. In the Atlantic City Casino one night in November 1982 he put some coins into a slot machine, pulled the handle and came out $1,250,000 richer.

A Tale Of Pearls

Two American women were on holiday in Britain, spending most of their time cycling from place to place, exploring the countryside and looking for inexpensive mementoes to take home.

They decided to go to Newhaven and found a cheap hotel to stay in overnight.

While wandering through the streets they came across a little junk shop and went in to buy some trinkets. The owner tried to sell them a little Bible and when this did not satisfy them, he picked up a string of beads which was hanging from a nail. The girls thought that these were just what they wanted and bought them for one shilling.

When they returned to London, they decided to have the beads re-strung as the cord was very frayed, so they took them to a jeweller.

The assistant said he would do the job that day and the beads would be ready the following morning.

When they returned to collect them, the jeweller asked them to step into his private office, where he introduced them to a stranger. The girls noticed their beads lying on the desk. They had been cleaned and polished and looked very beautiful.

The stranger, it turned out, was from the British Museum and was anxious to buy the beads from the two Americans. They had, he explained, belonged to Mary Queen of Scots, and had been missing ever since she was executed.

The beads were, in fact, a magnificent string of black pearls.

601

It Is Easier For A Rich Man...

A Shanghai millionaire, Woo Tai Ling, had a most disturbing dream one night. He dreamed that he was too overloaded with money to slip through the narrow gates into heaven. The next morning he gave all his money away and took a job in a market as an ordinary porter.

★   ★   ★   ★

. . . . .In 1902 St Pierre in Martinique was totally destroyed and 40,000 people killed when Mount Pele erupted. The only survivor was a prisoner who was being kept in an underground cell. No-one knows how he got out. .

★   ★   ★   ★

An Unfortunate Coincidence

Herr Keelsch of Seigen in West Germany made his living out of emptying cesspits – and, not unnaturally, after a day's work did not exactly smell of roses and violets. He drove around the town in a van which advertised his telephone number in large numbers. This so angered the makers of a certain well-known *eau de Cologne* that they took him to court to make him remove the offending numbers. As Herr Keelsch explained, it was not his fault that he had been given that famous number:

4711

Never Strike Twice?

In 1942 Roy Sullivan, a Park Ranger in Virginia, USA, lost a toe nail. Twenty-seven years later his eyebrows were damaged; the following year his left shoulder was burned and two years after that his hair was set on fire. It had grown again by the following year and then the same thing happened again. In 1976 his ankle was injured and in 1977 he suffered chest burns. The cause of all this misfortune? Lightning! All in all he has been struck seven times – and most people say that lightning never strikes in the same place twice. Tell that to the rangers.

Eccentricity Generating

*.................... Being matters of a kind concerning
freaks and eccentricities of behaviour or occurrence..*

Don't Meddle With The Ref

During a game between Catanzaro and Palermo, the score was one goal each when the home side, Catanzaro, had two penalties disallowed by the referee.

When the final whistle blew, the referee was chased from the ground. Fortunately, he was a fast runner and managed to dash into a restaurant, where he called a waiter and ordered some soup, hoping to give his pursuers the slip.

Unfortunately, when his meal arrived, so too did the owner of the restaurant, who had just come back from the match.

Recognizing the referee, the angry proprietor ordered him from the restaurant, throwing the soup after him. The furious referee, however, managed to get his revenge.

He found a telephone and called the restaurant. He told the owner that he was the manager of the Catanzaro team and he was bringing his players there for something to eat. They would, he said, be arriving in about an hour.

He then telephoned the Catanzaro manager and claimed to be the restaurant owner.

He told the manager that he was so upset by the result and so convinced that the local side had won that he was inviting the entire team to eat at the restaurant for a few pence each. Come, he said, in about an hour.

The footballers duly arrived and ate and drank their way through the menu.

When they were presented with an enormous bill they went crazy and broke up the restaurant.

The restaurant manager and the football manager had such a fight that the furious footballer was jailed for assault.

Quicker Clearance

A cinema manager once wrote to the *Daily Worker* (now the *Morning Star*) deploring the fact that the practice of playing the National Anthem was being phased out. He claimed that those who were lucky enough managed to leave the cinema before it started, and those left behind moved off more quickly, thus clearing the cinema in a shorter time than on occasions when 'The Queen' was not played.

Turn Up The Sound

A Los Angeles record company has produced an album entitled 'The Best of Marcel Marceau'. Each side has twenty minutes of M. Marceau in performance, followed by applause. M. Marceau is, of course, a well-known mime artist and never utters a word during his act.

A Short Time For 'A Long Way...'

The famous song 'It's a Long Way to Tipperary' was written by two friends, Jack Judge and Harry J. Williams, as the result of a bet. They were challenged by a group of actors to write a song and perform it the same day. So they sat down in a pub and did just that.

The song is still popular today, over seventy years later, especially in pubs!

★   ★   ★   ★

.... When a distraught widow saw a pair of bright, white false teeth grinning up at her from the funeral urn, she knew there was something wrong – her husband had never had false teeth in his life.............

★   ★   ★   ★

If Mr Marconi Had Only Known

The proud mother surveyed her children. There were eighteen of them – fourteen of whom had different fathers, and all of whom had been born after the mother had left her husband. The woman said that she neither smoked nor drank and that her only relaxation was the radio.

Over What Sea?

A North London man asked an official at Golders Green Crematorium if he could have the ashes of his deceased mother. He was asked where he intended taking them, and when he told the official, he was asked to pay £2, the usual amount if ashes were to be taken overseas.

The man was slightly puzzled and contacted the Home Office to be told that, under their regulations, the attendant had been quite correct.

'Scotland,' he was told, 'is officially overseas.'

The official could not say which sea it was over, but he had to stick by the ruling and charge the fee.

Small Is Beautiful

One of the most successful spies of the French Revolution was a thirty-two-year-old man who devised a novel way of slipping through enemy lines. He was so small that he was dressed up as a baby and was simply carried past unsuspecting guards by a female colleague.

A Cleveland Duel

A long-standing feud between two men who lived in a Cleveland apartment house came to a head one day.

Both men returned to their separate abodes and came back into the hallway each brandishing an antique pistol. Standing five feet apart, they took aim and fired, again, again and again – a total of six shots each.

When the police arrived, there were bullet holes all over the hallway but both men were alive. The detective in charge said that one of the contestants needed a stick to prop himself up while firing and the other had trouble seeing as he suffered from glaucoma in the eye. One of the men was 76 and the other was 77.

When did all this happen? Not during the last century as you may imagine, but in May 1981.

A Taxing Problem

Arthur Cox has one of the strangest food shops in Britain. He refuses to sell anything that carries VAT. He won't sell chocolate biscuits, but will sell chocolate-covered cakes. Cat food is not sold, but tinned fish is. But Mr Cox *is* registered for VAT. That way he can claim back the VAT on items that he buys for the shop, such as paper bags and till rolls. So the VAT man must pay him, without getting anything back from him.

High Speed Shopping

Villagers who live in the Oxfordshire hamlet of Finstock have to be the fastest shoppers in the world. Most of them do their shopping in the nearby town of Charlesbury, three miles away. The first available bus, run by the Oxford-South Midland Bus Company arrives in Charlesbury at 11.38 am. The last bus from Charlesbury back to Finstock leaves at 11.41 am. This gives the Finstock villagers three minutes to do their shopping.

Wednesday, Thursday, Thursday, Saturday...

In 1147, Pope Eugene III visited Paris. He entered the city on a Friday, although he knew that by doing so the people would be unable to celebrate his arrival, as Friday was an official day of fasting for all Roman Catholics. So a Papal decree was issued to say that that particular Friday was a Thursday.

Water Baby

Many people have managed to swim a mile, so there's nothing unusual in Simon Broadhurst doing it. Only it took him two hours – he was only three years old when he did his marathon swim at Saddleworth Baths near Manchester.

Hanging Upside Down
Excuse Me But That Painting's

A painting by the famous French impressionist painter, Manet, was lent to the New York Museum of Modern Art for an important exhibition, which ran from April through October. The painting showed a village reflected in a small lake. It was only after the exhibition had finished that one of the museum attendants realized that it had been hung upside down. No one had noticed, although many people had stopped in front of the painting and admired Manet's skill.

★ ★ ★ ★

. . . . In late 1981 a teenage couple who were anxious to get into the record books embraced each other and began to kiss – five days, twelve hours later they broke off. . . . .

★ ★ ★ ★

Coals To Newcastle

Abu Dhabi is one of the most desert-covered countries in the world. No matter where you look there is sand, sand and more sand. Yet a British firm once took an order to export 1,800 tons of sand to them.

The Rich Get Richer

Sutton Place was the home of J. Paul Getty, one of the richest of twentieth century oil millionaires. Weekend guests to his sumptuous home were astonished to find telephone boxes installed for their use. Despite his enormous wealth, Getty hated the thought of paying for other people's calls.

For Love of Guam

Yokoi Shoichi was stationed on the island of Guam when the Japanese surrendered to the Americans in 1945. Either no one told him or he refused to believe that the Imperial Japanese Army was capable of defeat, but for the next 27 years he lived in the jungle, eating small mammals and berries. He was found in 1972 and was returned to Japan.

A few years later he married and took his bride on honeymoon. Back to Guam.

One, Two, Three, Four...

Young Master Drew, a schoolboy in Waterloo, Iowa, ran home one day and told his mother, Martha, an amazing piece of information that he had learned that day in school. It was impossible, his teacher had said, to count up to one million. Martha Drew did not believe this, so she sat down at her typewriter and began to type out every number from one to one million. Five years and 2,473 sheets of paper later, she finished.

I HOPE YOU PASSED HER. SHE'S DRIVING THE CRANE!

A Long Way To Go For A Funeral

Mr and Mrs Richard Selley of Houston in Texas had almost forgotten that they had a wealthy cousin, until he died and left them one million dollars. Unfortunately, there was one condition they had to fulfil before they got the money – they had to arrange to have their benefactor buried on the moon.

The Gullible Burmese

There are many famous confidence trick stories ranging from shifty Frenchmen selling the Eiffel Tower, to the imposter who fooled the Albanians into believing that he was their king (for three days), but Lim Bim Sung, a Burmese man, came up with a winner. He convinced several people in Rangoon that he had bought an old American rocket and was organizing holidays on the moon. He was arrested as one potential customer was actually handing over the money for the fare.

★   ★   ★   ★

. . . .*It took Austrian Johann Hurlinger 55 days to walk the 871 miles from Vienna to Paris. Mind you, he was walking on his hands all the way.* . . . .

Have I Passed Then?

The unfortunate examiner who saw a nervous woman learner driver through her driving test in Guildford in 1969 ended up on the roof of the car along with the woman when she drove into the River Wey. The shocked examiner was sent home before he had told the driver if she had passed or failed her test. Ever-hopeful, the woman asked if she had passed and was told with remarkable British reserve that no one knew, as the examiner had not told anyone before he went home.

Distracting Credit

In the USA it is very common for sales assistants to check a customer's credit balance whenever a credit card is offered in payment. The assistant simply punches the card number into a counter computer terminal and the amount of credit available flashes up on the VDU. An ill-tempered queue was once formed in a shop called Broadway Bazaar in, where else, Broadway, New York. A female customer handed over ten credit cards until the cashier found one that had a sufficient balance left in order to pay for her purchases.

Long way away, a Texan woman found a novel way around the problem. Wearing only the briefest of bikinis to cover her shapely figure, she spent a morning in a large Dallas store paying by credit card, choosing youngish male assistants to serve her. It was only after she had run up a bill of over £1,000 that any of the men bothered to check her non-existent credit-worthiness – their eyes were obviously elsewhere.

★　★　★　★

. . . . An American woman insured her husband's life so that, if he died before she did, her lifestyle would not change too radically. Some lifestyle – when he died the insurance company paid up $18,000,000. . . . .

A Close Shave

Robert Hardie was anxious to publicize the barber shop he opened in London in 1909. He persuaded a friend to be shaved by him in public. The friend agreed and Hardie gave him a clean shave in 29 seconds – blindfolded.

A Fortune From Nothing

For their seven-year run on Broadway, which began in 1896 the Cherry Sisters earned $1,000 per week. When the show finished, although they had lived well during the run, they had managed to save $200,000. Their act? They played a sketch that was so bad it had to be acted behind a wire screen to avoid the rotten tomatoes and vegetables that were thrown at them every night. People were happy to pay, simply to bombard them.

I NEVER MISSED A SHOW EXCEPT THE TIME I WRENCHED MY THROWING ARM!

Quite A Bargain

The Russians first colonized Alaska in the 1780s but by the 1850s many Americans and Canadians had settled there, too. The Russians offered to sell the area to the Americans and agreed to take $7.3 million for it. That works out at around two cents an acre. At first the Americans thought the Secretary of State who had negotiated with the Russians was mad and called Alaska 'Seward's Folly' after him. But when gold, and later, oil were discovered there in huge quantities they changed their minds quite quickly.

Blow It

Susan Montgomery, an American schoolgirl, decided to blow a huge bubble with her gum. She chewed and chewed until she felt that it was just the right consistency. She began to blow and stopped when the bubble had reached a diameter of 19¼ inches.

Multiple Votes

Bessie Braddock, the tough but well-respected member for Liverpool Central, often told the story of driving through her constituency one polling day when her car had to stop at traffic lights. One of her constituents recognized her and knocked on the window. Mrs Braddock dutifully wound it down to be told by the woman that she was a life-long admirer and had voted for her, as usual. Bessie thanked the woman. 'Don't mention it,' said the Liverpudlian, 'in fact I voted for you three times. Two of my friends are ill, so I just took their cards to their polling stations and voted for you, just in case.'

Fortunately Mrs Braddock's majority was large enough for her not to have to worry about these three votes robbing her opponent of victory. But had it been in Ilkeston during the 1931 general election, three votes would have made all the difference, for the majority with which Abraham Flint was returned to Westminster was two.

615

Live Long, Live Loudly

Every year, the townsfolk of Montforte d'Alba in Piedmont hold a free-style Shouting Festival. In 1982, 2,000 people were in the audience enjoying watching and listening to lusty youngsters screaming at the tops of their voices to see who could register the loudest and most piercing yell.

A ripple of sympathetic laughter spread through the audience when an old man was helped on to the platform. Their laughter turned to cheers when he registered a scream of 124 decibels on the phonometer – equivalent to the noise a jet aeroplane makes on landing. The winner was ninety years of age.

Sweet Revenge

Carlo Gamba left home in southern Italy in 1913 when he was twenty-three. He never returned to Italy and never saw his family again. He worked as a shoe black in a San Francisco railway station. He worked seven days a week and most nights. Carlo never married, never smoked or drank, saved every penny he could and invested what he had wisely.

In 1962, he learned that his brother, Giuseppe, had sold the family home in Italy for $1,000. Carlo did not receive a penny from the sale. He neither said a word about it, nor did he forgive.

When he died in 1982, Carlo had amassed a fortune of $500,000. Giuseppe heard this news with delight, but the smile on his face did not last long. Instead of the vast fortune he expected to receive, Giuseppe got exactly $5.

The will read, 'I leave all my money except five dollars to the town of Verbicaro (his home town) to build a hospital. These five dollars I leave to Giuseppe so that he can buy a drink and remember that he should never have sold the family house without my consent.'

★　　★　　★　　★

. . . . The owner of a hotel in Chippenham, England, has a unique collection of drinks bottles. The contents are never sold in his hotel – the bottles are miniatures – all 19,000 of them. . . . .

Foiled

Mithradates, king of a long-forgotten realm, attempted to make himself immune to poisons by taking increasingly large doses of toxic substances. It is ironic therefore that when he was defeated by his enemies, the Romans, he tried to commit suicide by taking poison. None of the poisons available did the trick so he had to ask a soldier to hold a sword for him, and he killed himself by running into it.

★　　★　　★　　★

. . . . .The name Billy Jones is not to be found in any of the record books, although one day in May 1955, at Louisiana, he ran the hundred yards in nine seconds, smashing every previous record. Unfortunately, when officials checked the distance, they found that the track was ten yards short. . . . .

★　　★　　★　　★

An Odd Hobby

A man who works for Hertfordshire Social Services Committee has a very strange hobby. He traces twins who have no idea that they have twin brothers or sisters.

It all started more than twenty years ago when he became involved in the case of a boy who had been taken into care. He discovered that the child had been adopted and, before the boy left care, he said that his mother had told him he was one of a pair of twins. The boy went off to sea and the interested social worker decided to find out if this was true. He located the adoption society who put him in touch with the boy's grandmother. She knew where the other twin was. He had also gone off to sea.

Since then, the man has put 23 sets of twins in touch with each other. One set of twins found out that the only thing they liked to drink was advocaat and lemonade. Another set are both terrified of birds. Two boy twins turned up to meet each other wearing identical glasses, jackets and trousers, and other twins found that they lived within a mile of each other, drank in the same pubs and clubs and yet had never met until our intrepid investigator put them in touch with each other.

An Expensive Drink

In 1982, the Islay distillery of Bruichladdich decided to market a single malt whisky that had been maturing in oak sherry casks for fifteen years. They decided that such a fine old whisky should be treated with respect, so they commissioned Edinburgh crystal manufacturers to make special crystal decanters, plus a lock-fast Victorian-style tantalus, which holds two decanters of the precious liquid. The price of all this in the Italian shops where the 'cratur' was to be sold? The equivalent of £1,000. At normal pub measures that works out at £20 for a dram.

★　　★　　★　　★

. . . . A Portsmouth man who died recently left £250,000 in his will to . . . Jesus Christ, provided that he comes back to earth within the next twenty-one years. . . . .

★　　★　　★　　★

What A Shower

Some members of a Home Counties Soccer Club have complained to the London Football Association about one of their referees, who insists on taking a shower with them after the game. The referee, shapely Janet Walmsley, does not see what all the fuss is about. 'After all,' she says, 'I do keep my knickers on.'

A Close Run Thing

Willie Carson, the famous British jockey, was racing one day at Pontefract. He was happily leading on the rails, having made all the running. A furlong and a half from home he thought he heard something at his back and, glancing round, he saw the shadow of a horse coming up behind. Determined that he should not be beaten, he spurred on and was first past the post. He looked round and saw that the nearest horse was fifteen lengths behind – he had been racing his own shadow for the last part of the race.

How Have The Mighty Fallen

The Sri-Lanka tribe of Rodiya was once one of the mightiest on the island. They were in charge of collecting taxes and ensuring that whatever the king said was obeyed. One of their number was responsible for supplying the king's table with fresh game.

One day the king told his Rodiyan servant that he wanted freshly roasted venison for dinner. Unfortunately, deer was scarce in the forest and the hunters came home empty-handed. The terrified servant hit upon a substitute and the royal family pronounced the meal delicious until a human finger was found in the serving bowl.

The hunter was summoned before the furious king and confessed that he had slaughtered and cooked a human. He was instantly beheaded and, as punishment, all the Rodiyans were banished and denied all forms of work other than begging.

Although all this happened 1,500 years ago and the Sri-Lankan monarchy has long since died out, the Rodiyans still live by begging. The old royal decree has long been lifted, but the Rodiyans know no other way of life apart from that forced on them by the king.

Dance Of The Seven Veils — And Then Some

The vicar of a Sheffield parish was slightly perturbed when he heard that students at one of the local colleges were going to put on Oscar Wilde's famous play, *Salome*. The girl who was to play Salome heeded the vicar's warning about her role – for when she did the dance of the seven veils, she wore a flared skirt and tunic under her costume. Many of the men in the audience were slightly upset about this and did not applaud as Wildely as the happy vicar.

★ ★ ★ ★

.... Those who were lucky enough to see an early print of El Cid, *an epic film set in twelfth-century Spain, were amused when a large truck was clearly visible on the horizon during one sweeping camera shot. ....*

619

TOUR de FRANCE SOUP TO NUTS STAGE

. . . . *In 1977 a certain Frenchman was feeling slightly peckish – so he ate a bicycle, every last nut and bolt of it. . . . .*

★　　★　　★　　★

The Sausages Were Off

The foul smell that came from a Welwyn Garden City sausage skin factory so upset a local businessman that he went out and bought the entire works. It was only after he had done so that he discovered that the factory could only be used to manufacture certain things under a local by-law. The other uses included the boiling of blood, the breeding of maggots and the preparation of glue and manure.

Is The Old Way Best?

To try to teach her class of schoolchildren something about what life was like in Victorian England, a North London school teacher decided to put the clock back one hundred years. She raided the drama club wardrobe and found enough Victorian-style dresses for the girls to wear for one day and asked the boys to turn up wearing smart jackets, collars and ties.

When the teacher walked into the classroom on the morning of the lesson, the children all stood up and bade her good morning as rehearsed.

They then recited their tables in time to a metronome that had been installed in the classroom. Anyone who misbehaved was made to stand in the corner, a dunce's cap on his head. Lunch was served – a simple meal of gruel.

The pupils said it was the best day of school they had ever had and begged to repeat the experiment again and again – that is, apart from the lunch.

A Really Nervous Passenger

A Rotherham man had never flown before, but decided to fly to Bulgaria for a holiday. He boarded the 'plane and a few minutes later the engines roared into life and it began to taxi down the runway. It was then that he suddenly realized that in a few minutes he would be flying at supersonic speeds thousands of feet above the ground. He unfastened the seat belt and asked a stewardess to have the 'plane stopped. The girl tried to calm him down, but it was no good. The pilot took the 'plane back to the terminal and the man ran down the steps, rushed to get a taxi and went back to his house in Rotherham. What happened to his baggage, that's what I want to know?

★　　★　　★　　★

. . . .*In 1910, the eccentric Polish aristocrat, the* ***Princess Radzewill, drove a chariot pulled by a lion and a*** ***leopard.*** . . . .

★　　★　　★　　★

Help! My Baby's In There

Tony Stellato was only too pleased to help the hysterical lady who stopped him in the street, pointed to a blazing building and told him that her baby was trapped in the fire. He battled his way through a wall of smoke and flames and frantically searched for the child. But he could find nothing. He stumbled back into the garden, gasping for breath.

The lady pleaded with him again to go and find her baby, so he ran back into the conflagration, broke through a locked door, and still found nothing. Suddenly a blast of smoke hit him in the face and he began to lose consciousness. He stumbled outside and managed to make it into the fresh air before passing out. He was rushed to hospital and treated for severe smoke inhalation.

When he was fully recovered the doctors told him that he was a real hero, although they did not understand why he had risked his life to try to save a cat called 'Baby'.

It later turned out that the cat had left the house as soon as the fire had started.

Luckless Heirs

During the American Civil War, New York society was dazzled by a beautiful woman called Ida Mayfield. She married a congressman, Ben Wood, who showered her with money and jewels. When she travelled to Europe she was introduced to the Empress Eugénie of France. She danced in London with the Prince of Wales, and back home she entertained President Cleveland.

Then, in 1901, Ida mysteriously vanished. In 1931 the *New York Daily News* stated that she had been discovered living in a shabby state in New York's Herald Square Hotel. Her room looked like a hamster's cage. There were mountains of yellowed newspapers and hundreds of letters scattered across the floor. Trunks and boxes were stacked from ceiling to floor. Ida was blind and deaf and wore two of the hotel's towels held together by safety-pins as a dress.

She was pronounced to be mentally incompetent and made a ward of court. The judge ordered that the boxes be opened. They contained securities worth hundreds of thousands of dollars, as well as a magnificent emerald and diamond necklace of priceless value. But it was the nurse who came to look after Ida who made the real discovery.

Around the old woman's waist was a canvas and oilcloth pouch containing $500,000 in ten-thousand-dollar bills.

When this was taken from Ida, the shock was so much that she had a stroke and died, leaving no obvious heirs.

Soon every Mayfield in Louisianna seemed to have arrived in New York claiming to be a relation of Ida's. It took four years for the courts to make a decision – and when it was announced the Mayfields were horrified.

Ida Mayfield, the court decreed, had never existed. The woman who claimed to be her was, in fact, Ellen Walsh, the impoverished daughter of an immigrant textile worker. Though poor as a church mouse, Ellen had brains as well as beauty.

She borrowed a ballgown and journeyed to New York, adopting the name of Ida Mayfield when she arrived there. She soon became the toast of the town, after gate crashing a party in her one borrowed frock. Because she looked the part of a rich, elegant lady, fashionable clothes shops gave her credit, which was soon paid off when she married Ben Wood. Not even he knew the truth about his wife.

The fortune that she left was divided among a handful of descendants who were located after quite a search. They did not even know that their ancestor had ever existed.

★　　★　　★　　★

. . . . *Gary Trench of Phoenix, Arizona once sleep-walked to his place of work and did a three-hour shift packing toys before he woke.* . . . .

★　　★　　★　　★

A Little Overdue

The librarian of Cincinnati Medical Library thought his eyes were deceiving him when he checked the return date of the book in front of him. It was due back in 1823 having originally been taken out by the great-grandfather of the returner. The fine of $2,646 was waived under the circumstances.